PRAISE FOR A SONG OF LIGHT & FIRE

Stunning! Absolutely riveting!

By the time you turn the final page of this book, you'll have ascended to the radiant heights of Heaven and plummeted into the searing depths of Hell. You'll roar with laughter, weep with raw emotion, recoil in shock, and catch your breath in awe. This journey will transform you. *A Song of Light & Fire* ignites vivid, heart-pounding adventure while remaining steadfastly anchored in sound biblical doctrine.

— RAYMOND REED, THE INDEPENDENT

A Song of Light & Fire is unlike anything you've ever read. It's not a theological textbook, although it effectively reflects Christian theology. It's not a novel, a fantasy, or an illusion. It's a storied journey through Heaven and Hell that will draw you in and make you feel as though you're actually there.

— DR. WOODROW KROLL, BACK TO THE BIBLE INTERNATIONAL

Cory Rosenke has expertly married a compelling narrative with extensive scriptural, historical, and theological support to provide readers with the most eye-opening and accurate depiction of Heaven and Hell I've ever encountered. Heaven's radiance and joy left me longing for that day, while Hell's contrasting grayness—void of any beauty or goodness whatsoever—left me wanting to shake my unbelieving friends and family awake. I guarantee that no one will walk away from this book unchanged.

— CORTNEY DONELSON, OWNER OF VOCEM LLC, SPEAKER, AND AUTHOR

Too many books about Heaven and Hell simply fill the mind with distant facts. This one fills the heart with joy. It doesn't just point you toward eternity—it stirs the soul with an excited anticipation of glory.

— DR. JOEL KING, LEAD PASTOR, TRINITY CHURCH OF SUNNYVALE

I was deeply moved by the historical, theological, and biblical richness of Cory's work, all brought to life through his vivid imagination and compelling characters. The story draws you in and leaves you contemplating the reality of eternity. For me personally, it awakened a renewed longing to know Jesus Christ more deeply. Yet as I read and reread, my heart also ached for those who have not placed their faith in God or experienced the boundless love of Christ. I closed the book more determined than ever to love, to pray, and to help others taste and see how beautiful Jesus truly is.

— KAMEL H. SHALHOUB, THE NAVIGATORS, MENA REGIONAL DIRECTOR EMERITUS

A SONG OF LIGHT AND FIRE

AN UNCENSORED JOURNEY
THROUGH HEAVEN AND HELL

CORY ROSENKE

CONTENTS

AUTHOR'S WARNING
READER DISCRETION
IS STRONGLY ADVISED.

A Song of Light & Fire ascends to the heights of Heaven and descends into the shadows of Hell. It portrays death, violence, and defilement—not for spectacle but for truth. Every haunting image, every cry of agony, every glimpse of wonder serves a single purpose: to confront what is real, what is ultimate, and what awaits beyond the veil.

- You will witness indescribable beauty.
- You will encounter unimaginable suffering.
- You will be encouraged, challenged and transformed.

These pages were written with reverence, not indulgence—with trembling hands, not careless ones. Yet truth, when unfiltered, is never tame.

Proceed at your own risk—but if you do continue with the journey—may courage sustain you, and may the Light of life guide you safely to the other side.

PART I
AN UNCENSORED JOURNEY THROUGH HEAVEN

INTRODUCTION
THE GREATEST TRUE
STORY NEVER TOLD

∞

A childhood memory still glows clear in my mind. I was nine or ten, caught in the grip of a nightmare so terrifying it shook me to my core. In the dream, a giant spider chased me across a gray field, its legs thundering closer as I ran. My heart pounded as I sprinted for the protection of my grandparents' house in the distance. I pushed myself harder, desperate to reach the front door, but as I glanced back, the spider morphed into a snarling wolf. Rounding the corner, I scrambled up the porch stairs, only to feel the predator's weight slam me to the ground—just inches from safety. With one paw pinning my chest, the other—eerily hand-like—drove claws through my cheeks as haunting eyes bore into my soul.

I woke in a cold sweat, my small body trembling, too scared to move. My parents' room was down the hall, a forbidden sanctuary I wasn't permitted to enter. But that night, fear overpowered rules. I stood outside their door, heart racing, and dared to knock. My father's gruff, sleepy voice answered, "What is it?"

I stammered that it was me, that I was scared. They invited me in, and what happened next changed everything. My parents welcomed me onto their bed, where I snuggled between them, still shaking. Then they began telling me about Heaven. They spoke of a crystal sea, a place with no sadness or fear, where animals roamed as friends, not threats. As a child, those words wrapped around me like a warm blanket, banishing the wolf's shadow. I returned to my room and slept peacefully.

That night opened my eyes to the awe-inspiring reality of Heaven —and the contrasting verity of Hell.

Comprehending the true nature of these eternal realms can reorient your life in ways you may not expect. Even now, as a grown man, I can say this with confidence: When you rightly understand Heaven, it stirs a hope and assurance deeper than anything this world can offer. And when the stark truth about Hell is revealed, it compels you to speak—with urgency, with warning, and with a heart full of compassion.

Yet, most people, including many Christians, know very little about eternity. The word itself is a mystery, a vague notion tied to jumbled rumors. They've heard that "Jesus went to prepare a place for them" (John 14:2). They know God will "wipe away every tear" (Revelation 21:4) and that there will be no sadness or sickness. But these fragmented snippets are too thin to anchor their souls, too frail to bring the peace that transformed a terrified boy into a man of faith. They also know that Hell will be a place of "the gnashing of teeth"— whatever that means. It's a consequence too vague to inspire any urgency.

So, after all these centuries, why has our understanding of Heaven and Hell remained so limited? One reason may be that the true story of eternity is so extreme, so utterly beyond human comprehension, that serious theologians often shy away from it, fearing their words might sound fanciful or speculative. This hesitation, I believe, has been to our great loss, depriving us of both the vibrant hope and dire warning that Scripture offers. With this book, I seek to break that barrier, offering a broad and unfiltered glimpse of eternal life—and death.

After carefully considering how best to present a biblically faithful, vivid, and relatable depiction of Heaven and Hell, I chose a narrative format, inviting you into a story that lets you experience their respective glory and terror up close. However, don't be misled into believing this book is merely a fairytale—or a nightmare. This is not fiction. It's a sneak peek at your future existence, contingent upon your personal decisions.

With *A Song of Light & Fire: An Uncensored Journey Through Heaven and Hell*, I hope to inspire and inform, presenting eternity with clarity, urgency, and relevance. My mission is to unveil Heaven's splendor and Hell's agony in a way that captivates your heart, sharpens your perspective, and draws you closer to the good God who calls to you.

As a pastor and theologian, I've devoted years to this task, poring over Scripture, from Genesis to Revelation, mining every passage that reveals the nature of eternity, tracing each truth claim to its logical conclusion. I've consulted with fellow theologians, probing their interpretations of complex texts like Revelation 21–22, Isaiah 6, and Ezekiel 1. I've studied the testimonies of those who say they've glimpsed the other side—individuals who've died and returned—testing their words against scriptural truth. The result is a comprehensive, biblically rooted vision, woven into a lively narrative that captures the raw reality of our everlasting destiny.

I conclude with a detailed appendix section, outlining the interpretive process and reasoning behind my conclusions, followed by a glossary to help you understand key terms and concepts—like "common grace" and "Shekinah glory"—especially if you're new to these ideas. I encourage you to refer to the appendix or glossary as you encounter unfamiliar words, phrases, or descriptions. In addition to exploring Heaven and Hell, I introduce "The Choosing Ground," a concept that may transform your understanding of earthly existence.

We begin now with an odyssey into Heaven. But I warn you, dear reader—this is not a gentle tale. *A Song of Light and Fire* is an uncensored journey. It begins in the brutal shadows of a Roman dungeon, where the air reeks of sweat, urine, and blood, and the clink of shackles echoes with despair.

You will walk with Perpetua—a young mother and Christian noblewoman—and her companions as they face the horrors of martyrdom in Carthage in 203 AD. The opening chapters are unflinching, depicting the physical and emotional toll of their stand for Christ with intense, gut-wrenching detail. You will feel the sting of irons, hear the roar of a bloodthirsty crowd, and witness the savagery of beasts and blades. This is not gratuitous violence; it's the historical reality of early Christian sacrifice, rooted in Perpetua's own writings and the accounts of her time. It is also a necessary prelude to contrast Heaven's triumph, for as Jesus declared, "In this world you will have trouble. But take heart! I have overcome the world" (John 16:33).

The dungeon and arena are only the beginning. From the ashes of earthly suffering, you will ascend with Perpetua into a realm of indescribable beauty—a Heaven alive with the presence of God Himself.

This is the real thing, the culmination of all that Scripture reveals about eternity. Drawing on hundreds of scriptural passages, I have crafted a narrative that brings to life the New Jerusalem, the River of Life, the Tree of Life, and the Throne of the Lamb. Every detail is intentional, rooted in the creative richness of God's Word.

My goal is not to speculate but to synthesize, to pick up the scattered pieces and complete the puzzle. The heavenly chapters are a tapestry of Scripture's promises, from the garden of Eden to the eternal city—woven into a story that invites you to authentically experience God's Kingdom.

As an author, I know that compelling storytelling generally requires a strong antagonist or adversarial component to create tension, drive the plot, and keep the reader hooked. This is commonly referred to as the principle of opposition. But in Heaven, no such adversary exists, and inventing one would be unbiblical. Instead, I will rely on curiosity and a sense of wonder to keep you engaged. This shouldn't be difficult, as Heaven is positively brimming with astonishing wonders—so many, in fact, that they have tested my limits as a writer. Truly, this book is my attempt to accomplish the impossible: to imagine the unimaginable and describe the indescribable. I suspect I shall fail gloriously, but in this case, even my failure will be a transcendent delight.

As an international Bible teacher, I have witnessed a rabid hunger for answers about eternity. My previous work, *The Magnetic Heart of God: Understanding the Five Cravings of Your Soul*, explored how our deepest longings point to the Creator. This book answers the ultimate craving: to dwell in God's presence forever. It is not a theological essay, though it is grounded in rigorous study. It is not a novel, though it is written in story form. It is a vision—a call to fix your eyes on the Lamb who prepares a place for you (John 14:2–3). For believers, this is your future—a home where every tear is wiped away and every wound healed. For seekers, this is an invitation to discover a hope beyond your wildest dreams.

So, brave the dungeon, brace for the arena, and let your spirit soar into Heaven's light. This is the truth of eternity, revealed in Scripture, embodied in Christ, and awaiting all who trust in Him. Prepare to be swept away into the greatest true story never told—the crescendo of everything. May Part One of *A Song of Light and Fire* stir your heart, deepen your faith, and bring you the peace that once calmed a frightened boy—and still sustains me today.

—Cory Rosenke

CHAPTER I
THE DUNGEON

The dungeon reeked of despair—sweat, urine, and the faint, musty odor of blood embedded in stone. Beyond the iron bars, a distant torch flickered, its frail light struggling to pierce the heavy, damp cold, leaving the huddled prisoners cloaked in shadow. Five of them, arrested together in Carthage, sat among a scattering of other captives, all condemned by the same charge: refusing to honor the emperor as a god. Their breath filled the space—shallow, uneven, broken by sobs or murmured prayers. Shackles clinked softly as they shifted, waiting in darkness for judgment to descend upon them.

Perpetua, her beauty striking even in the gloom, sat with her knees drawn up, arms wrapped about them, a thin tunic clinging to her damp skin. At twenty-two, she was a mother, a daughter, a Christian—a woman of prominence and position. Now, she was just a prisoner, her noble name stripped away by Rome's brutal grip. *I'm terrified, God. Please, strengthen me.*

Her wrists burned where the irons bit, each pulse a reminder of a world she might never see again. She bowed her head, and memory swept in like a tide. She saw the sunlit courtyard of her family's villa, her son's laughter as he toddled after a stray kitten, his tiny hands grasping at her tunic. She'd sung to him then, a psalm of David, as he buried his sleepy face in her long dark curls. That was before the soldiers came, before her father's shouts and her mother's tears, before the irons. *Lord, keep them safe,* she pleaded silently, her soul a knot of love and dread. The dungeon's chill yanked her back, the stench of misery coiling tight around her. The pain echoed the panic rising in her chest as she prayed to a God who, in this moment, felt distant and unreachable.

The cell was a grave, its walls slick with moisture that dripped like tears. Perpetua traced a finger along the stone, feeling the grooves where countless others had clawed or prayed or wept. *How many before us?* she wondered, her mind drifting to the stories her teacher had shared—martyrs who'd faced the arena, their voices ringing with psalms as teeth tore flesh. She shivered, not from cold but from the weight of that legacy.

To her left, Felicity curled against the wall, ebony skin glistening with sweat, her swollen belly a stark contrast to her thin, trembling frame. Eight months pregnant, the former slave clutched herself, breath ragged with stifled sobs as the cold stone pressed against her spine.

"Perpetua," she whispered fearfully, "do you think my baby will make it?"

Perpetua turned, her face softening with love and helplessness.

"God is with us," she promised, though her voice wavered. *Is He? This place is swallowing me whole.*

Felicity nodded, lip quivering, hands tightening over the unborn child slumbering beneath her tattered clothing. Perpetua had known her since childhood—braiding each other's hair in the courtyard, their laughter ringing out as they played. A servant turned friend, Felicity had followed Perpetua into faith, her face glowing with the same fire. Now, that fire burned low, struggling to stay lit against the unrelenting wind of despair.

Perpetua shifted closer, ignoring the weight of her bonds, pressing her shoulder against Felicity. The contact was a lifeline, a reminder of their shared past. She remembered the day Felicity first heard the gospel—her face alight as their teacher spoke of a kingdom where slaves and nobles knelt as equals. They'd prayed together that night, under a Carthage moon, vowing to follow Christ no matter the cost. *The cost is here*, she thought, her throat tight. Felicity's hand found hers—fingers cold but fierce—and Perpetua squeezed back, willing strength into them both. "We'll sing to your baby," she murmured, and for a moment, they hummed softly—a gentle lullaby.

Across the cell, Lucius rocked on his heels, his aged frame hunched awkwardly, gray streaks threading his hair. Calloused hands, hardened by decades of labor, clasped together as he muttered, "The Lord is my strength," over and over. Perpetua had met him hauling grain at the market, his back bent under heavy sacks. She recalled his warm, contagious smile when she offered him water. Later, he joined the catechism classes—shy but eager—absorbing their teacher's words with quiet hunger.

Perpetua studied him, recalling the night he'd shared his story over bread and oil: a widower, his wife lost to fever, his children grown and scattered. "I found Christ late," he'd said, in a frank and honest manner, "but He found me first." That night, he'd taught her a prayer from his youth—one his mother sang. Simple, raw, a plea for courage. She murmured it now, hoping it would steady her as it did him. Lucius caught her look, nodding faintly, a flicker of recognition in his weary expression.

Beside him, Marcus slumped, his powerful shoulders sagging, muscles taut beneath a worn tunic. A wet stain darkened the floor beneath him. He'd lost control, and his face burned with shame as he turned away. Perpetua glanced at him, her brow tightening. *He's not weak. None of us are. This dread—it's eating us alive.* A former slave like Felicity, Marcus had attended catechism classes with her. A kind soul, he would often linger to ask questions about forgiveness in a deep, earnest voice. "Can God forgive a man who's really, really failed?" he'd once asked, downcast, as if dreading the answer. She'd told him yes,

11

and he'd smiled—a crack in his doubt. Now that doubt seemed to swallow him whole. *I won't let it,* she vowed, her resolve hardening despite her fear.

These men were her brothers now—bound by faith, but struggling under the weight of cruelty and uncertainty. She wanted to reach out, to bridge the gap between them, but her own bonds held her back.

Mago sat apart, his thick blond hair glinting in the faint torchlight, his countenance lifted upward, as if piercing the stone and staring into the heavens. At thirty, he possessed a rare gentleness blended with an unshakable calm. Even now, as blood and filth clung to him, he appeared unfazed. The last to join their group, Mago's quiet presence resonated with them instantly. He had come to Carthage from a coastal village, his hands rough from fishing nets, his mind alive with spiritual curiosity. He'd hounded their teacher with questions about faith, perseverance, and the martyrs—his persistence unveiling a soul already forged to endure this terrible hour. Perpetua watched him pray alone, and she coveted his quiet strength.

She tilted her head toward him, whispering, "Are you afraid?"

His steady look met hers, clear and unwavering. "No," he replied frankly, leaning his head against the cold stone wall. "Not anymore."

How? I crave that peace.

She found his calm to be both comforting and unsettling.

Across the cell, another prisoner coughed—a hacking, wet sound that cut through the murmurs. Perpetua squinted, making out a gaunt young man, barely older than a boy. He hadn't spoken since they'd been thrown together, but his eyes darted like a trapped animal, haunted by whatever he'd seen before the dungeon. She wondered who he was—a merchant's son, a laborer, a believer like them? The young man's silence gnawed at her, a mirror of the apprehension she fought to bury. *Lord, reach him,* she pleaded, heart stretching toward this stranger she might never know.

Just then, a sharp cry cut through the din. A woman with wild, unkempt hair wailed in shrill panic. "They're coming for us," she hissed, rocking violently. "The beasts—I saw them tear my cousin apart..."

12

Her voice broke into sobs, loud and ragged.

Lucius scowled at her. "Shut up!" he snapped, patience fraying. "You'll get us whipped."

The woman was lost in terror and couldn't hear him, the sound of her agony echoing off the walls. Perpetua's stomach twisted. *Her panic is drowning us.*

Stirred by the agitation, another prisoner, a thin man with a scarred face, leapt to his feet and began pacing near the bars, muttering curses at the guards. Perpetua watched him, pondering what had brought him here. Was it faith, rebellion, or something else? His anger was a fire, burning hot, while her fear chilled her bones. She envied his defiance, even as it unnerved her. What good was rage against Rome's might? Her teacher's voice echoed within her. "Not by might, but by My Spirit." She clung to it, a thread of hope in the gloom.

Stiff with discomfort, Perpetua leaned her head back, lids fluttering shut against the suffocating turmoil unfolding around her. The sound of her son's laughter flashed through her mind—a melody now out of reach. She'd given him to her mother when the soldiers came to take her. Her mom had screamed while her father desperately pleaded, "Perpetua, stop this Jesus madness!"

They'd begged her for months, but she couldn't turn back—not from the faith that defined her. The memory stung, bitter as a lash. She pressed her palms to her face, fighting tears that burned with loss and dread. *What will happen to my son now, Lord? Will he know You?*

She turned toward Felicity again. *You poor sweet soul.*

When Perpetua's son was born, Felicity had held her hand through the pain, singing to him when Perpetua couldn't. Now, she was carrying her own child through this hellish nightmare.

Sensing her stare, Felicity leaned close to Perpetua, as if to tell a secret. "What if we die?" Her hushed tone was thick with alarm.

Perpetua met her eyes. "Then we will see our Lord." She forced the words out, willing them to be enough. *But where are You now, Lord?*

Felicity, unaware of Perpetua's inner turmoil, nodded faintly, accepting the comforting words, though her hands still shook.

The stranger's sobs grew louder again, finally erupting into a scream. "I can't do this!" she shrieked, clawing at the air.

Her panic spread like a contagion in the room. Shackles rattled as prisoners shifted and moaned, some weeping, some murmuring incoherently, others banging their heads against the stone wall as they teetered on the brink of madness. Marcus groaned, burying his face in his arms, his broad frame hunching tighter.

"Quiet, you fools," Lucius growled, rough with exhaustion, but the plea fell on deaf ears. The gloom was slowly eating them alive.

Perpetua watched Marcus rock back and forth, staring desperately at the floor, as though willing a hole to open up and swallow him. *My dear friend.* She remembered laughing with him in the courtyard, his strong hands tossing her boy playfully into the air, making him squeal with delight. Marcus had often asked questions about grace—about second chances—as if he needed them most.

"Hey," she called softly, leaning toward him, "it's okay. We're in this together."

He summoned the courage to meet her look, tear-stained cheeks glistening in the torchlight. "I'm not strong like you," he murmured, thick with defeat.

"I don't feel strong," she whispered frankly, shaking her head.

Marcus blinked at her, a flicker of relief crossing his face—a small bridge between their shared fragility.

Perpetua's lids fluttered shut again, images flooding in—her parents' pleas, her son's giggle, and these dear friends: Felicity with her baby, Lucius with his prayers, Marcus with his fear, Mago with his indomitable spirit—her family in faith under pagan Roman rule. Her teacher's voice echoed again in her mind. "They overcame by the blood of the Lamb and the word of their testimony—they didn't love their lives so much as to shrink from death."

That scares me, Lord. Is this it?

A harsh clang shattered her thoughts. The dungeon door rattled and swung open. A guard loomed in the threshold, his bulk framed by torchlight, his armor dull and stained. A sneer twisted his face as he stepped in, boots crunching on straw. The air thickened with dread.

"You scum," he barked, spitting near Perpetua's feet. "Sentence is set. Tomorrow, you're arena meat—beasts and blades for the emperor's big day."

He laughed—a cruel, hollow sound—then slammed the door shut. Gloom flooded back, heavier now.

Felicity gasped, "No."

The wild woman wailed, and prisoners erupted in panic. Marcus trembled. Lucius' mutters quickened. Mago gave a slow nod, lifting his face again toward the heavens, his calm demeanor a beacon of light amid the chaos.

Perpetua sat frozen. *Could this really be happening? Tomorrow? Lord, help me—help us!*

Felicity grabbed her hand, pleading. "What do we do?" she whispered desperately.

Perpetua squeezed back, her shoulders bowed under fear's crushing weight, until a pulse of divine resolve steadied her—raw and unyielding. It surged within, a strength not her own. The words came, just two of them: "We trust."

It was enough.

Even in the valley of death, Lord, You're all I need.

Perpetua's words hung in the air, a faint spark against the despair. She looked at Marcus, then Felicity, Lucius, and Mago—their faces dim but dear, bound by nights of shared bread and whispered hopes. Her spirit stirred, heavy with love. *We're not broken yet, Lord.*

She slid nearer to Felicity. "Let's pray."

Reaching for her friend's hand, their fingers tightened together.

Perpetua turned to Marcus, his head still low.

"Brother," she called, softly but firmly. He lifted his gaze, shame fading in the torchlight. Lucius paused his muttering, his gray eyes catching hers—a nod passing like a vow. Mago smiled, his expression urging her on.

A reverent hush washed over the cold cell as Perpetua drew a deep breath. "Our God sees us," she began, meeting the weary look of each one of them. "He's here, even now."

She bowed her head, and memory flooded in—not of her son this time, but of hours spent in prayer and study with her spiritual family. The laughter, the tears, the questions, the soul-sharpening debates. They'd sung psalms together, voices rough but true, promising to stand for Christ.

"Lord," she prayed, "You walked the dust, bore the whip, faced the cross. You know this place—its stink, its pain. Hold us, Jesus." Her voice rose, thin but fierce, like a hymn cutting the night.

Felicity's grip shook, but she murmured, "Amen," her breath steadying.

Marcus' shoulders eased, his whisper joining—"Lord, forgive."

Lucius' hands unclenched, his prayer blending in, "Strength, O God."

Mago's voice came last, soft as a breeze. "Your will, Lord, always."

The cell felt less heavy, the air less thick, as if their words carved space for hope. Perpetua looked at her friends, their faces clearer, etched with a fire kindled anew. *We're still Yours.* Her heart swelled, dread loosening its hold.

She saw the young man in the corner, his cough quieter, watching them with a curious expression. The scarred man's pacing slowed, as if their prayer touched even him. The wild woman's sobbing relented.

Perpetua's chest ached, not with panic but with love. They weren't just prisoners. They were brothers and sisters now, bound by a truth stronger than stone. *They overcame by the blood of the Lamb, and by their testimony.* She felt it—a certainty no beast could steal.

We'll stand, Lord. Together. Whatever comes.

The moment held, fragile but real, a flicker of eternity in the gloom. Perpetua squeezed Felicity's hand, nodding to Marcus, Lucius, and Mago.

Their eyes met with a silent oath. *We're not alone.*

The cell's stench lingered, and the shackles still rubbed, but something had shifted—a warmth no cold could quench. They were ready—not fearless, but faithful—for whatever dawn would bring.

CHAPTER 2
THE ARENA

Night dragged slowly, shadows twisting under the faint flicker of the torch. Perpetua prayed, her whisper raw and trembling. *Lord, give me strength.* Her pulse beat like a drum. At times, terror gripped her, but she pressed on, palms flat against the floor. *Courage, God—please.* She saw her son's face—his tiny hands grabbing her hair—and tears burned. *Keep him safe, Jesus.* She prayed for Felicity, her baby's fragile life, for Lucius' old bones, Marcus' broken spirit, for protection over Mago's steady calm. *Hold us, Lord.* The words spilled, a plea for faith to stand, to face the arena without shame. *I'm Yours—make me ready.*

Hours bled away, her voice hoarse, knees numb. She prayed for Rome's blind crowd, for guards with hard eyes, even the beasts waiting to tear. *Show them You, God.* Her lips moved, psalms rising—*The Lord is my shepherd*—soft, like a hymn, binding her to hope. *Don't leave me, Jesus.* Fear gnawed, but faith held—a thin flame in the dark. She felt Him—distant, but there—His cross a promise she clung to.

As night waned, a strange quiet fell over the room. The wild woman's wails, the scarred man's curses, the young man's cough—they all faded. Perpetua glanced up, eyes burning with exhaustion. Felicity slumped, head on her knees, breathing slowly. Lucius leaned back, tension released. Marcus' big frame sagged, lids shut, shame softened. Mago rested, his expression serene. Even the strangers slept, fear drowned by fatigue just before dawn. *You gave them rest, Lord,* she praised.

Perpetua's lids grew heavy as exhaustion pulled at her, sudden and deep. Dreams swirled—vague yet sharp with meaning. Teeth flashed, lion's jaws dripping red, snapping close. Claws raked air, heavy with death. Swords gleamed, cold steel slicing shadows. Her son's cry pierced, and his hands were torn from hers before fading into mist. Images churned, chaotic, like paint spilled on canvas. Crimson sand, a cross glowing in the distance, a voice she couldn't catch. *What's this, Lord?* The dreams felt heavy, pointing somewhere—truth, maybe—but also strange, tangled—leaving her gasping. She stirred, the cell's chill snapping her back, heart racing, meaning just out of reach.

Suddenly, the door crashed open with a thunderous clang. Torchlight spilled into the cell like a jagged wound, stark and blinding after hours in shadow. Three guards stormed the cell, armor clanking, faces etched with scorn. The prisoners jerked awake—some whimpering, others stiff with terror.

The lead guard roared, "Up, you filth! Time to face your reckoning!" His boots kicked up straw as he seized Lucius by the arm, wrenching his aching old frame upright.

Perpetua pushed herself to her feet, shackles dragging with a mournful clink, her legs trembling from the cold stone. *It's here. God, it's here.*

Felicity struggled beside her, dark skin slick with sweat, panicked hands clutching her swollen belly, face ashen. "Perpetua, I can't—" she gasped, but a guard silenced her with a rough yank, hauling her up.

Marcus staggered to his feet, quaking with fright. Mago rose quietly and stretched as if it were just another morning. In contrast, the wild woman clawed at the floor like a trapped beast. A guard kicked her forward, her cries bouncing off the damp walls. A fourth guard, younger, appeared near the door, holding his spear loosely, a confused expression on his face.

With brutal hands, the guards shoved the prisoners into a ragged line, driving them from the cell—all but the young one, who trailed behind, as if reluctant to follow. The corridor extended before them, narrow and grim, its stones slick from the damp air. In the distance, an ominous sound grew—the swelling clamor of a bloodthirsty crowd. The prisoners stumbled forward, spear tips jabbing at their backs. Perpetua's shackles scraped with each movement, her wrists raw and stinging.

The lead guard, a pockmarked brute with a greasy beard, struck Lucius' shoulder with a dull thud.

"Move, old fool!" he snarled, a cruel glare glinting under his dented helm.

Lucius grunted, his old knees buckling, but he bit back a cry.

Perpetua's heart raced. *Hold him, God.*

The guard laughed—a harsh bark—his meaty hand shoving Lucius again.

Felicity gasped, steps faltering, her face gray with pain. A second guard, lean and wiry, grabbed her arm, his nails digging into her skin.

"Keep up, sow!" he spat, breath sour, teeth yellow and jagged.

He yanked her forward, careless of her trembling frame. She whimpered with terror. Perpetua reached for her, but the guard's spear jabbed close, its tip grazing her side, sharp and cold. *Lord, shield her.*

Marcus' big frame hunched, heaving with ragged breath. The third guard, squat and bald, cracked his whip—the lash snapping near Marcus' ear with a vicious crack.

"Coward!" he roared, thick with scorn, his small eyes squinting with delight.

Marcus flinched, a low groan escaping, shame burning his cheeks red. The whip snapped again, grazing his back.

Perpetua's stomach knotted. *Give him courage, Jesus.*

Mago walked steadily, head high, but the lead guard swung his boot—kicking him in the leg with a thud.

"Wipe that smirk off your face, blondie!" he growled, spit flecking his beard.

Mago staggered, catching himself, gaze fixed ahead. The guard cursed and raised his fist, but Mago's courage held—quiet and sure.

He's Yours, Lord, Perpetua prayed, awe threading through fear at her friend's steady defiance.

The wild woman's wails grew shrill, her hands clawing desperately at the stone. The wiry guard kicked her ribs—a sickening crunch—his cackle high and cruel. "Scream louder, hag!" he jeered.

The fourth guard continued to trail behind, looking uneasy. His helm sat crooked, too big for his head, and his lips pressed tightly with apprehension. Perpetua caught his glance. *He sees us, Lord.*

They emerged in a holding area—a cramped cage of splintered wood and rusted iron. Through the slats, the ragged prisoners glimpsed their final destination: a colossal stone bowl rising tier upon tier, packed with thousands of faces, their cheers a thunder that shook the ground.

The arena floor stretched vast and unforgiving, its sand marred with uneven stains, raked but not cleansed of gore. Towering columns flanked the rim of the bowl, carved with images of emperors and gods. Across the expanse, an iron gate loomed, its jagged teeth glinting with menace. The spectacle was breathtaking—its grandeur almost divine— yet the air pulsed with a corruption that twisted the beauty into something grotesque.

Perpetua stared, breath shallow, her features tight with dread. *I can't stop this!*

Felicity pressed close, grasping her hand. Marcus stood still, mouth agape, eyes wide with dread. Mago tilted his head, taking it all in with indomitable silence.

A horn pierced the air with a sharp, commanding blast, and the gate—the final shield between them and their inevitable doom— groaned mournfully on its hinges as it swung wide.

The guards shoved them forward, out of the holding area and onto the sand. The heat struck first—a blazing sun searing their skin— followed by the noise, a wall of sound crashing over them like a tidal wave. Faces leered from the stands, jeering, laughing, some hurling scraps of bread that bounced off the sand.

Perpetua stumbled, catching herself with a shaky step, her gaze sweeping the chaos.

They're here for our blood!

Cages rattled along the arena's perimeter, snarls and growls spilling out—lions, bears—something bigger. The restless pacing of the beasts rumbled beneath the frenzy of the crowd.

The guards herded them to the center of the arena where, on some unspoken cue, a man in a purple tunic strode forward, raising his arms, silencing the crowd with a sweeping gesture.

"Citizens of Rome!" he bellowed, his voice rich with pride and scorn. "Today, we gather in the shadow of our eternal empire, beneath the gaze of our divine Emperor Septimius Severus, whose birthday we honor with blood and spectacle! Behold these wretches—traitors, blasphemers, deniers of our sacred gods! They spurn Jupiter's altars, mock Mars's might, and reject the emperor's divine favor, choosing a crucified man from a distant province. Their insolence stains our honor, and their rebellion threatens our peace. For this, they face justice, swift and unyielding—a lesson to all who dare defy Rome's glory. Let beasts and blades purge this filth, let their screams echo as a song to our power, and may their deaths bring joy to our people and reverence to our ruler!"

The crowd erupted—a deafening roar that shook the stands.

Perpetua's group tightened together, a fragile knot of five against the vastness. *We're nothing here, Lord. But we're Yours.* She glanced at Felicity, her face streaked with tears, hands still clutching her belly. The young guard lingered on the perimeter, face pale, cheeks glistening—a silent mourner amid the chaos.

Suddenly, the first cage swung open, and a lion burst forth, its eyes glinting with feral hunger. The crowd howled as it prowled, muscles rippling under its tawny coat, pacing toward them with menace. Lucius stepped forward, his voice rising above the din.

"The Lord is my strength!" he shouted, fists clenched, his elderly frame trembling but defiant, just as it had been in the market under heavy loads.

The beast lunged. A blur of gold and teeth slammed Lucius to the sand with a sickening thud. His scream cut off as claws raked his chest, blood spraying in a vivid arc, soaking the ground red. The cheers of the crowd drowned out his last breath.

Perpetua flinched, her stomach turning. *He's gone—my brother who shared bread and psalms.*

A second gate rattled open, and an enormous brown bear lumbered out, its growl low and guttural, a hulking mass of fur and fury. It moved first toward Lucius' lifeless body, threatening to steal the lion's kill. The lion snarled, springing to defend its prize, and the beasts clashed—claws swiping and teeth bared.

The bear retreated, thwarted, its dark intent swinging back toward the group. It charged Marcus, massive paws slashing through the air. Marcus screamed as he was struck, his thick chest caving under the blow with a crack of bone. He crumpled to the ground in a broken heap, blood pooling fast. The bear bit his shoulder violently and dragged his body away, unwilling to share its prize with the lion.

Perpetua's head swirled. *Marcus—my gentle giant, who asked for grace.*

Felicity grabbed Perpetua's hand, desperate fingers digging in. "I don't want to die like this," she sobbed, belly heaving.

Before Perpetua could answer, a guard shoved Felicity forward, laughing cruelly. "A fitting end for the expectant mother!" he sneered, his face a twisted mask.

A third cage sprang open, and a leopard leapt free, sleek and deadly, its spotted coat glinting in the sun. It circled Felicity, tail flicking, then pounced. Its claws tore into her side as its jaws clamped her throat. She fell hard, a dark halo seeping into the sand beneath her, failing hands still grasping her unborn child as life faded.

Perpetua choked on a sob. *Fel—my shadow—my sister.*

The wild woman snapped, her cry a piercing shriek. "You've forsaken us, God!"

She bolted, legs pumping, sand kicking up as she sprinted for the arena's edge. A guard cursed, hurling his spear. The shaft whistled, striking her back with a thud. She staggered, a guttural wail ripping from her throat, her arms flailing as she collapsed face-down. Crimson bloomed around the spear's tip, staining the sand red, and the crowd laughed, a cruel cackle of malevolence.

A sharp blare split the air—not quite a trumpet, but a raw, bone-shaking bellow of rage. An elephant thundered from a hidden gate, massive, its gray hide cracked like dry earth and tusks gleaming wickedly. Its trunk curled, eyes wild, as its legs pounded the sand into clouds. The lion snarled, leaping aside. The bear lumbered back, their growls drowned out by the beast's piercing rage. The crowd gasped, then cheered with delight.

The elephant charged straight for the gaunt young man and the scarred rebel, cutting them from Perpetua and Mago like a wall of wrath.

Lord, no! Perpetua prayed, choking on dread.

The young man stumbled and fell, his face frozen in terror. The elephant's foot slammed down, crushing his chest with a sickening snap, his body shattering like a broken doll beneath unimaginable weight. The scarred man turned to face his doom, fists raised in hot defiance. The beast swung its trunk, smashing his skull with a wet crunch.

With gruesome violence, the rabid elephant crushed him, flinging his twisted body across the arena as a man might throw a small stone. *God, receive them!* The elephant trumpeted, then wheeled away, leaving death and gore in its wake.

The stands thundered with the echoing approval of the crowd, their revelry washing over the carnage like a relentless tide.

Only Perpetua and Mago remained, standing close, the sand slick beneath their feet.

Mago looked at her, calm and unshaken, even now. "It's almost over," he smiled gently, his voice steady with divine resolve.

A final gate screeched open, and two gladiators marched out, their swords gleaming like ice, their armor cold and unyielding under the sun.

23

Mago faced them first, chin high, his stance resolute. "Christ is my king." His words rang clear—a challenge to the roaring mob.

A gladiator advanced, his sword slashing in a brutal, downward arc. Mago twisted, raising an arm to shield himself, but the blade hacked through flesh and bone, slicing deep into his side. Blood gushed as he grunted, staggering back. Mago's left arm lay severed in the sand, his rib cage slashed open. He looked from his gaping wound to the gladiator, then spoke, his voice steady despite the pain. "You can know Him too," he declared. "God's grace is yours; find it in Jesus."

The gladiator thrust again—a fierce strike to the chest. The blade plunged in, twisting. Mago dropped, his knees buckling, sand puffing around him. Blood pooled, a dark mirror on the sand.

Perpetua's pulse raced, breath shallow. *Mago—my rock, who saw this coming.*

The second gladiator turned to her, his face a mask of duty.

The crowd chanted, "Kill! Kill!" in rhythmic savagery. He hefted his sword, its edge catching the light.

Perpetua straightened, her voice trembling but clear. "Jesus, I'm coming," she shouted, lifting her chin in a posture of acceptance and resolve.

This is it, Lord. I'm Yours.

Her gaze drifted past the gladiator, locking on the eyes of the young guard still watching in horror from the arena's edge. In that breathless moment, something passed between them—a shared thread of humanity amid the brutality.

He sees me. Lord, draw him to Yourself!

The gladiator lunged, sword slashing down. Pain erupted—white-hot, searing, ripping through her neck as the blade bit deep. Blood spurted, splashing her chest as she gasped, a choked cry tearing from her throat. She clawed at the air, legs buckling as the gladiator twisted the blade deeper.

The crowd's thunderous applause faded to a distant hum, her vision blurring at the edges. A faint pulse stirred within, beyond the pain. Even as her body convulsed on the sand, peace washed over her, soft and warm, wrapping around the agony like a gentle hand.

It burns, but I'm not alone.

Her sight dimmed, then went black, and the world slipped away. Blackness swallowed her, thick and absolute. Silence fell like a heavy curtain.

Then—a shift.

Her body was gone, the pain a faint echo, but she was still here, still somewhere!

A new sense of awareness bloomed, light and unfamiliar. She felt herself moving, not walking exactly, but drawn forward through a vast, black tunnel. Ahead, a light glowed—small at first, a pinprick in the void, then growing, warm and alive, whispering with a quiet promise that tugged at her soul.

Her consciousness sharpened—wonder threading through her like a golden strand.

This isn't the end. It's the beginning.

The light swelled around her, bright and boundless, filling the tunnel with a radiance that felt safe...like home! She leaned into it, the darkness falling away behind her, the tunnel dissolving into memory.

Peace and light washed over her, all-consuming. Whatever lay ahead, she was ready.

CHAPTER 3
THE GLORY

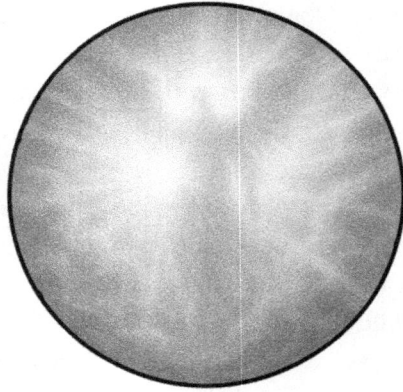

H er body lay broken on the arena floor, a lifeless heap amid the churned sand, her blood pooling dark and still beneath the gladiator's blade. The crowd's roar lingered, a fading echo of Rome's cruelty, but it could not touch her now. Perpetua was gone from that place, her flesh a discarded husk, her soul alive, soaring—drawn irresistibly toward a light that beckoned with promise. The tunnel of blackness stretched behind her, its cold weight unraveling like a dream. Ahead, a dazzling pulse drew near, warm, alive, calling her forward with a gentle pull. *I'm here, Lord.*

Peace enveloped her, soft as a loving embrace yet vast as the heavens themselves. It was not the fleeting calm of a quiet moment, but a living wholeness, a tide that washed away the sting of chains, the sear of the sword, the screams of her brothers and sisters. The darkness of the tunnel frayed, its edges dissolving like mist before dawn, and the light swelled all around—marvelous, boundless. It wasn't merely light, but a Presence, holy and transcendent, a splendor that hummed with the heartbeat of eternity. *Shekinah*, she thought, the word rising unbidden, a whisper from psalms sung in secret. The glory of God Himself.

The darkness fell away completely, like a curtain torn aside, and she stood—or floated, or simply was—in a realm glimmering with splendor. The light was not a fog, yet it moved like fog, swirling, shifting, alive with flashes of color she could not name. Sapphire bled into gold, crimson danced with emerald, every hue shimmering beyond the spectrum of Earth, each throbbing with a melody she could feel in her soul. Her senses sharpened, heightened beyond mortal limits, as if she tasted the warmth, heard the colors, saw the song of creation itself. *I can't describe this. Words are too small!* Yet the glory was no mere spectacle; it was a Presence that knew her, held her, loved her with an intimacy that pierced to the core. It was holy, yet tender, folding her into its embrace like a child returned home.

She was weightless, yet grounded, her consciousness blooming into something new—a clarity she had never known. The pain of the arena, the grief of Lucius' fall, Felicity's cry, Mago's blood—all were echoes, faint and distant, unable to penetrate the wholeness that now clothed her. *I'm not broken anymore. I'm whole—more than whole.*

Amazingly, the light pulsed even brighter, its beam so intense it should have blinded her, yet her new sight drank it in, unburned, unbowed. It was not a thing to be seen, but a Being to be known, the Source of all that was good and true. *Lord, is this You?*

Suddenly, through the heavenly mist, an immense shape emerged, passing through the light like a breeze through flame. It drew near, vast and beaming, its form both solid and fluid, a paradox of power and grace. Perpetua's breath—if she still breathed—caught in awe. It was unlike anything she had ever seen, towering yet gentle, its essence a thunder of holiness that echoed through the atmosphere. Its form shimmered, not flesh or metal, but light woven into being, swirling like fire yet not fire, a cascade of brilliance that defied her understanding. Wings—massive and sweeping—unfurled from its back, not feathered or scaled, but forged of light's own essence, their edges rippling with sparks that sang as they moved. Eyes gleamed within its face, countless yet one, seeing through to the core of her being.

Overwhelmed, Perpetua fell to her knees—or what felt like knees—in a surge of worship. *This must be God!* Before she could bow lower, a voice rang out, clear as a bell, deep as a mountain's root, yet gentle as a whisper.

"Rise, daughter of the Most High." The words reverberated within her, each syllable a chord of truth. "Do not worship me. I am sent by He who sits on the throne, the Alpha and Omega, to guide you through this dawn of eternity."

She looked up, trembling, not with fear, but with wonder. No anxiety existed here—only awe.

"Are you...an angel?" she asked, her voice feeling small in the vastness.

The being tilted its head, eyes sparkling like stars reflecting off moving water. "I am what my Maker formed me to be," it replied, a trace of mirth in its tone. "But yes, you might call me an angel, for that is a name your heart knows."

Perpetua stared in astonishment, for the angel was a marvel beyond words. Its presence glowed like star-forged crystal, sharp-edged yet fluid—like a dawn-soaked sea frozen mid-surge. It was radiant, as if eternity's breath had shaped it—for indeed it had. Its frame loomed, colossal and mysterious, its shoulders carved like cliffs smoothed by sacred winds. She felt safe in its presence, wrapped in a haven where dread dissolved. Yet beneath the angel's calm, a fire lurked—terrible and fierce—a storm's wrath coiled tightly, ready to shatter God's foes with a glance. Its visage could strike terror in the bravest devil's heart, yet the smallest child could play without fear in its shadow. Its hands—if indeed they could be called hands—moved gracefully, yet held the strength to crush darkness.

It's awesome, she gasped, paralyzed in amazement.

The angel studied her, its regal face lined with interest. "What do you see, daughter?"

For a moment, Perpetua struggled to find words. Nothing in her vocabulary seemed sufficient. "In you...I...I see the artistry of God Himself." Her voice was raw, spellbound.

The angel paused, its many eyes sparkling like a reservoir of insight, as though it had spent long ages contemplating the depths of divine wisdom. When it spoke, reverence gripped its mighty tone. "I see that same divine artistry in you, Perpetua. You are precious to the Lord of Hosts. That is why you are here, and why I accompany you now."

Pure joy swept across her face. "You know my name, but what's yours?"

"I am Neriah," it answered with a boom, the name resonating like a note struck on crystal, its meaning—*light of the Lord*—blooming in her mind unbidden. "I am here to guide you, Perpetua. For your soul has crossed the veil, and this new realm is vast beyond your current vision."

She stood—or rose, or simply became upright—her gaze fixed on Neriah's brilliant form. The Presence, the *Shekinah*, shone fiercely about them, an atmosphere so intense it pressed against her senses, yet lifted her into rapturous joy. She tried to see through it, to grasp the shapes or borders of this place, but her sight faltered—not from weakness, but from newness. *It's too much—too grand! My eyes aren't ready.*

Neriah's countenance softened, as if discerning her struggle. "You are like a child newly born," the angel empathized. "When an infant leaves the womb, its sight is dim, its mind unformed to the world's expanse. So it is with you now, born anew into the Kingdom of God. The glory you see—the Presence of the Almighty—is your new air, your new truth. Your soul must adjust, as eyes to light, as lungs to breath. I am here to walk with you until you see clearly."

"Where are we going?"

"To the River of Life." Neriah gestured ahead. "It flows from the throne of God and of the Lamb, a crystal stream that washes away the old and ushers in the new. When you cross its waters, the last shadow of The Choosing Ground will fade, and your sight will be clear, your soul fully one with Him who made you."

Perpetua tilted her head, eyes flaring with interest. "The Choosing Ground?"

Neriah's form pulsed softly as it spoke. "It is the place you call 'Earth'—a sacred stage crafted by the Creator. There, each soul faces a choice: to reject the ruinous path of Adam and Eve and choose life, or to persist in rebellion and defy their Maker's love."

Perpetua's spirit stirred. "Earth—a choosing ground?"

"Yes, daughter. It's a sacred space, a fleeting season of decision—brief enough to spare humanity the endless toil of mortality, yet long enough for hearts to make their choice. Many squander their days battling over empires or chasing pleasures. But The Choosing Ground was never intended for eating, drinking, or simply being merry. Its true purpose is far greater—and more urgent. While mortal bodies decay, the souls of mankind are eternal. The Choosing Ground offers each one the opportunity to reconnect with their Maker—or persist in defiance. The death of the body is not the end of existence; it's the finish line of decision, sealing the soul's choice forever."

Neriah fell silent, its form tensing, as if roused by ancient and shadowed memory. Perpetua's gaze sharpened, her breath catching as she noticed, for the first time, the battle-worn armor cloaked beneath the angel's quiet presence. Formidable plates, scarred by countless nicks, now pulsed with a silvered glow. The marks raised no alarm of danger, but praise for complete victory.

Neriah continued speaking, rumbling in a low, serious tone. "A primeval enemy—dark and cunning—weaves lies to lure souls toward destruction, promising empty joys. Sinister and beautiful, this adversary sets traps of deception, seducing the weak and flattering the proud, wielding despair and selfishness with cruel precision."

The angel's voice lifted, its words swelling into a boast of pure joy—almost laughter. "But the Creator is relentless, Perpetua, never forsaking His own." Neriah's eyes danced with holy mischief, its armor fading again beneath a cloak of triumphant light. "God sent His Word to reveal truth, His Son to forge a path to life, and His Spirit to awaken and empower. Even creation itself—sunsets, seas, whispering winds—testify to His glory. Every soul matters to Him, Perpetua. The

Choosing Ground is His gift, a divine invitation to cast away darkness and choose differently than Adam and Eve."

Perpetua marveled as the revelation sank in. She had lived and died on Earth, yet never grasped its purpose so clearly. Memories washed over her in a rush. She recalled the internal tug-of-war she had sensed throughout much of life—the pull toward what was right against the lure of what was easy. Voices of fear had breathed despair into her weakest moments, and false promises had beckoned her to trade faithful conviction for the world's acceptance. Yet through every temptation and trembling breath, another Voice had called her by name. Jesus whispered courage when doubt pressed in. And the Holy Spirit never gave up on her—steadfastly drawing her into the embrace of her Heavenly Father.

This truth redefined everything. Earth wasn't about mortal survival or fulfilling temporal dreams. It was a hallowed stage where every moment offered the opportunity to choose an eternity with God—or one apart from Him—a battleground where each soul determined their allegiance.

"I never knew," she whispered in awe. "Every heartbeat, every trial —even the pain—it was all to awaken me, to call me toward life."

"Yes, daughter. The hardships and temptations inherent on The Choosing Ground reveal the heart's true devotion. But God's love is relentless—chasing each soul with mercy. You chose life, and here you stand, on the threshold of His fullness. When you cross the river, its waters will seal your union with the One who made you."

Perpetua's heart blazed with fresh clarity. *A gift—a choice—a road home—He wove it all for us.*

"Lead on," she beamed, eager for the river's embrace.

Neriah turned, its form glistening as it moved. Perpetua followed, her soul drawn forward as naturally as breath, the glory parting around them like a living veil. The Presence palpitated stronger now— filling her with a joy that felt like flight. As they moved, she sensed the edges of this realm teasing her vision—shapes and sounds flickering through the light, still too vibrant for her new sight to hold.

A breeze stirred, not wind but something deeper, carrying the rush of water, the sigh of leaves, the hum of voices lifted in song. Through the swirling mist, she glimpsed hints of form—trees, their branches heavy with fruit that sparkled like jewels; mountains, their peaks piercing a sky that was no sky but light itself; a towering wall in the distance, shimmering with colors that danced like flame. Yet these were mere shadows of truth, outlines her soul could not yet grasp—like a dream half-remembered.

"Do you see it, Neriah?" Her voice trembled with excitement. "The shapes, the sounds?"

"I see all," the angel stated matter-of-factly. "But you see as through a glass darkly, as your apostle wrote. The wall is a band of light, cradling the fullness of His Kingdom, where all who love Him will gather. The mountains sing His praise, the trees bear His fruit, the voices rise to His throne. In time, your sight will sharpen, and you will walk its paths, taste its bounty, join its song."

"When?" Perpetua wasn't impatient, but eager, her soul hungry for more.

"When you cross the river," Neriah answered. "Its waters are life, flowing from the throne, clear as crystal, pure as His love. It will wash away the last veil—the fears, the pains, the half-seen truths—and you will see Him as He is."

Her spirit surged, a tide of longing. *To see You, Lord—not in part, but face to face!*

"How far is it?" Her new eyes searched the mist, seeking the river's gleam.

"Not far. Distance here is not as you knew it. Your soul moves by desire, by love, and your love for Him draws you swiftly."

They moved on, the glory dancing around them, its colors swirling in patterns that felt like worship—crimson for sacrifice, gold for divinity, white for purity—each hue a note in a symphony she could almost sing. The sounds grew clearer now, weaving through the light: the rush of water, steady and strong; the rustle of leaves, a whisper of promise; voices, countless yet one, lifting a chorus of "Holy, holy, holy" that trembled her soul.

I know that song. We sang it in the cell, in the dark. Now, it's alive!

33

She turned to Neriah. "Do they all sing? Lucius, Felicity, Mago—are they here, praising Him?"

"All who love Him are here, Perpetua, their voices joined in the everlasting hymn. Your brothers and sisters rest in His presence, their wounds healed, their joy complete. You will see them, when the time is ripe, beyond the river's flow."

Her throat tightened, not with sorrow, but with a fullness too vast for tears. *They're here—whole. Thank You, Lord.*

"And the guard?" The young one's face flashed in her mind, his look heavy with sorrow. "The one who watched—will he find this place?"

Neriah's tone softened, a note of hope. "His soul was moved, even in the arena's shadow. The One who sees all knows his path. Pray for him, Perpetua, as you did in life. Your prayers rise like incense, and grace pursues those who seek."

She nodded, lifting a silent plea. *Draw him, Lord. Let him see Your goodness.* The act felt natural—as if prayer was her breath now, woven into her being.

The glory pulsed brighter, the sounds swelling as they drew near the river. Its rush was louder now, a melody of power and peace. Through the light, she glimpsed its edge—a ribbon of crystal, sparkling, radiant, as if the presence of God poured through its current, as indeed it did.

I'm almost there. Her heart raced with joy. *The old is fading. The new is so close!*

Neriah stopped abruptly. "Here is the River of Life."

The bank of the river sloped gently, covered with soft white stones. "Step into its flow, Perpetua. Let it carry you to Him who waits."

She peered into the water—its clarity a mirror of truth, its movement a dance of immortality. No fear touched her soul—only awe and a longing so deep it burned. *This is it—the end of the veil, the start of forever.*

She turned to Neriah, moved with gratitude. "You brought me here. Thank you, Neriah—light of the Lord."

The angel's form shimmered; its eyes warm as a hearth. "I am but a servant. The One who sent me is your true Guide. Go now, daughter. Cross the river, and see."

She stepped forward, the glory parting like a curtain, the river's song filling her ears. The water lapped at her feet—or what felt like feet—cool yet warm, alive with a touch that tingled her soul. *It's not water. It's life!*

She waded deeper, the current gentle yet strong, tugging her forward with love's own pull. Light swirled around her, brighter now, the colors blending into a white so pure it sang of Him. Her vision sharpened, the shapes beyond the river teasing her sight—forests stretching toward a boundless horizon, a band of brilliant color rising like a flame, their promise vast and near. *I'm coming, Lord!*

Halfway across the river, she pause, the water surging to her waist, its flow washing away the last whispers of Earth—the arena's sting, the blade's bite, the heartache of loss. They were nothing now, shadows burned away by glory. *I'm new!*

She turned, glancing back at Neriah, who stood on the bank, a sentinel of light.

"Goodbye, Neriah," she called out, waving in a gesture of thanks and love.

Neriah's wings stirred—a final ripple of light. "Not goodbye," it called back. "We meet again, in His presence, where all are one."

She smiled, her heart full, and turned back to the river. The current beckoned, and she stepped deeper, letting it carry her forward. The light swallowed her, not blinding but embracing, and she knew—knew with every fiber of her being—that she had come home.

CHAPTER 4
THE GATE

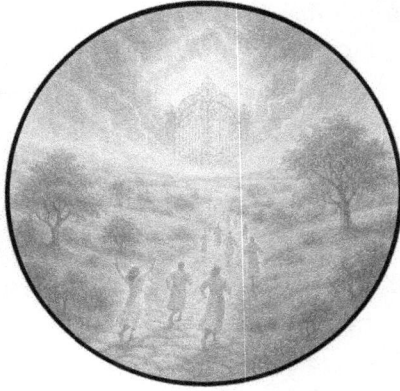

The River of Life surged around Perpetua, its crystal tide rising past her waist, her chest, her shoulders. She surrendered to its pull, letting the current draw her deeper until it closed over her head, submerging her wholly in its living flow. No breath faltered; no panic stirred. She was not drowning but being reborn. The water—that was not water but life itself—coursed through her, scouring away the last shadow of Earth's pain. The arena's blood, the blade's sting, life's heartaches dissolved like ash in a flame, leaving her fresh, vibrant, whole.

She emerged—not stepping but rising—as if the river itself lifted her to its bank. Her sight, once dimmed by mortality, now burned clear, sharp with a vision that drank in eternity. A horn sounded within her, its warm tones resonating like a divine summons. She felt a shift, as if her spirit had rejoined a body, now perfected, free of corruption, unbound by earthly limits. She longed to consider herself more closely, but the wonders around were too exhilarating to pause.

Before her stretched a landscape of unimaginable bounty. Fields rolled like waves of light, trees swayed with fruit twinkling like stars— each blade and branch alive with God's splendor.

She tilted her gaze upward, and there it was: a luminescent wall soaring skyward, lightning flashing within it like a storm of color in a crystal cloud. At its center stood a majestic golden gate, its surface gleaming with a warmth that beckoned her heart, tall as a mountain's peak, its edges etched with patterns of resounding grace.

A path wound from the river's edge to the gate—a ribbon of smooth cobblestone peppered with figures—travelers, countless yet distinct, each moving toward the same promise. Some ran, their laughter ringing out like children at play, their movements a dance of joy. Others walked slowly, faces lifted, tears of joy blessing cheeks bright with awe. No shadow touched their steps—only anticipation, a shared longing that tugged at Perpetua's soul. *We're kindred spirits— called, chosen, free in Him!*

She moved forward, her heart racing with excitement. The air hummed with happy voices and rustling leaves, all woven into a gentle song that whispered, "Holy, holy, holy."

Turning onto the path, she brushed against a blossoming shrub, and a strange warmth kindled within her, a curious sensation she couldn't yet understand.

Some nearby travelers drew her attention. They looked human enough—flesh and bone in appearance, yet beaming with spiritual sheen, all mortality washed away. Technically, they were strangers, yet instinctively she claimed them as family, their shared laughter binding them as one.

The garments they wore intrigued her—not robes but seals of light, unique to each soul. One was a mantle of red and gold, rippling like flame. Another bore a cloak of sky blue, glistening like dew. A third's raiment swirled like white snow, not covering impurity but revealing goodness—all woven by the hand of God Himself.

It's their faith, their story, their love for the Lamb!

Perpetua looked down, gasping at her own form clad in pearl and gold, flowing like water, a mirror of her sacrifice. She touched the fabric—or whatever it was. Its warmth pulsed like a heartbeat.

The beauty of it all was overwhelming—filling her soul to bursting. As she joined the throng, an old proverb surged within her: *Joy is not complete until it is shared.* Alone, Heaven's marvels were a gift beyond words. But now, surrounded by these travelers—strangers yet family— it multiplied, as if their elation wove with hers into a greater tapestry. *They're mine. My heart knows them!*

"Do you feel it?" Perpetua asked, turning to a woman near her.

The woman's face glowed with euphoria, her seal a swirl of purple and cream. "I do feel it."

The woman's words flowed in a language unfamiliar to Perpetua— yet their meaning bloomed clear in her heart. She flashed back to Carthage—to catechism lessons on the gift of interpreting tongues. *Does everyone here share this gift?*

The woman continued, "We're all connected in spirit. It's Him I think—in us and through us. We are one here, bound by His love."

Perpetua laughed—freer than she'd ever felt. "What's your name?"

"Miriam," the woman chimed. "And you, sister?"

"I'm Perpetua."

Strangely, her own name sounded new, as if polished by the river's touch. "The gate—what happens there?"

Miriam gazed toward the golden portal. "It's the Judgment," she answered, with no hint of concern in her tone. "Not the wrath we feared, but a welcome—a reckoning of His grace. The Lamb paid our price, and He affirms our love, our faith, opening the way to His King- dom. It's a celebration, Perpetua, a song of 'Well done.'"

Her heart leapt—Matthew's parable echoing in her soul. *I'm ready, Lord. Yours always!*

Perpetua walked faster, her steps light as a breeze, weaving through travelers. Some nodded—their smiles a shared secret; others clasped her hands in celebration. *We're all His—my family in faith!*

A man on the edge of the path drew her attention. He was tall, his seal a cascade of blue and gold—shimmering like a river under starlight. His face was lined yet youthful, as if age had touched him—and withdrawn in defeat. He walked slowly, eyes tracing the wall's flashes and flares, tears of thanksgiving glistening on his cheeks.

She slowed her pace, drawn to his quiet awe, soul stirred with a strange familiarity.

"Brother," she called gently, "may I walk with you?"

He turned to greet her, his expression kind—like a shepherd tending his flock. "Gladly." His voice was accented with a cadence she couldn't place. "I'm Thomas. And you?"

"Perpetua." She fell into step beside him. "This place—it's more than I dreamed. Are you...from Rome, like me?"

Thomas laughed, a sound rich with delight. "No, not Rome. A place called Chicago, long after your time. But here, it's all one, isn't it?"

"Chicago?" she echoed, her brow lifted in curiosity. The word was a riddle—foreign yet intriguing. "How did you come here, Thomas?"

His face softened, a shadow of memory passing across it, yet no pain lingered. "A car accident," he stated flatly. "Metal and glass, moving too fast. One moment I was driving, the next—here. No pain, no sorrow. I'm still trying to wrap my mind around it. How about you?"

Confusion swirled in her mind. "Car?" The word was clumsy on her tongue. "A chariot?"

Thomas chuckled, not mocking but warm, like a brother explaining a mystery. "No chariot, Perpetua. A machine, from my time—wheels, engine, speed. But it doesn't matter now. You died in Rome, didn't you? How?"

She nodded, the arena faint as a dream. "A gladiator's sword, for Christ's name. But it led me here."

His hand rested on her shoulder, a bond forged in faith. "Brave sister," he murmured softly. "My death was quick, yours fierce. Yet we're both here, standing in His splendor."

"But your time—" she pressed, her mind grappling with the mystery. "You speak of machines, places I don't know. Is your world so different?"

Thomas paused, his face gleaming with truth. "It is, and it isn't. On The Choosing Ground, time flows like a river, one moment after another. But here, Perpetua—on this side of the veil—time is not as we once knew it. Past, present, future—they overlay, happening at once. Heaven holds all moments, like a song where every note sounds together. Our Great Father exists apart from the constraints of time, as does His home—now our home."

He smiled, continuing, "Your Rome, my Chicago—they're threads in His tapestry, all woven together. Clearly, time or waiting exists here in some fashion, but not as it does on The Choosing Ground. There's a big difference between things happening in His timing versus things happening under the governance of a twenty-four-hour clock or a lunar year."

Thomas paused again, thoughtful. "Earthly theologians might interpret Scripture closer to God's intention—especially eschatology and divine foreknowledge—if they more readily embraced the mystery of timelessness in eternal design."

Perpetua's breath caught—the idea both shocking and exciting, even to her expanded senses. *All at once and in His timing? Lord, Your ways are deep!*

"So we're all here," she clarified, "from every age—in His timing, which isn't limited to a sundial?"

"You got it," Thomas confirmed, smiling. "Eternity, by definition, is the merging of beginning and end into one infinite present—just as the Alpha and Omega is One. Look around—sisters from deserts, brothers from cities yet unborn. We're one family—no divisions."

"All at once and waiting too!" she stated, considering the idea. "It's new to me, but it makes sense." Perpetua smiled at the thought, then shifted topics. "What's it like? The Judgment? What do we say?"

"We don't plead or prove. He knows us—knew us before we were born. The Lamb's blood speaks for us, and He shows us our lives: our love, our pain, our faith. Then He gives rewards. Not wages, but gifts —crowns, roles, joys we can't yet dream."

"Crowns," she whispered, Paul's words echoing—incorruptible, eternal. *You're too good, Lord!*

"Well, you certainly have been a fountain of information for me, Thomas. Thank you." She nodded sincerely.

Thomas chuckled. "I asked my angel a lot of questions before I crossed the river. Now I'm just passing it on."

She smiled, remembering Neriah. *How long ago since I crossed the river? An hour? A year? Longer?* It didn't matter. Her eyes twinkled. *All at once, and in His timing.*

Perpetua glanced at her fellow travelers—some sprinting up the path, laughter ringing like bells, others pausing to embrace each soul they met.

They reached the gate where a platform of gleaming crystal rose, its edges quivering with light. A vibrant crowd had gathered—a happy blend of diverse expressions: radiant joy, reverent awe, and eager expectation. The sight rekindled memories of harvest festivals from her childhood, when the streets of Carthage burst with life—musicians playing, jugglers twirling, markets brimming with olives, grapes, flatbreads, and salted fish. Stalls overflowed with colorful dresses, bronze jewelry, oil lamps, and spices, treasures to her young heart. Voices filled the air: shopkeepers boasting, neighbors swapping tales, cousins calling as they raced past.

Those festivals were fleeting moments of unity and abundance, yearly highlights of her youth. Now, at Heaven's gate, her spirit soared —not for temporal blessings that fade, but with an everlasting promise. She stood among a heavenly throng, celebrating, not *for* the harvest but *as* the harvest—the harvest of God Himself.

As her heart swelled with thanksgiving, a sudden hush fell over the bustling crowd—like a faucet turned off.

Silence.

Perpetua caught her breath, stirred by the abrupt quiet. This was no common stillness. It throbbed with adoration. Every heart slowed —poised for a sacred moment. Then, whispers sparked, gentle at first, like a breeze catching flame.

"Jesus is here," a woman across the path murmured, trembling with amazement. "The Lamb comes," a man up ahead echoed, his tone rich with wonder.

The whispers grew to shouts—a crescendo of joy that shook the path. "Jesus is here! Our King, our Savior!"

The crowd buzzed with excitement—their seals of light shining like stars, faces etched with longing. Hands clasped, tears streamed, laughter rang out, and songs of praise erupted in a surge of "Worthy is the Lamb!" and "King of kings!" that thundered through the divine atmosphere.

The sound swelled—voices weaving into a symphony, each note a heartbeat of worship that lifted Perpetua's soul to dance.

He's near—my Redeemer!

The air itself seemed to dance—the wall of light pulsing faster, as if Heaven itself had joined the cry.

Then, the crowd hushed again, the reverent stillness returning, every heart gripped in awe—waiting, anticipating.

A presence mounted the platform. It was not an angel, but Jesus Himself—a vision beyond imagining, clothed in radiant glory. His eyes burned like molten stars, piercing every soul yet brimming with boundless love. The hair on His head gleamed whiter than purest snow, crowned with unapproachable splendor. Light poured from His very being, weaving holiness, grace, and majesty into a melody too marvelous for words. All the beauty and power of creation was sourced in His awesome presence. Where Neriah glowed like a star, Jesus was the cosmos—infinite, holy yet tender, transcendent yet near —a song of light and fire that shook Perpetua to the core. Her breath stilled—heart bowing low.

His voice rang out, clear as crystal, deep as the river's roar.

"Come, you who are blessed by My Father," He invited—echoing His own words from dusty scrolls. "Your works are known, your love is seen, your faith is weighed—not for wrath, but for mercy. My blood speaks your name, writing it in the Book of Life. Step forward, and receive what I have prepared."

Perpetua's heart soared, tears of joy spilling down her cheeks. *It's You, Lord. Your grace, always.*

The travelers gathered closer, a family bound by faith, yet each stood within a personal moment, their lives flickering in the air.

Perpetua saw herself in the arena, her voice unbroken as she declared her King. Yet now, with luminous clarity, she saw more—her sins, vast and heavy; moments of pride, sharp words, and faltering trust—each a stain only the blood of Christ could cleanse. Gratitude swelled, not shame, for His grace had washed her clean. Miriam's alms to the poor beamed, each coin a seed of love; but her failures—neglect, bitterness —flashed too, forgiven by the Lamb's mercy. Thomas' kindness shone forth, his compassion to strangers; yet his anger and doubts loomed large, redeemed only by Jesus' sacrifice—his rewards unearned but freely given.

No disgrace lingered, for Heaven held no guilt—only thankfulness as hearts sang of the grace that outshone their flaws.

A woman saw her care for orphans, generous despite her own hunger, but her envy and lies stood revealed—covered forever by love unending. A man beheld his prayers of faith, his sacrifice for others, but he also saw his bitterness and lust—each transgression absolved in mercy's tide. Every soul stood, not condemned but grateful—their sins a canvas for God's grace—their lives woven by love divine.

Though together, they faced Him alone—their hearts laid bare, each scene a thread in their story, refined by fire, a celebration of the Lamb's redeeming power.

"Well done, good and faithful servants!"

Jesus' presence wrapped around them like a father's arms, each word a caress of goodness. "Your faith, offered in love, is gold, silver, and precious stones. Enter the joy of your Lord."

A cheer rose—not from the travelers alone, but from Heaven itself —voices, unseen yet near, singing, "All Praise to the Redeemer!"

Crowns appeared—not heavy, but light—shimmering on each brow, not in boast, but as seals of His delight. Perpetua felt hers, a circlet of silver and fire, placed gracefully over her dark, flowing curls.

I'm Yours, Lord—forever Yours.

The gate swung wide, the wall of light parting like a veil. Beyond lay not a city—not yet—but a promise—a path stretching further into Paradise.

Perpetua turned to Miriam, to Thomas, and to countless other faces—family, known and new. They clasped hands, their seals of light blending, their laughter ringing like a song.

Together, they stepped through the gate, the ground swelling to meet them.

And this was only the beginning.

CHAPTER 5
THE VALLEY

The travelers stepped through the gate, its towering frame fading behind them as the path sloped into a valley unlike any Perpetua had ever dreamed of. Mountains rose on all sides, their crests jagged with celestial gleam, painted in shades of violet, blue, and bronze—forged from the dawn of creation. The air thrummed with a vitality that tingled her soul—a timeless breath that carried no trace of dust or decay.

The group moved as one, yet apart, with some linking arms in quiet delight, while others glided alone—faces bright with wonder, each soul free to revel in the sacred expanse that unfolded before them.

Perpetua's spirit soared, peace and joy coursing through her. The valley stretched vast and alive—a cradle of meadows bursting with wildflowers: poppies, bluebells, lupine—the petals swaying as if caught in a dance. Streams carved through green hills, their waters flashing like silver paths winding through unending adventure. The land unfolded with limitless places to explore, to climb, to discover, to rest—a sanctuary of promise and wonder, untouched by any shadow of harm.

Enormous trees dominated the landscape, with trunks broader than thirty men abreast, their bark etched with patterns that glowed faintly, like veins of light. Some bore leaves of green, violet, and pearl, murmuring like happy whispers. Others bristled with needles—long, soft, in shades of emerald and bronze—their shapes and colors as varied as Earth's own forests, and more: a chorus of towering giants swaying in harmony.

Perpetua tilted her head back, scanning the thick branches that wove a canopy above. Beyond the canopy, the sky, or what resembled a sky, danced with heavenly splendor. It burst with hues beyond naming —sapphire and lavender swirling like rivers of light, streaks of marigold quivering as if the breath of God stirred them. Stars danced —not fixed but alive—twirling in joyous arcs, their radiance singing with joy.

Birds wheeled above, wings flashing in colors too bold for earthly names, their songs a tapestry of beauty that wove through the breeze.

Along the trail, Perpetua spotted Thomas, his tall form gazing at a meadow below, joy rippling across his face.

"Look, Perpetua."

She followed his eyes, and there they were—deer springing across the field, their coats dappled with flecks of gold, bounding not in flight but in gleeful play, serene in a haven untouched by fear.

"Our God has thought of everything, hasn't He? This is more than I could ever have imagined."

She nodded, her spirit echoing his awe. The valley's beauty stood as a testament to the Creator's infinite care, its vibrant nature untainted by stress or danger. Here, worship came effortlessly—not as a duty but as a tide rising with every breath—praise pouring out as their souls sang without sound.

"Thomas," she pondered, "does it ever stop—this feeling? This...fullness?"

He turned to her, warm and certain. "No," he responded flatly. "It grows. Every moment here—it's like He's unveiling more of Himself.

Back in Chicago, I would pray to experience the warmth of His presence, even an ember. But here? Now? It's fire, Perpetua, a blazing fire —and it doesn't burn out."

Joy bubbled up inside her. "Fire," she echoed, savoring the word. "Yes, fire as it was intended to be. As painful as the journey was—even the arena—it was worth it."

Thomas nodded. "You stood for Him there. I read about you—your courage. It's part of you, here, shining in that seal." He gestured to her pearl and gold light. "What was it like—persecution?"

She paused, the memory distant yet clear. "Heavy," she admitted, "but light, too. His strength held me—His voice speaking peace to my soul. You, in your accident, did you feel Him then?"

"Like a hand pulling me up," Thomas murmured. "One second, chaos—metal, noise, fear—then peace, brighter than anything. He was there, Perpetua, before I even saw this place."

They stood in silence, bound by shared amazement, the valley humming around them. Perpetua looked down, drinking in the canopy of trees below—a mosaic of divine artistry. Leaves shimmered like polished gems, interwoven with blossoms that flickered like embers in a breeze. Emerald needles gleamed, soft as velvet, beside boughs draped in light, their textures a masterpiece—smooth, silken, rugged, yet tender. Each branch alive, whispering praise.

She could hear travelers up ahead laughing, their voices bubbling over as some ascended onto the lower limbs of massive trees. Perched high above the ground, they swung gently, their joy a melody that rang through the valley. The cool, welcoming shadows beneath the branches stretched like an invitation to rest.

This is paradise, she breathed, her soul swelling with awe. *A realm where every glimpse unveils my Father's boundless heart.*

"Ever climb trees as a girl?" a voice called, breaking her reverie.

A woman nearby—her seal a swirl of violet and snow, grinned from a branch, her face dancing with mischief.

Perpetua laughed. "All the time—until my mother scolded me!"

"Then come up!" the woman urged, patting the limb beside her. "No scolding here!"

With a spark of delight, Perpetua surged upward, her soul lifting her effortlessly to the branch. The bark felt warm, alive, pulsing under her touch. She settled beside the woman, their seals blending in the dappled light.

"I'm Ramona," the woman greeted, her tone singing. "From a small town in Alberta. You?"

"Perpetua, from Carthage," she replied, her spirit warmed by the ease of kinship. "This tree—it feels...alive, doesn't it?"

Ramona nodded, examining the luminescent veins. "It's His handiwork—every leaf, every root, singing to Him. Back home, I tended a garden, coaxing life from the prairie soil. I loved its colors—wildflowers, wheat fields, sunsets. But this? This is beauty that breathes, Perpetua, pure and unending."

Perpetua leaned back, looking through the branches at the sky again. Its tone and texture had shifted; deep violet and cobalt tides now swirled with stars that danced like joyous children.

"It's like He's showing us His heart," she murmured.

"Right?" Ramona agreed enthusiastically. "And it's everywhere—every branch, every breeze. There's more waiting, too. Those streams? They babble like they're alive with His laughter."

"Laughter," Perpetua echoed, her smile softening. "I can't wait to hear it."

Talk of laughter woke a rush of memory in Perpetua—bright moments of joy that shaped her: her mother's merry laugh as she wove at the loom, her voice lifting in song; her father's hearty chuckle as he tossed grain to chickens, delight spilling over like sunlight; her son's giggles as he chased a breeze through the fields. Here, no sorrow dimmed the memory. Each sparkled with joy, polished by Heaven's light.

My little boy, she reminisced, hearing his laughter echo in her soul. *We'll laugh again soon.* The certainty bloomed, free of loss, only with promise.

Then came a gentle tug upon her soul—a holy summons, urging her toward a sacred meeting yet unseen.

She smiled at Ramona. "Something calls to me." Gathering herself, she prepared to move on. "Till we meet again, sweet friend."

Ramona's expression beamed with understanding. "Follow it, sister. He's leading you to gladness."

Perpetua descended, drawn toward something ahead.

The path curved, leading to a bridge spanning a babbling brook. Its arch rose in mighty timbers—powerful beams hewn with smooth precision, their grain glowing with divine craft. Yet it stood unfinished, its far side still rough, planks awaiting a master's touch.

Two men worked, their skilled hands steady on their tools, faces beaming with joy. One, clad in tawny brown, drove a mallet against a peg. The other, wrapped in sable, sanded a plank with care. Perpetua paused, drawn to their task.

"What do you build?" she inquired.

The man with the mallet looked up, his face sincere with a father's kindness.

"This bridge," he proclaimed with joyful contentment. "On The Choosing Ground, God gifted me with a love for crafting things— homes, benches, tables. Here, He lets me shape beauty for Him, forever." He hammered the peg, the wood humming under his strike. "It's never done—always more to create."

The man's countenance was lit with the pleasure of doing exactly what he was designed to do: worshiping in the precise manner he was created to worship.

Perpetua nodded, admiring his artistry.

"My name is Joseph," he continued, "and this rascal with me is Hubert—though I call him 'Hoo-bert' to keep him humble." He flashed a teasing grin, and Hubert rolled his eyes, chuckling.

Hubert introduced himself. "You can call me Hugh if you like. Time here is strange, if it exists at all. I'm from an age of electric saws and steel nails, whereas Joseph here, well, he was whittling logs with a stone 'til I showed up."

Perpetua giggled at their playful banter, noting the two men looked to be of similar age. "My name is Perpetua," she smiled, performing an equally playful curtsy. Then her eyes widened as she considered Joseph's name.

"Your name is Joseph...and you're a carpenter? Not—the father of Jesus?" she teased, half-laughing.

Elation danced across Joseph's face. "The very one," he declared proudly.

Her jaw dropped in astonishment, but before she could speak, Hubert groaned. "Oh no, Perpetua, you've started it now. Once he starts talking about his 'son,' there's no stopping him." Hugh pressed his face into both hands in mock despair.

Joseph leaned close, eyebrow lifted. "I raised Him, Perpetua." She could sense the cheeky amusement alive beneath his solemn tone. "I like to think I taught Jesus everything He knows about creating things."

There was a brief moment of silence before they erupted in collective laughter. Perpetua clutched her sides. "I can't escape dad jokes—even here!" She shook her head in amazement.

Joseph winked. "Keeps eternity lively."

Suddenly, a grouping of butterflies burst overhead, gliding upstream, their wingspans as wide as a raven's, swirling in a flurry of yellow and orange.

"What's up there?" Perpetua gestured upstream. The lure within her tugged again, urging her onward.

"Go see," Hubert encouraged enthusiastically. "There's so much joy in discovery, and here, it never ends."

Drawn by the divine pull, Perpetua followed the butterflies into a forest. Trees stood as sentinels—branches arching like a cathedral of light, the shadows cool and gentle. The ground was blanketed with moss and blossoms, soft as a whisper, guiding her steps.

As she moved across the forest floor, she experienced the same curious sensation as when her hand had brushed the flowering shrub near the river. The feeling was strange, connective, beautiful. It was like a riddle she could not yet answer.

The butterflies floated ahead, the soft fluttering of their wings a beckoning force. Then the trees parted, revealing a pool cradled by a gentle cliff. A waterfall tumbled, its spray a prism of light kissing the water's surface—peaceful, vivid, enchanting.

At the pool's edge sat Felicity, vibrant and youthful, her dark skin glowing with warmth beneath the shimmering mist. She peered at a butterfly resting on her hand, tracing its design with tender awe.

"Felicity!" Perpetua shouted, joy bursting like flame.

Their eyes met—recognition shining. They rushed together, colliding in a fierce and euphoric embrace. Laughter spilled, shouts and tears mingling in a surge of celebration.

"You're here!" Perpetua stepped back, drinking in her friend's radiance. "*You're* my divine appointment!"

"I'm here!" Felicity sparked, arms wide. "The river brought me—light broke, an angel spoke, then this place. Time is strange here, Perpetua. Like I just arrived, yet always belonged. It's a joy far beyond our songs."

Perpetua and Felicity danced gleefully by the pool's edge, their laughter mingling with the soothing hum of the waterfall, its tender spray casting fleeting rainbows across their happy faces. The serene beauty held them, echoing the sunsets they'd shared as girls.

They leaned close, hands clasped, and stories poured forth in bursts of eager delight, recounting their paths to this moment. They spoke of earthly pains—the weight of trials, the sting of loss—yet no shadow dimmed their telling, only amazement at the blessing that had broken through.

Their laughter rang, pure and unrestrained, as they marveled at the river's cleansing tide, the angels' guiding voices, and the tranquility that now enveloped them. Each shared gasp, each shocked expression, wove their journeys tighter, their souls thrilling at the grace that carried them here. The butterflies fluttered nearby, wings catching the light, as if joining their celebration.

Felicity inhaled sharply, eyes flaring wide. "Have you seen the city?"

"Not yet."

She squealed excitedly, pulling at Perpetua's hand. "I have to show you!"

They surged through the forest, weaving past rocks and leaping logs like girls, hands linked and spirits free.

Crossing the bridge, Felicity called out, "Joseph—Hoo-bert, are you coming to the big event tonight?"

The two men paused their work, grinning. "We wouldn't miss it!"

They waved as the girls raced on.

The valley sprawled, wild, flawless, meadows stretching to unseen horizons, dotted with blooms of every hue. *It's Eden reborn,* Perpetua gaped, soaking it all in—vast, perfect, alive with Him. They flowed down the path with wild abandon, fellow travelers laughing, shouting encouragement to them as they sped on. Every moment unveiled a melody from beyond, hinting at blessings yet unseen.

"Perpetua, look!" Felicity pointed to a stream where fish darted, scales flashing like jewels—ruby, sapphire, gold—leaping in arcs of delight, as if praising with their dance.

They paused for a closer look, and a traveler joined them, his seal a swirl of bronze and gray, marking him as one who guides souls to hidden splendors.

"First time seeing the valley?" he inquired warmly.

"For me it is," Perpetua smiled. "It's...everything."

"I'm Ezra," he said. "From Jerusalem, long ago. Been here, or feels like it, forever, but also like yesterday. That stream? Follow it later; it leads to groves where the fruit tastes like light."

"Fruit that tastes like light?" Felicity laughed, intrigued.

"You'll see," Ezra winked. "Every bite's a gift—His joy in your soul. The lumora fruit is golden and soft as a sigh. And the grove is home to a family of miulumes, tiny cat-like creatures, no bigger than a hand. They've got shimmering fur and live in holes in the trees, purring tunes that blend with the grove's song. Always scampering after the fruit."

Perpetua's eyes danced. "Miulumes and lumora fruit? We'll visit after the city."

Ezra nodded. "There are countless other creatures to enjoy as well. All that existed on The Choosing Ground, plus many more—each lovingly shielded within the eternal expanse by the Maker of all things. A gift, blessing His children with the joy of unending discovery."

Ezra stepped to the side, making room for them to pass. "The city is calling you now, I can tell. But when you're ready, the grove is just past the silver reeds. You'll hear the miulumes' purring before you even get there." He waved them on. "Go, find that light!"

Felicity grinned, nudging Perpetua. "I'm coming back for those miulumes!"

Perpetua laughed, turning toward the path again. They moved on, restless with excitement.

Then—she saw it!

The valley widened, revealing the great city beyond the mountains' curve—its walls glimmering with crystal and gold. Its gates were open wide, throbbing with Heaven's heartbeat. Spires soared, tipped with a brilliance that defied sight, and a sound rolled forth—voices, countless yet one, singing a song of triumph.

Perpetua halted, her breath stolen. "The city," she whispered in amazement.

Felicity squeezed her hand, staring in wonderment at its oscillating glow. "Our home," she breathed. "Where He waits."

They flowed forward, the laughter of fellow travelers echoing about them, and Perpetua knew—knew with every fiber of her soul—the adventure had only begun.

CHAPTER 6

THE CITY

Perpetua and Felicity stood breathless at a cliff's edge, their hearts filled with enchantment as the city unfolded below—a stunning palace of unimaginable grandeur, reminiscent of the sacred vision in Revelation. Its towering walls, crafted from jasper, pure as crystal, captured Heaven's radiance in a symphony of fiery colors: gold, scarlet, emerald—each stone pulsing with ethereal brilliance. The walls hinted at hidden layers, levels of glory ascending high into the sky beyond sight, revealed only to those drawn deeper into the city's divine embrace. Twelve gates shone, three per side, each carved from a single pearl, their entrances adorned with sapphire, ruby, and topaz—a mosaic of God's covenant. Even from afar, the streets were visible—golden threads reflecting the Lamb's light.

Meandering through the heart of the city flowed the River of Life, clear as glass, its waters sparkling with timeless purity. From the Throne it poured—a life-giving current that nourished all. Spanning the river stood the Tree of Life, its vastness beyond imagining—like a mountain of living color, crowning the city in splendor. Thick roots gripped both banks, twisting upward to form a grand arch over the water, woven together into a single trunk that pierced the heavens.

Perpetua trembled with awe, her gaze tracing the tree's ascent. "Felicity," she whispered, voice quaking, "it's beyond John's words—beyond all imagining."

Felicity gripped her hand. "It's Him," she spoke with amazement. "His heart, His palace—our home."

A winding path beckoned them, and with hearts ablaze with passion, they hurried to the valley floor. The descent was quick, their steps light on a trail cushioned with moss. Wildflower meadows flanked the happy lane, releasing a rapturous chorus of fragrance. Nearby, creatures akin to stags bounded freely, their nearly translucent coats speckled with gold. Majestic antlers shone with a soft luster, reflecting the light of God's presence in a joyful dance. Streams sang around them, weaving melody through the valley, while birds fluttered overhead in flashes of blue and yellow.

Perpetua felt the city's pull, a lure swift and sure, as Neriah had said: "Your soul moves by desire, by love, and your love for Him draws you."

Their route led past a grove of trees laden with fruit—red and green apples, sapphire plums—their rich scent lacing the air with sweetness. Perpetua stopped to admire a stunning star-shaped leaf. She touched it gently, and the leaf responded, as if reaching to touch her back. Startled, she pulled her hand away. Suddenly, she understood the riddle—the strange sensation she had experienced first with the shrub by the river and then on the forest floor while following the butterflies: She wasn't merely passing *through* Paradise—crossing its rivers, stepping on its stones, gliding through its grasses—she was moving *with* Paradise, connected with creation in a unified rhythm of worship.

Perpetua was astonished. Neriah had taught her that distance was distinct here. Thomas had explained how time was different. Now, nature itself offered a fresh insight into the transcendent purity of Heaven's creation. The delightful sounds of nature surrounding her weren't merely reverberations of beauty; they were songs of worship.

She had known people on The Choosing Ground who made false deities of trees and animals, bowing down to worship creation. But here, she worshiped *with* creation—together—lifting praise to the God who is over all, through all, and in all.

"Everything here worships Him," she whispered in amazement. "The rocks, the water, the trees, the light, the animals—they cry out in adoration, like Jesus said they would if we didn't."

It explained so much—the connection she felt with everything and everyone—the melody she sensed in every sound, from the rippling of waters to the rustling leaves.

"It's like Eden," she murmured in hushed reverence.

Felicity nodded, plucking a ripe plum, her bite rewarded with a burst of juicy flavor. "Better," she retorted, alive with joy. "Eden was a shadow. This is the substance."

As they neared the city gate, its magnificence brought them to a halt. A single pearl loomed, vast as a mountain's face, its surface alive, etched with names—Judah, Reuben, Benjamin—each a note in Heaven's refrain. At the threshold of the gate, angels hovered like sentinels, their presence both awesome and terrible, a breathtaking embodiment of divine power and grace. Their wings, vast and unfurled, were woven of pure light, shimmering in a cascade of prismatic hues that flowed like living flames. These were no mere appendages, but extensions of celestial might, capable of rending the heavens or sheltering the meek with equal ease, their edges blazing with a brilliance that hinted at untamed strength restrained by infinite love. Towering yet approachable, their forms appeared to flicker between the tangible and the ethereal, as if they straddled the veil between God's Throne and the city's streets. Their armor, if it could be called that, shone with a luster that defied earthly metals, marked with patterns that told of battles won in realms unseen, each line a testament to victories over darkness.

Their eyes, kind and welcoming, burned with a depth that pierced the soul, twin flames of compassion and wisdom that saw every heart's longing and every tear shed in faith. To meet their gaze was to feel both exposed and cherished, as if they knew Perpetua and Felicity by name, their journeys carved in divine memory. These were not the gentle cherubs of earthly art but warriors of the Almighty, their grace a paradox of tenderness and terror—like a storm held at bay by a whispered promise. Each movement was deliberate, infused with a dancer's elegance, yet carrying the weight of worlds, as if a single step could shake the foundations of creation.

Perpetua's heart trembled, for these guardians radiated a love so fierce it could only flow from the Throne of God.

They crossed excitedly into the city, its atmosphere bursting with vibrant life, a song of bliss echoing through golden avenues. Architecture soared—spires of crystal, domes of gold, arches of white—each a marvel of heavenly craft, blending all cultures in perfect harmony. Pyramids, towers, aqueducts, bridges, and columns—fashioned from stone, pearl, wood, reed, clay, and countless other hallowed elements —all stood resurrected in exalted form, not as a reflection of human designs but as their divine source. Each structure, perfected by the Lamb's glory, shone in testament to His everlasting reign.

A sudden swooshing sound caused Perpetua to look up. High above, an angel—or a great white eagle—was gliding gracefully. As she gazed upward, she sensed the presence of additional layers, boundless dimensions and hidden heights. These mysterious levels were not visible from the path she currently followed. Instead, adjacent alleys contained portals and staircases that seemed to offer access to these unseen tiers of the city. Such unearthly engineering was beyond Perpetua's ability to comprehend. *Maybe this is what Paul meant when he referenced the third Heaven?*

Laughter, melody, and chatter filled the air—voices of all ages, tongues, and tribes as one. A child dashed past, shrieking gleefully as a man in a white robe playfully chased after her.

Felicity nudged Perpetua, her smile beaming. "Do you know who that was?"

Perpetua blinked, puzzled. "Who?"

Felicity grinned. "Jesus!"

Perpetua stopped abruptly, dumbfounded.

Felicity continued, her voice bright with adoration. "Sometimes He shines as at the gate, all majesty and power, but other times, He walks among us—laughing, playing, like a Father with His children, or a friend. He's everywhere, Perpetua, in every smile and every laugh. His presence is woven into all things, yet He chooses to run with us, to share in our delight as if He's never apart."

Perpetua's eyes widened. "How can He be so close, yet so distant as to fill everything?"

Felicity chuckled. "That's His heart—always with us, always beyond us, holding all of Heaven at once."

Like time, Perpetua thought, *held together in His presence and unfolding as He wills it.*

They wandered the golden streets, their translucent depths revealing currents of light below. Markets brimmed with fruit—golden apples, purple berries—all offered freely. Fountains sprayed, waters arcing in diamond sheen, children splashing, laughter ringing out like starlit chimes. Perpetua paused by a plaza where elders shared tales of trials turned triumph. A woman recounted a desert trek; a man answered with a city's fall, both ending in praise: "Glory to the Eternal King."

They meandered through courtyards where artisans worked, their hands shaping wonders. A potter molded clay that glowed, each vessel sparkling as it formed. A weaver spun threads of light, her loom crafting translucent floral patterns. Perpetua watched, captivated. Felicity tugged her sleeve, pointing to a cobblestone square where dancers twirled, their seals swirling in patterns of praise, their movements a prayer that lifted the air itself.

Amid the plaza's vibrant hum, a flash of blond hair glimmered through the crowd. Perpetua's breath halted, then leapt.

"Mago?" she cried, voice breaking.

Felicity spun, eyes wide, and there he stood—their brother in faith, his seal a blaze of green and gold, his countenance alive with elation.

"Mago!" Felicity shouted.

They surged forward, parting the crowd, colliding in laughter and tears. His arms held them close, a memory reborn.

"Sisters!" he laughed, stepping back to look at them. "I knew you'd come."

"You're here!" Perpetua clapped, flooded with happiness. "After the arena—"

"Light broke through," Mago inserted, flashing a radiant smile. "The river carried me. No pain remains—only this." He gestured to the city's brilliance. "The Lamb's mercy has gathered us here—into love without end."

Felicity wiped tears, laughing. "Still leading us, aren't you?"

"More like keeping up with you two," he teased. "But there's more —come!"

He led them down avenues, past orchards where luminescent trees bore shimmering fruit that cast light into the breeze. They passed a square where another storyteller held a crowd, his voice rising and falling, narrating a storm crossed, a mountain climbed—only these were new stories, recounting heavenly adventures. Perpetua lingered, her soul stirred, but Mago urged them on, the river's flow growing louder.

They wove through paths where children played, tossing spheres of light that chimed, their laughter echoing through vibrant lanes. Eventually, they emerged near an elegant wooden wharf that extended into the river like a ribbon of light. Boats of various shapes and sizes bobbed gently, secured by silver ropes.

There on the dock stood Marcus and Lucius, hands waving, their grins as bright as the city itself. Lucius' once gray head was now covered with a shock of thick brown hair, all traces of age erased by wonder-working power. The shame that had long burdened Marcus was completely lifted, replaced by an aura of strength and joy.

They rushed forward in a whirlwind of shouts, embraces, and tears. Marcus' laughter rang out, and Lucius' wit sparked: "Took you long enough!"

Perpetua stuck out her tongue playfully. "All at once and in His timing," she quipped.

"What?" He chuckled.

Their reunion was a dance of happiness.

Lucius stepped back, his arm around a woman with long blonde hair, her seal a soft gold and rose.

"Perpetua, Felicity, this is Sabina." His voice was warm with pride. "She was my wife, who left The Choosing Ground before me."

Sabina's smile was jubilant, her eyes twinkling as she joined the embrace.

Felicity tilted her head inquisitively. "You were married on The Choosing Ground—but what does that make you here? There was much debate about that, wasn't there?"

Sabina lay her head on Lucius' shoulder, her voice soft but sure. "The debates fade here. I'm not sure of the answer, but I know this: Jesus brought us together as soulmates there, and we remain soulmates now."

Lucius' face beamed, and they all embraced again.

Marcus grasped Lucius' shoulder, grinning. "The only downside to this place is that we can't tease you about being old anymore." They laughed, their timeless youth a shared miracle.

Lucius turned to Perpetua and Felicity. "We waited for you. Mago knew you'd find us."

"By the river," Marcus added, grinning.

"Speaking of the river," Sabina chimed in cheerfully, "we have something to show you."

They boarded a small boat carved from a single pearl, its bow pulsing as it glided into the celestial flow. The water's clarity was shocking—its depths a window into captivating aquatic wonders. Beneath the surface, vibrant life thrived in ceaseless worship. Fish darted in bursts of color, their scales flashing like jewels, their swift movements forming radiant trails of praise. Schools of smaller creatures swirled, their playful dance a joyful offering. Massive leviathans glided with gentle grace, flowing through the deep in noble adoration.

Perpetua leaned over the side of the boat, peering into the depths. She recalled the arena's darkness, her chains, the lion's roars.

"All that suffering," she whispered, "led to this—the Lamb's river, His light." Her heart raced at the sight of such splendor. This was no mere water but a sacred current, flowing from the Throne, alive with worship.

Marcus steered the boat while Lucius pointed ahead, narrating with a grin. "Wait till you see it!" His voice brimmed with excitement.

"What is it?" Perpetua asked.

"You'll see." They all answered as one, their voices blending in a single, exuberant chord. Laughter erupted at their unified reply.

The boat passed an elegant plaza where a choir sang—reverent voices lifted in a cascade of "All Hail the King of Glory."

Perpetua's spirit swelled. "It's so beautiful," she gasped in awe.

Marcus glanced back playfully. "They're practicing."

"Practicing?" Perpetua wrinkled her nose skeptically. "If practice is this beautiful, what does the real thing sound like?"

Again, they all responded in unintentional unison. "You'll see."

Their laughter continued, happiness ringing out like bells, a shared spark lighting their faces as the boat glided on.

The river carried them through the city, guiding them forward on a winding silver strand. Buildings rose—crystal walls etched with stories: Noah's ark, David's harp, Esther's crown—each a triumph of faith.

Children ran along banks, waving as they glided past. Felicity watched them closely, remembering her unborn child who had died in the arena with her.

"He's here," she murmured, examining each young face. "Somewhere."

Mago gently squeezed her shoulder. "I'm certain of it," he asserted with assurance. "You'll find him. God's timing will be perfect. I have no doubt."

Nearing the city's center, the Tree of Life loomed—its enormity breathtaking. Roots plunged deep into both banks, merging above the water in a majestic arch, uniting into a single trunk that soared beyond sight. Its canopy spread wide, a regal crown of emerald and gold. Each leaf quivered, lush with healing power. Fruit hung like jewels—ruby, amber, jade. Homes flickered within its mighty branches, souls abiding in the tree's embrace, a testament to the Creator's matchless design.

Perpetua's soul was caught up in reverence. "It's...everything."

Mago nodded. "More than our dreams. Remember those nights in the cell?"

"I do," Felicity breathed. "We never could have imagined this."

Marcus looked up, overwhelmed by beauty, his face a canvas of complete peace. All shame, striving, and fear had been forever washed away. "Every prayer," he marveled, "every tear—He heard them."

As their boat glided beneath the Tree of Life, its warm, enveloping shadow washed over them. Countless lanterns hung merrily in the branches overhead, flickering in golden hues. The fruit, the leaves, the homes—all swayed in a gentle rhythm of praise, glistening with welcoming warmth. The Tree's inhabitants moved along paths within the colossal branches, their seals glowing like beacons. Even below the boat, the riverbed sparkled as living corals danced with prismatic sheen.

Suddenly, their moment of quiet awe was interrupted by shouts of complete joy. High in the expansive canopy above, adventurous thrill seekers gazed down with mischievous intent—their colorful seals sparking against the shadowy backdrop. With jubilant cries, they leapt, twirling through the air, light trailing like comets as they plunged into the river. The water swelled around them as they surfaced, laughing, shouting to their friends above, "Jump, jump, jump."

Perpetua rejoiced, her laughter mirroring theirs.

The river pulled them onward, each twist revealing new wonders—so many that no heart could hold them all, nor tongue recount them in full.

The boat drifted past a plaza where banners of light hung, shifting in the breeze like living flames. Each fabric was embroidered with names—Abraham, Ruth, Paul—a litany of faith everlasting. Perpetua's breath caught, recognizing her own name among them, etched in silver, a gift of grace she could scarcely fathom.

"Look," she pointed, and Felicity nodded, her own name gleaming in crimson, a testament to their shared journey.

Then Perpetua felt a shift, a deepening of the city's pulse.

The river turned, and Lucius pointed ahead, his voice pitched with excitement. "We're almost there."

A crowd gathered, hands raised in fervent worship, their chant— "Holy, holy, holy"—a tide that pulled the boat forward. Beyond the crowd, a matchless brilliance shone, brighter than all. It was the King of creation, seated on His throne.

Perpetua's spirit raced. "It's Him," she stammered, burning with anticipation.

Closing her eyes, she joined the chant, her voice rising, "Holy, holy, holy," a trembling offering to the Lamb.

The boat surged forward, drawn by a call to worship. As they approached the throne room, the atmosphere grew dense—like sailing into the heart of a storm. The tempest erupted with unimaginable force, fierce and untamed, yet enveloping the worshipers in complete security.

The River of Life roared, waves leaping high in fervent praise. Lightning flashed, cutting through the sky with brilliant streaks, illuminating countless faces in glory. Thunder resounded, proclaiming the throne's might.

The boat glided to the shore, its hull resting against a welcoming bank. Perpetua, Felicity, Marcus, Lucius, Sabina, and Mago stepped forward, hand-in-hand, their hearts seized by overwhelming wonder. The storm's raw power echoed about them—every boom a call to worship, every flare a glimpse of eternity. The crowd's fervor intensified, drawing them toward the throne's radiant heart, where all of Heaven bowed in trembling awe.

CHAPTER 7

THE THRONE

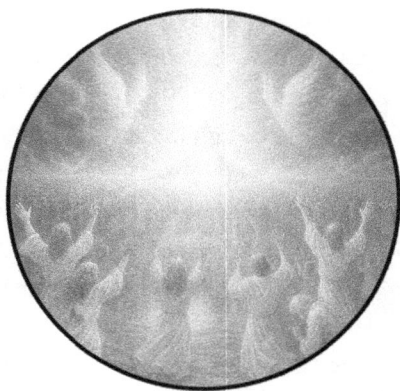

The storm surged, billowing with a mighty roar that shook the heavens. Brilliant arcs of lightning flashed through the air as a holy dim settled over the worshipers. Vast wings, white beyond mortal conception, unfurled like clouds in boundless majesty—each wing ablaze with celestial fire. Lightning flared within them, every bolt a thunderous declaration of sovereign might.

Perpetua's heart soared, her soul gripped in adoration. A psalm of David echoed in her spirit: *I will sing under the shadow of Your wings.*

Felicity's hand tightened in hers, their breaths shallow in the electric air. Marcus stood tall, eyes wide with awe, while Lucius and Sabina leaned together, faces bright with wonder. Mago's breathing joined the storm's cadence—a call to worship that pressed against their spirits, urging them to bow before unrivaled glory.

At the storm's center rose the throne—a seat of indescribable splendor, forged from jasper and crystal, rippling with a resonance beyond description. An emerald rainbow arced above, its verdant haze a vow of everlasting covenant.

He who sat upon the throne was the Maker of all things—supreme in power—the source of life, love, mercy, and justice. His presence burst forth, a fierce light that would have filled His worshipers with terror had He not already driven fear from their hearts.

His form flickered, not shifting but pulsing with divine unity—first in appearance of magnificent light, vast and all-consuming. Then the Lamb—Jesus—His nail-scarred hands outstretched, eyes like fire, feet glowing like burnished bronze. Next, the Spirit—a swirling tempest of majesty, a wind that took form—breath and power woven together as Father, Son, and Spirit—seated, reigning as One.

Around the throne were four creatures, their shape a heavenly mystery, echoing with ceaseless praise. The first, lion-like, roared with a voice that shook the air, its mane a torrent of molten flame—proclaiming the unyielding sovereignty of the Most High. Another, ox-like, bellowed with a deep throbbing power—its strength a call to steadfast devotion. The third, human-faced, spoke with piercing wisdom—its words a melody of truth that captivated Perpetua's heart. The fourth, eagle-like, rose with wings of fire—its cry an anthem of purity.

Their eyes—countless, gleaming—saw every moment, every heart, their gaze alive with adoration. Night and day they chanted, "Holy, holy, holy, is the Lord God Almighty, who was and is and is to come!"

It was the song woven into every dimension of Paradise. Perpetua had first sensed its soft refrain when traveling with Neriah through the Shekinah Glory, across the river. But here, it thundered—a wave that crashed over her, flooding the senses with such force it stole her breath.

A vast expanse stretched before the throne—a sea of crystal glass, translucent, yet alive with hints of color: emerald, ruby, sapphire—dancing beneath, as if unseen creatures praised in its depths. Countless souls now gathered upon it, a growing throng from every tribe, nation, and tongue. Their seals—once unique with the hue of their own stories—now glowed alabaster white as they assembled in praise. The pure light of their adornments throbbed in unison as they worshiped, a testimony to God's gift of redemption.

Then, a final roll of thunder boomed and faded, echoing in the distance.

An awesome silence descended—holy and profound. A hush that was not empty, but alive—a gripping pause that held the worshipers in quiet reverence, every breath a prayer, each heartbeat a metronome of praise.

In that sacred stillness, the silence deepened, and a warm essence wrapped around Perpetua. Her eyes fluttered shut, not in sleep but by divine lure. The Throne Room faded, replaced by a soft, familiar light.

She stood—or seemed to stand—in the courtyard of her family's villa in Carthage, the air thick with the scent of olive trees and sunbaked stone. She was no longer flesh but spirit—an unseen witness, her heart trembling in wonderment.

Lord, what's this?

A scene unfolded before her, vivid yet dreamlike.

The villa was quiet. Its vibrancy now dimmed. She saw her mother, kneeling in the garden, hands clutching the soil, face streaked with tears. Grief hung heavy, a shadow over her once-bright eyes. Perpetua wanted to reach out and comfort her. *Mother, I'm here. Safe!*

She saw her father pacing the courtyard, his noble frame taut with anger, fists clenched. "Why, Perpetua?" he muttered, his voice raw. "This Jesus—He took you!" His words pierced her, not with pain but with love, for she saw their source: a father's broken heart, raging against a God he didn't know.

They blame You, Lord, she prayed, yet her soul quickened, sensing a divine hand at work.

Time shifted, fluid as the River of Life. Night cloaked the villa, and her mother slept, face troubled. In her mother's dream, a glow filled the room, soft as moonlight, and Perpetua saw herself—not as she was in the arena, but beaming, clad in pearl and gold, laughing by the Tree of Life.

Her mother woke, eyes wide, the dream's light lingering in her gaze. She rose, clutching her chest, disturbed yet comforted, whispering, "Perpetua—alive?" The Spirit of God hovered—unseen but warm —a gentle breeze that kissed her mother's tears.

Night after night, the Spirit returned, whispering truth, drawing her heart to the One who held her daughter.

Perpetua's spirit beamed. *You're chasing her, Lord. You never stop!*

Her mother spoke, tentative at first, sharing her dreams over bread and oil. "She was happy, Cassius," she said, voice trembling. "In a city of light."

Her father scoffed, his laugh bitter. "Foolish dreams!" But his eyes betrayed him—searching, haunted.

The Spirit moved again, a quiet fire in his chest, softening his heart of stone. Perpetua saw him pause one evening, staring at the stars, his anger faltering. "If You're real," he whispered, "show me." Tears welled, not of rage but of longing, and Perpetua's soul sang. *You're breaking through, Lord. Your love is relentless!*

The vision swirled, years melting away. Her son—her little boy, no longer small—stood tall, a young man of twenty, his dark curls like hers, his eyes alight with faith. He sat in a modest room, teaching a catechism class, his voice steady, rich with joy.

"God is good," he said, hands gesturing, "even in loss. My mother, Perpetua, stood for our God, and He holds her now."

The listeners leaned in—young and old—their faces etched with hunger for truth. Her son smiled, recounting God's mercy, his words a melody of hope.

Perpetua's heart swelled, tears of gratitude spilling over. *My boy— he's Yours, Lord, fully Yours!*

She saw the threads converge: her mother, now gray but radiant, praying with clasped hands, her faith a flame kindled by dreams; her father, kneeling beside her, pride humbled, his heart claimed by the Spirit's patient call; her son, leading others to the cross, his life a testament to the God who pursued them all.

They're Yours, she marveled. *You didn't just save me. You chased them, loved them, refused to let them go!*

The vision burned with truth—God's mercy, vast as the throne's light, relentless as the river, weaving her family's pain into a story of redemption. Her soul trembled, praise rising like a tide. *Worthy are You, Lord, for Your love never fails!*

As her family's redemption glowed within, the villa faded, and the light of the throne came rushing back. Perpetua's eyes opened, her spirit still tingling from the weight of the vision. Felicity's hand was warm in hers; Marcus' awe mirrored hers. Lucius and Sabina's faces shone, and Mago's gaze met hers with knowing joy. *Thank You, Lord, for Your endless grace.*

The sacred silence held as glory pulsed around them. The chant of the four creatures had not ceased, but dimmed, holding space for what was about to happen next.

Then—a sound, low and resonant. Soft at first, but growing. A man had stepped forward—not onto a stage, but out of the crowd, before the throne. He held a golden horn, its gleam alive with Heaven's light. He breathed through it with the breath of the redeemed. The tone was rich, pure, and honest, a note that hummed with joy. Perpetua sensed the Lord's delight in it—a gift of praise from this one man, with his singular note.

Another soul stepped forward, clutching what appeared to be a wooden lyre, its strings shimmering like dew. A second note joined legato—clear and bright—weaving with the horn's resonance. The sound swelled, a harmony that tugged at Perpetua's soul.

Then, a choir surged forward, their voices lifting in a song she'd never heard yet knew by heart: "Amazing Grace, how sweet the sound..."

The words poured forth—each syllable a declaration of truth, binding her to the Throne's goodness. Her lips moved, singing, tears of joy falling.

More musicians emerged, offering gifts of praise. Lutes, flutes, and drums—earthly instruments perfected—joined with heavenly ones: cymbals of starlight and pipes of woven flame. Each note rang true, honed by Heaven's touch.

The worship grew, rising to a crescendo that shook the crystal sea. Voices soared—"All Glory to the Lamb!"—a thunder of triumph. The sound washed over the worshipers, spirits trembling, caught in its resounding embrace.

Angels descended—not merely playing instruments but embodying

71

music itself. One, its wings a living harp, strummed chords that split the heavens. Another's wings beat like drums—a cadence of divine might. A third spun overhead, its form a flute, its breath a melody that danced like wind. The harmonies wove together—the angelic and the redeemed—merging in thunderous worship. The music surged—"O the wonderful cross!"—a cry of sacrifice and victory. Perpetua's heart burned with holy fervor, longing to bow yet yearning to dance.

The crescendo peaked—a roar of praise—then dropped again to a reverent hush.

Silence trembled, alive with the throne's presence. Soft as dawn, a new song began—"Endless Hallelujah…"—tender, piercing, a balm to every soul. The choir's voices blended, countless yet one, joined by strings, horns, and angelic chimes. The worship climbed, a spiral of praise that stirred the air, lightning flashing in rhythm. Souls swayed —some kneeling, others spinning in joy, hands raised to the throne.

Overcome with excitement, Mago caught Perpetua's hand. "Let's get closer," he shouted. She couldn't hear his voice but could read his eyes.

Perpetua nodded, heart racing, and grasped Felicity's hand. Marcus, Lucius, and Sabina joined them, their hands linking—a chain of faith forged in the arena's fire. Together, they wove through the throng.

The air hummed with anticipation—a sacred pull that guided their steps, as if the heart of God was magnetic, drawing them forward.

They stepped onto the crystal sea, its surface gleaming.

Sabina gasped, pointing down. "Look!" she cried, bubbling with joy.

Beneath the glass, lights danced—emerald, ruby, sapphire—living sparks of praise, swirling like creatures in a celestial waltz. Perpetua felt weightless, her soul singing, caught up in boundless joy.

They arrived at the front of the crowd, the throne looming tall before them. The One seated on the throne shimmered with threefold brilliance: a consuming Fire, fierce with creative power; a scarred Shepherd, hands marked by wounds of love; a breath of Light, swirling with eternal promise—united in majesty.

As worship rang out, the gaze of the Almighty settled directly on Perpetua and her friends. Awe enveloped her—a holy reverence mingled with a peace that surpassed all understanding. The gaze lingered—a blessed moment that seemed to last a lifetime. Perpetua felt seen, known, cherished beyond measure. As she poured out her heart in worship, she felt the King of kings pouring right back into her: strength, joy, purpose, love, acceptance.

Her friends stood with her, their faces radiant as they shared the holy communion.

The crowd's voices lifted, singing, "I Exalt Thee," a melody of devotion that shook the air. Countless angels swooped overhead, their wings trailing light, weaving through the heavens like living stars.

Worshipers surged past—a wave of redeemed souls yearning for their Heavenly Father. Every heart was seen as limitless love blazed forth from the throne of grace.

The song shifted, voices and languages blending—"O Praise the Name..."

Perpetua sang out, joined by Felicity's clear tone, Marcus' deep hum, Lucius and Sabina's woven duet, and Mago's steady chant. The throne's light bathed them in warmth—a promise of eternal nearness.

Then, a familiar presence stirred beside her. Perpetua turned—and there stood Neriah, wings glistening, deep notes of adoration rumbling from a mighty chest.

"Neriah!" she cried, flinging her arms around the angel as a child might hug an enormous tree.

"I told you we would meet again, daughter," the angel spoke tenderly, "in His presence, where all are one."

"Neriah, these are my friends!" Perpetua was brimming with excitement.

Neriah's eyes gleamed. "Felicity, Marcus, Lucius, Sabina, and Mago," the angel named each of them, its voice a melody of welcome. "Blessed are you, faithful ones."

They smiled, awe-struck, hearts full.

"Come," it instructed in a warm yet commanding tone. "I am sent to guide you to your heavenly homes."

Perpetua's heart swelled, tears of gratitude falling. She had completely forgotten about that part—Jesus had promised to prepare a place specifically for her—for each of them.

The six friends clasped hands again, ready to follow. The throne's light bathed them—an eternal promise of rest and glory.

Perpetua looked at Neriah, then her friends, and knew—this love, this moment, was forever.

"Lead us," she whispered, her voice trembling with praise.

CHAPTER 8
THE ETERNAL HOME

Neriah guided them through the crowd of worshipers onto a path that led back toward the city's center. As the Throne Room receded from view, their seals—which had all turned alabaster white—regained their vibrant colors, each symbolizing their distinct journeys of faith.

The city spread out, its streets alive with energy—a divine melody infused into every breath. Spires rose about them, cast from crystal and gold, their peaks stretching into the clouds. Smaller streams—offshoots of the River of Life—meandered through the city, sparkling as they flowed, nourishing happy gardens.

Perpetua's heart brimmed with song, her hands still clasped with her friend's. The atmosphere echoed with laughter, voices, and the hustle and bustle of contented creation.

They passed dwellings that were not mere houses, but marvels of architectural brilliance—each one distinct. Some were crafted from starfire, others sculpted from living stone, crystal, or celestial timbers.

Grand stadiums emerged, where souls and angels engaged in playful games, their laughter rising like a wave. Immense libraries ribboned the skyline, filled with books and ancient scrolls from across the ages. The authors—prophets, apostles, poets, martyrs, dreamers—often read or recited their literary works to eager listeners. Perpetua spotted a scribe, quill of light in hand, narrating tales of God's grace to an enthralled audience. Her soul yearned for such stories, but Neriah's gentle guidance urged them forward, its starry eyes filled with purpose.

As they reached the top of a small hill, a golden dome caught their gaze, its silver spire gleaming like a star.

Lucius paused, his eyes wide with interest. "What's that?"

Before Neriah could speak, Sabina—who had been there longer than the rest—answered.

"It's an observatory," she chimed with delight. "A place to look into The Choosing Ground and its timeline—seeing past, present, future before they unfold. We offer prayers and thanks to the One who judges rightly, holding all in His hand. There are also pools in the forest reflecting similar visions."

Perpetua's breath caught, imagining her son's life unfolding, her prayers rising like incense. Neriah nodded, and they moved on, each expressing their excitement about returning to learn more about these observatories.

The city opened into a district of towers and villas—a community of timeless homes, each crafted to celebrate unique personality and design.

Sabina squealed, running ahead with excitement. She paused beside a white stone tower with huge wooden doors and a breath-taking flower garden surrounding its base.

"Hurry!" she called out—not with impatience, but overflowing with jubilant anticipation.

"Lucius, we live here! Each with our own space, yet close. Remember your dream—a place with a city view? You've never seen anything like this!"

Lucius laughed and ran toward her. The tower doors opened,

revealing halls of light.

Sabina's rooms were beautifully furnished, with easy access to the garden. Lucius' quarters were higher up, with wide windows framing the city's glow in every direction. The walls were layered with patterns of limitless horizons, reflecting their shared love and faith.

Already, their laughter filled the rooms.

Neriah's voice resonated, rich with joy. "Blessed are you, soul-mates of faith."

Perpetua's heart swelled with gratitude, happy tears falling, as they left Sabina and Lucius to settle into their forever home.

The remaining five travelers continued down a hill. All about them fountains sprayed in arcs of crystal water, reflecting the city's light, while vibrant awnings fluttered over busy pathways.

Marcus stopped at a street-level home, its warm amber walls facing a lively market. Stalls overflowed with fruit—golden peaches and sapphire plums—the air rich with pleasant aromas.

"This is mine," Marcus stated, trembling with amazement. "I dreamed of a place like this—alive and full of voices."

The door opened, revealing a space decorated in earthy tones, its windows facing the market. The walls were adorned with soft scenes of eternal festivity, whispering of his kindness and open heart.

Perpetua embraced him. "My dear brother, it's perfect for you."

Marcus smiled, envisioning the people he'd welcome. Neriah's wings stirred—a sign of approval—and they moved forward.

The path led to a vast park, a sprawling forest at the city's center, where towering trees—their bark illuminated with light—swayed in a gentle breeze. Leaves of emerald and coral rustled as streams chimed, their waters shimmering like silver. Birds fluttered about with blue and gold wings, their calls casting a melody of delight. Deer bounded, and butterflies danced in the air.

At a meadow's edge was a cabin, crafted from timber and crystal, its wide windows framing the trees, its roof dappled with light. Mago's steady gaze traced the woods. "This one's mine," he murmured in quiet awe.

The cabin's interior glowed with warmth, its walls adorned with patterns of endless exploration—reflecting his quiet strength and curiosity.

Perpetua squeezed his hand, remembering his resilience in the dungeon. "You'll watch the deer forever," she smiled. "Be sure to invite me over often."

Mago laughed, deep and heartfelt. "Absolutely!"

Neriah gave a gentle nod, blessing his rest.

The path curved upward, out of the forest, to a street lined with villas, their courtyards blooming with everlasting spring. Across from each other stood two homes—radiant and distinct.

To the left, an archway led to a villa of soft ivory, its yellow door adorned with a wreath, inscribed with the words: "For my beloved daughter, Felicity."

Felicity paused, her voice quivering. "That's mine?"

To the right, Perpetua's villa gleamed, its courtyard graced with trees of lavender and green, swaying in a tender breeze. A deep purple door displayed a wreath with illuminated words: "To Perpetua—my fierce one."

Wonder washed over Perpetua, her breath catching. "Mine," she whispered, hands trembling, eyes fixed on her purple door.

Neriah's expression changed—not with alarm, but a sense of duty. "I am summoned to the gate," the angel stated. "More of the redeemed arrive. Enjoy your homes, my friends. I will return."

The angel's magnificent wings spread wide and, with a powerful swoop, it soared into the air. Diamond droplets cascaded down, forming a dazzling arc against the sky. The girls exchanged glances, their hearts overflowing with praise.

"Just another day in Heaven," Felicity remarked playfully.

"I'm gonna learn to do that," Perpetua laughed, wiping a droplet from her cheek as she looked up.

They hugged, overwhelmed by God's many blessings.

"Go explore your home, dear friend. I'll drop by soon," Perpetua said.

Felicity nodded—then dashed to her villa, Perpetua to hers—their steps swift with anticipation.

Felicity pushed open the yellow door, heart pounding. The villa unfolded before her—room after room filled with light and promise. The walls were adorned with visions of paradise: gardens in perpetual bloom and skies painted in blended colors. It was a home designed to be filled with the laughter of many kindred spirits. Once a slave, now a daughter of the King, Felicity marveled at the space. Light streamed through tall windows, revealing a courtyard teeming with life.

She traced a wall with delicate fingers, tears falling as she whispered, "Is all this really mine?"

A soft knock interrupted her thoughts. *Who could that be?*

She crossed to the door quickly, expecting to welcome Perpetua. Instead, she found a boy—eleven or twelve in appearance—his dark eyes reflecting her own. He held a purple daffodil.

"Hello, Mother," he said, a warm smile flashing across his face.

Her son—once lost in the arena—now stood before her, whole, his tender face glowing as a testament to God's promise.

Felicity gasped, tears streaming down her cheeks as she embraced him.

"My boy," she sobbed with joy, holding him tight.

He laughed, leaning back to offer her his daffodil. She received it, pressing the flower to her heart.

"I dreamed of you," she breathed, "and here you are."

Catching her hand, he led her inside, showing her his room—filled with sketches of the city. Their souls connected immediately, the walls of their home echoing with the sound of shared delight.

They clung together, telling stories—her faith, his waiting—their reunion a blessing of grace. Felicity's heart sang, praising the One who restores and redeems.

Across the street, Perpetua stepped into her villa. The parlor shone with marble and gold, the scent of blossoms washing over her as she entered the room. She paused, her breath catching as the space unfolded. It was a sanctuary crafted by Jesus—each detail a testament to His intimate knowledge of her heart. The air hummed with melody, as if the walls sang of His glory. She wandered deeper, eager to explore the haven designed for her by the Lamb.

The courtyard beckoned first, its open expanse bathed in light. There, beds of jasmine and roses—her favorites—bloomed in vibrant white and crimson. Among them grew heavenly flowers: sapphire petals blazing like divine flames, iridescent whorls cascading like water. She brushed a quivering petal, its warmth pulsing under her touch.

Lord, You wove my past into eternity's undying present.

Fragrance wafted about her, awakening pleasant memories of the sunlit gardens she'd danced in as a little girl.

Inside, the rooms glowed with elegance. Heavenly-positioned furniture decorated the space: delicately crafted chairs, cushioned couches, florid rugs spread across mosaic floors, ornate chests and cabinets filled with happy surprises. A carved olivewood table, like the one in her family's villa, stood ready for feasts with friends.

A glint caught her attention, and she looked up. A sword hung on the wall—its blade broken, rusted, a relic of decay. *What's this, Lord?*

She stepped closer, curiosity drawing her. The pitted steel, fractured at the hilt, was unmistakable. It was the gladiator's sword that stole her mortal breath in the arena. No fear stirred; instead, her heart quickened with wonder. Etched faintly on the blade, glowing through the rust, were four words: "My grace is sufficient."

Your victory, Lord! The broken blade—once a tool of death—now hung as a trophy, a triumph over the grave, its earthly decay dwarfed by Heaven's boundless joy. *This sword ended my trial, but You began my eternity.* It stood as a beacon for all, proclaiming that Earth's fiercest pains fade before the Lamb's unimaginable goodness.

A gentle yet firm knock sounded. Crossing to the parlor, Perpetua opened the purple door.

Jesus!

He stood waiting on her porch—not the majestic King on His throne, nor the Light at the gate, but as He was in Galilee, with warm eyes and rustling robes.

"May I come in?" He inquired softly.

Perpetua felt a surge of wild emotions—shock, bewilderment, awe.

She struggled for words, sputtering before they finally came out. "Please do."

She stepped aside as He entered, His presence filling the room—awesome yet familiar. The King of kings and the Lord of lords visited her now, as a friend.

What happened next would become blurred in Perpetua's memory from dizzying wonder and excitement. Seated side by side on her garden bench, they talked: Redeemer and redeemed, Creator and creation, Father and daughter, brother and sister. Words flowed—conversations about her villa, the city, the forest, and His choice of flowers for her courtyard. They spoke of her journey—her stand in the arena and the River's cleansing tide.

"You were never alone," Jesus said, taking her hand in His. The nail scars that themed the crescendo of countless songs touched her now—skin to skin.

"Each step led you here." He smiled, gesturing to the warm villa around them. "This home is yours, fierce one. Fill it with joy."

She nodded, tears flooding her eyes.

After a long, enthralling conversation, He stood to leave. "Tonight, a feast awaits in the Garden Hall. Your companions will be there."

He gave directions and turned to depart. As He neared the door, Perpetua cried out, "Jesus!"—her voice breaking with adoration.

He turned around, smiling, seeing her heart. After the briefest hesitation, she ran—and jumped. Jesus opened His arms to receive her as she leapt wildly into His embrace with blissful abandon. She clung tightly, tears soaking His robe as He cradled her—a hold of redemption and intimacy.

I'm home! she breathed.

How long did she cling to Him? A minute? A thousand years? It didn't matter—time no longer had any form or relevance.

She stepped back, releasing Him.

"Sweet daughter," He whispered, caressing her cheek with tender fingers. "I'll see you at the feast."

He left, His soft footsteps crossing the street to Felicity's villa.

Perpetua closed the door, trembling. Then, erupting with joy, she danced through the halls—arms flung wide—singing at the top of her lungs, praises to the Father who graces His children with more than they can ask or imagine.

CHAPTER 9
ABUNDANT LIFE

T he Garden Hall glowed with life—cherry blossoms and jasmine trees arching overhead, their petals drifting softly through the air. Along the great table, ivory cloth and gold trim shimmered in the light. Crystal goblets sparkled, silver cutlery gleamed, and centerpieces overflowed with golden apples, ruby pomegranates, and sapphire berries—arranged like artwork, their mingled fragrance rising like a hymn of abundance. Warm, fragrant breads rested beside jars of amber and rose honey.

Perpetua entered, jittery with excitement, taking a seat among her friends. Miriam and Thomas were there as well, and many others from her journey—all smiling, all embracing, all amazed that this could be real.

Jesus sat at the head of the table—not as the Alpha and Omega, but as a gracious host, His eyes sparkling with kindness.

The feast, they learned, was a recurring event, welcoming new arrivals to their eternal home. The garden was alive with souls laughing, toasting, and sharing tales of faith.

Jesus rose to His feet, and the garden grew quiet. He spoke, His voice familiar—like that of a father and a friend.

"Well done, faithful ones," He praised, His eyes encompassing every soul in attendance. "You are home, united forever in Paradise. Heaven is yours—without barriers, time limits, or restrictions. Discover its many wonders, from the city's shining spires to the mysterious beyond. Create with hands liberated by grace, crafting beauty that reflects My Father's heart. Love endlessly, as I have loved you. Your journeys—through dungeons, arenas, temptations, and trials—have brought you here, where every tear is wiped away, every wound healed. Walk the river paths, climb the mountain peaks, dive into crystal blue oceans, for all are yours to enjoy. This is My ever-lasting promise: you are Mine, and I am with you always—in every song, every step, every thrill."

The hall erupted with cheers as people raised their goblets in surreal thanksgiving. Fruits, breads, cheeses—a culinary spread of various delights—were savored by all, just for the thrill of it. No one needed food to survive, only to revel in the blessing of taste and texture.

Stories flowed. Perpetua giggled with Felicity over their mischievous childhoods. Lucius teased Sabina, who snorted uncontrollably—infectiously. Marcus and Thomas stood up from the table, imitating Neriah's mighty movements, causing Jesus to throw His head back in laughter.

The feast was glory—love, unity, satisfaction—every longing fulfilled.

Eventually, a divine cloud, like night, descended—not from the turning of a planet away from a sun, but as a warm, comforting dark-ness, a veil crafted by the Creator's hand. It gently embraced the city, causing golden spires to shine brighter and blossoms to sparkle like jewels.

The River's tributaries glowed, their waters dancing in the sacred dim, a symphony of light.

The garden guests gradually turned toward their homes, carrying ornate silver lanterns. They rested—hearts brimming with memories of laughter, Jesus' words, and the blessed reality of happy eternity.

In the timeless flow since the banquet, the only method of measure was the endless parade of discoveries. The companions roamed the city's paths with childlike zeal.

Felicity and her son wandered meadows where blossoms sang, meeting her great-great-grandfather. She had not known him on The Choosing Ground, yet their embrace was a joyful reunion—bound not by mortal blood but unending grace. They walked together by a stream, and he recounted his life in a distant province. He spoke of his faith, which began in childhood, the day an apostle came to his village —boldly sharing Jesus in the town square. Felicity told her story as well, their laughter mingling with the rustle of leaves and blossoms. She felt her heart expand, woven even deeper into Heaven's vast family.

Marcus explored bustling marketplaces, stumbling upon Apostle Paul by a fountain. Their exchange sparkled—Paul's wit meeting Marcus' earnest questions about grace, leaving him beaming with inspiration. Paul's eyes twinkled as he spoke of the road to Damascus, his words painting a vision of God's relentless pursuit.

Marcus later returned to his amber-walled home, sketching plans for a bakery stall—his hands itching to knead dough that would delight the city's souls.

Sabina bumped into Queen Esther in a radiant courtyard—literally bumping into her. "Oh, sorry!" she laughed before gasping, "You're the queen?"

Esther grinned. "I was down there. But here, we're sisters!"

On The Choosing Ground, Esther ruled, and Sabina toiled. Now, they swapped tales of courage and faith like old friends.

Lucius marveled at theaters where souls and angels competed in playful games. He also joined a choir, his rich voice weaving with others in a hymn of triumph and praise, the sound rising like thunder toward the throne.

Mago traced forest paths, deer bounding beside him, his calm spirit eager to discover. Each step deepened his awe—a quiet vow to explore as much as he could and, eventually, to write a series of books about his ongoing adventures through God's unending provision.

Perpetua roamed the libraries and was finally able to listen to storytellers share tales of goodness and faith—as she'd longed to do when Neriah first urged her onward. One speaker in particular, a tall man named Charlie, held her attention as he told of his life on The Choosing Ground—sharing grace and truth with young people who had been led astray by godless ideologies. Every word he spoke lifted glory to the Savior who'd strengthened him—even through martyrdom. His testimony, fervent yet warm, echoed her own stand in the arena, stirring memories of the guard who'd watched her death, his face pale with grief. A quiet assurance bloomed in her heart, causing her to smile—certain she would see him again in God's perfect timing.

All of them had explored the Tree of Life, a forest city unto itself—treading paths through its mighty branches, crossing bridges woven between boughs, gazing down at the River's crystal shimmer below. They made regular treks to the throne, joining the vast throng in ceaseless praise.

The companions reunited often, their homes filled with love and laughter. Felicity hosted new friends in her ivory villa, her yellow door always open. Marcus' stall took shape in the marketplace, his first loaves—golden and fragrant—shared freely with passersby, their smiles fueling his joy.

Now, outside a beverage shop by a sparkling fountain, Marcus had gathered them all together, hoping to spot Paul or Peter again. They settled around a table, sharing tales of their adventures.

"Paul's wit is sharper than a blade," Marcus said, grinning. "He told me grace is a river—deep, endless, always flowing."

Sabina's face lit up. "Lucius and I visited an observatory. We saw our children on The Choosing Ground—not living for God yet, but He's pursuing them."

Lucius nodded. "Their hearts are hard, but the Spirit is relentless. We saw a moment when our eldest son paused under the stars, questioning. God's there—whispering to them."

Perpetua's heart quickened, her thoughts turning to her family.

"When Neriah was leading me to the river, it was suggested that I should continue praying for the salvation of others, as I did on Earth, and that our prayers rise like incense to the Father."

She paused for a moment, recollecting. "Then, in the Throne Room, the first time we joined in worship, I had a vision of God pursuing my family."

"He's relentless," Sabina agreed. "The observatories show His pursuit—patient yet fierce."

Mago looked at each friend, his brow furrowed in thoughtful expression. "After all we've seen and experienced—dungeons, arenas, sickness, this city—if you could speak to your loved ones on The Choosing Ground, just for a moment, what would you tell them?"

His question hung in the air, its weight settling over the group. Lucius sipped his drink, considering. Perpetua gazed at a colorful awning fluttering in a light breeze, pondering.

Sabina spoke first. "Our boys—they chase wealth, power, pleasure. I'd tell them, 'If you gain the whole world but lose your soul, it profits you nothing.' Jesus offers eternal joy. Choose Him, and find life. I understand their temptation to think The Choosing Ground is all there is. I've experienced that, but it's a fleeting season."

Lucius nodded, his eyes distant. "I'd say the same. Their hurts and ambitions blind them, but the Lamb's love sees through. I'd urge them to seek the treasure that lasts."

Marcus' voice was low, raw. "My brother, Hanno—we were troublemakers, stealing, fighting, and worse. I'd tell him, 'No sin, no shame, can outrun Jesus' blood. It washes clean. There's an eternity where you can walk tall, head high, in His light. Seek Jesus, my brother. He's calling to you.'"

There was a pause as they considered the question further.

Then Felicity spoke. "To my family—slaves, taken to Gaul, lost to me long ago. I'd say, 'No chain, no pain, is forever. Trust Jesus. He's preparing a better day.' I'd share what I learned in catechism: 'For the joy set before Him, He endured the cross.' Like Jesus, set your mind on the joy that's coming."

She laughed. "I know that's easy for me to say now. I remember how fearful I was in the arena, but looking back, it was nothing by present comparison. I would want them to know what I know now."

Perpetua's heart swelled, her thoughts on her parents and son. "My family grieves, thinking I'm lost. I'd tell them, 'I'm home, in a place beyond dreams. Don't mourn but seek Jesus—and join me here.' I'd point them to the city, the river, His love."

Their eyes turned to Mago, who sat silent, the last to speak.

"My mother—she left me when I was young, chasing dreams that broke her. I'd say, 'I forgive you. The love of Jesus heals every wound. Come find Him—find us—in this eternal home.'"

They sat silently, the weight of their words a prayer. Perpetua reached for Felicity's hand, then Marcus'. The others joined, forming a circle.

"Let's pray," she said, trembling with love. "For our families—for all on The Choosing Ground."

Lucius led, speaking slowly, his simple words poured out with deep conviction. "Lord, pursue them—our children, brothers, mothers, fathers. Let Your Spirit awaken their hearts, and Your light break their chains. Draw them to Your cross, Your city, Your love. Amen."

Amens echoed—soft but fervent. They continued holding hands, praying silently, individually, together. The sound of the fountain seemed brighter, as if Heaven joined their plea.

Mago smiled, breaking the hush. "So...what's next?"

Marcus grinned. "My bakery is opening soon. I'll have breads, cakes, and scones. Come by, or I'll chase you with a loaf!"

The group burst with laughter.

Sabina leaned forward. "Lucius and I—we want to guide newcomers, like Ezra does. Show them the groves, the observatories. I want to see their faces light up at the Throne Room."

Felicity's eyes danced. "Speaking of Ezra, my son and I—we're off to that grove—to taste the lumora fruit and hear the miulumes purring. Then I'll weave light, spinning stories in thread—for a while at least. Maybe I'll make you all scarves!"

They chuckled, and Mago spoke next. "I'm going to explore. Then, I'll start writing my books. There's so much to discover: deserts of diamond sand shifting under fiery skies; oceans, clear as blue crystal, filled with islands; coral palaces with pearl caverns, and creatures of light swimming through deepest deep. There are distant jungles that pulse with color, plains where grasses sing, mountain ranges piercing clouds, canyons of unimaginable depth. Cloud kingdoms, fire kingdoms, realms of light and shadow—all open to a heart that seeks."

Mago spoke with passion, his words painting a vivid picture that stirred their collective spirits.

They sat silently, enjoying Mago's vision together. Then Marcus cleared his throat. "Don't forget to take a loaf with you."

They burst out laughing again, promising they would visit his booth regularly. Sabina requested blueberry scones.

"And you, Perpetua?" Felicity inquired, lifting an eyebrow.

Perpetua sat silently for a moment, the unending possibilities swirling. She thought of their journey—dungeon prayers, arena courage, the throne's light.

"I think...I think I'll explore for a while too." A contented smile graced her cheeks as she reached her decision. She glanced at Mago. "Want a traveling companion?"

He grinned. "The more the merrier."

Laughter erupted, mingling with the joy of countless other souls—all blending with the city's song, the river's chime, the forest's rustle.

The countryside stretched, unending—meadows of starlit blooms, mountains singing glory, streams dancing with light. Heaven's bounty unfolded: a tapestry of love, discovery, and worship, waiting for all who seek the One who spoke it into existence.

It's there now, waiting for us—a home where every heart is known, and every longing is fulfilled. It's an eternity of joy with each other—and with the Lamb who calls us His own.

He's at your door now, knocking. I encourage you to open it.

A LETTER
ADDRESSED TO YOU

Dear friends,

What a thrill it's been to share this adventure with you! I pray your heart is brimming with hope and your imagination soaring after journeying with Perpetua through Heaven's dazzling city. Writing Part One of A Song of Light and Fire was a wild ride—pouring over Scripture from Genesis to Revelation, sparring with theologians over the mysteries of Isaiah and Ezekiel, and chasing the spark of God's eternal truth. There were many late nights, lively debates, and moments when I felt like I was trying to bottle a sunrise. But oh, the delight! Every word was like uncovering a treasure, and I pray this book has lit a spark in you—a rapturous glimpse of the home Jesus is preparing for you.

You might be tempted to believe you've just read a fairytale, a whimsical story spun from dreams of Narnia or Middle-earth. But dear friends, this is no fantasy. It's the realest reality! Or, as I call it: The Greatest True Story Never Told.

Heaven is the future God desires for you, alive with golden streets that shimmer underfoot, the River of Life sparkling like crystal, the Tree of Life heavy with fruit, and happy discoveries that never end. It's a place where every tear is wiped away, every wound healed, and Jesus Himself greets you with a smile that feels like home. Cherish this truth! Let it sink deep into your bones, for it's realer than the sunrise you'll see tomorrow.

Rejoice in it with all you've got! Sing of Heaven's wonders like the redeemed, their voices shaking the crystal sea with "Holy, holy, holy." Let psalms bubble up—Psalm 23's gentle shepherd and Psalm 100's shout of joy. Share it with your family, your friends, and the barista at your coffee shop. Tell them about the river, deep and purifying, or the trees, vibrant beyond imagination, each a spark of God's boundless creativity.

And yet, as we lift our voices, let's not miss the full glory we proclaim. Too often, we herald the resurrection of Jesus with trumpets and hallelujahs, yet sideline the glorious promise of Heaven itself. Friends, that's like rejoicing over a door without stepping into the home it opens! The true wonder of the resurrection isn't solely that Christ lives, but that we can live too—in an eternal home—where life and joy never fade. This is the heart of all Christian triumph: the destination that makes every sacrifice worthwhile. Never allow this truth to slip through your fingers but embrace Heaven's reality every day, with every breath! Don't let this hope stay locked in your heart like a hidden gem—paint it bold and bright so that others may feel its magnetic pull.

When I was a boy, trembling from a nightmare, my parents' words about Heaven wrapped me in peace. Let this truth do the same for those you love.

Heaven isn't just a far-off promise. It's fuel for today's journey. Jesus faced the cross because He knew the joy that awaited all of us— and that same joy can carry you through life's storms. When bills pile up, picture a home where every debt has been paid in full. When grief stings, envision loved ones laughing by the River of Life, whole and radiant. When fear creeps in, think of Perpetua's broken sword and the words engraved upon it: My grace is sufficient. Let Heaven's reality anchor you, giving strength to love fiercely, to endure bravely, and to shine brightly. Share it boldly, like Mago's cry amid the arena's roar, inviting others to the Wedding Supper of the Lamb—where love never fades. Your joy is a lighthouse, guiding others to the Savior who's crafting their place.

So hold this vision tightly and let it spill over. Chat about it over dinner, whisper it in prayer, live it in every kind word. Heaven's not just a destination; it's a melody to sing now, a hope to share with a world that's hungry for hope.

Let's meet one day by the Tree of Life—swapping stories and

singing "Amazing grace, how sweet the sound," our hearts bursting with His love. Until then, keep celebrating, keep sharing, and keep your eyes fixed on the Lamb who calls you His own!

With boundless joy,
Your brother,
Cory

PAUSE.

TAKE A DEEP BREATH BEFORE
DESCENDING INTO PART TWO.

PART 2
AN UNCENSORED
JOURNEY
THROUGH HELL

PRAYER

Lord, protect our hearts and minds
as we confront the reality of Hell.
May we look confidently to You, our joy
and our salvation.

INTRODUCTION
A WORLD WITHOUT DAWN

∞

I hope and pray that Heaven's radiant light has filled your heart with courage to endure the darker journey ahead.

Admittedly, the following pages were agony to write, leaving me torn by conflicting emotions. Part of me wants to warn you, dear reader, to close this book now. What lies ahead is real, raw, and unsettling—truths about Hell you can't unlearn, images that may haunt your nights. On the other hand, I urge you to press on. You owe it to yourself to face this reality, for the stakes are unimaginably high, and understanding the truth about Hell could change your path forever.

Some interpreters have attempted to declaw and defang Hell, both literally and metaphorically, reducing its horror to an unnamed discomfort, or even the absence of life and happiness. But Scripture does not allow such softening. Texts like Luke 16:23–24 and Revelation 20:14–15 reveal an existence fraught with torment and despair, demanding that we face it head-on and acknowledge its terrifying truth. Yet, we do so trusting the God who judges justly (Romans 2:5–6), His perfect mercy and justice ensuring no soul faces Hell undeservedly. This book confronts that reality boldly, urging you to heed its warning.

As the narrative deepens, you may wonder if these pages draw from ancient myths of shadowy underworlds or the chilling anguish of horror films. I assure you, I've drawn no inspiration from such depictions. In truth, the reverse holds: dark fables and cinematic terrors are mere whispers of Hell's true essence, fleeting glimpses, like crude, subconscious sketches of a nightmare too vast to fathom. They spring from humanity's deepest apprehensions—primal echoes stirring an intuitive sense of the dread to come, a doom Scripture unveils with piercing clarity. Far from mimicking these innate glimpses, I've stubbornly anchored my vision in the only authoritative source: God's Word, which reveals the uncensored truth of divine judgment and eternal separation. So, pray for God's peace to sustain you before pressing on—not to linger in purposeless fear, but to confront an impending darkness deserving of your unwavering attention.

Imagine now a world where dawn never breaks, where the sweet sound of a child's laughter or the soft rustling of leaves sparks no warmth in your soul. Picture a reality where love, connection, and goodness wither to ash, leaving a gnawing ache that never ends. This isn't just a place, but an existence so devoid of God's presence that your heart chokes on despair. This is Hell, in its first, insidious form: the absence of God's common grace—the light sustaining even the most rebellious. In Part Two of *A Song of Light and Fire*, we embark on a vivid, unflinching odyssey through Scripture's stark warnings, tracing souls like Emperor Septimius Severus from Hades' emotional desolation to the Lake of Fire's eternal suffering. Our path isn't fiction but rooted in divine truth, anchored in God's unchanging Word. It's not meant to terrify, but to awaken—to call you back from the ledge before it's too late.

Years ago, in my early twenties, I had a life-changing experience that shattered my comfortable assumptions about the spiritual world. I was with a friend, sharing an evening of ordinary camaraderie, when something shifted. Their breathing grew heavy and ragged, their expression contorted, with froth forming at the corner of their mouth. Their eyes held no trace of the person I knew—only a void, a chilling malevolence. A guttural voice spoke, naming itself Pan, sneering murderous threats against my children with ancient, unrestrained hatred. Stunned, my mind reeled. I had no training, no playbook for this surreal moment, yet the danger was real. In desperation, I grabbed my Bible, and the entity shrieked, as if God's Word burned it. Exercising authority I didn't know I had, I declared my family safe in the Savior's blood, commanding the demon to leave in Jesus' name. It wailed—a piercing, otherworldly cry—and my friend collapsed, dazed, remembering nothing. The memory blurs now, but one truth shines clear: spiritual forces, holy and demonic, are real, whether or not we acknowledge them. That moment forced me to confront Hell, not as a distant idea, but a real place where evil reigns unchecked, where no Bible can be raised and no Savior's name invoked. It's a place we must not choose, and this book reveals its impending reality, not to instill fear, but to offer a path to redemption.

To fully understand Hell, we must grasp what is lost when God's presence is removed—an unimaginable devastation. It's not a mere absence, like a friend slipping away, but the embodiment of existence unmade—where all virtue, life, love, and goodness are eviscerated in an instant, leaving us exposed to ourselves: depraved, swollen with pride, gripped by terror, bereft of the grace that presently holds our self-annihilation at bay (Romans 3:10–18).

On The Choosing Ground, God's common grace sustains us, His benevolence poured lavishly on all, believer and unbeliever alike. It's rain falling on the just and unjust (Matthew 5:45); breath in our lungs; the glow of a sunset stirring awe in hardened hearts (Acts 14:17). It's the moral law etched in every soul, urging justice, mercy, and truth, even in those ignorant of God's name (Romans 2:14–15). It's the voice whispering, *We're made for more*, reflecting God's character, nudging us toward His holiness despite rebellion. Common grace restrains evil, sparing humanity from overwhelming chaos (2 Thessalonians 2:7). It's why flawed societies seek justice, why the godless love their children, and why kindness breaks through darkness (1 Corinthians 13:4–7).

Now, imagine an existence stripped of this grace we so easily take for granted. Picture a reality where the moral law no longer whispers, where love, connection, and compassion aren't just absent but unthinkable. In Hell's first stage, Hades, the soul plunges into a void where God's mercy vanishes. The joy of shared meals, a mother's touch, a friend's loyalty—these aren't merely gone; they're incomprehensible (Psalm 88:3–6). Love, defined as patient, kind, and selfless (1 Corinthians 13:4–7) becomes foreign, as no one in Hell gives of themselves. Connection, once a spark of God's image, dies, leaving isolation (Isaiah 59:2). Alliances form, but they're animalistic, driven by survival. A companion is a shield against betrayal, discarded without remorse when useless. Pride and desperation fill the vacuum left by love's death, swelling the heart with false defiance that promises strength but delivers anguish (Proverbs 16:18). The soul, stripped of divine grace, becomes a shadow, clawing for survival in unyielding gloom. This is the first Hell: God's absence revealing humanity's true nature—not noble-seekers but creatures bound by sin, their vanity mocking the glory they could've known (Romans 3:23).

This point is worthy of reemphasis: Hell will not be a place where evil souls revel in their wickedness, for no pleasure exists in its depths. The best parts of us—our kindness, empathy, and compassion—were never ours, but God's divine imprint, stripped away at His departure. Left behind, we stand unmasked as selfish, corrupt, and cruel, our true selves laid bare. Without His presence, all virtue dissolves, unveiling a heart of darkness that plots its own ruin.

But Hell isn't static. This book traces its progression through six harrowing chapters, grounded in Scriptural truth. Early chapters follow souls, like Severus, into Hades' psychological torment. No demons or boiling rivers yet—just internal flaying—pride collapsing under an unchangeable fate (Ecclesiastes 9:10). Scripture warns: "The wicked are like the tossing sea, which cannot rest" (Isaiah 57:20). Without grace, there's no peace, only anguish preparing the soul for what comes next.

The journey deepens into judgment, deeds laid bare before God's throne (Revelation 20:12). For those rejecting mercy, the final Hell awaits—the Lake of Fire, its agonies echoing Scripture: "a lake of fire burning with sulfur" (Revelation 20:14–15). Demons and rebellious souls co-inhabit this realm, their eternal suffering fulfilling Jesus' warnings of an "eternal fire prepared for the devil and his angels" (Matthew 25:41). These chapters don't flinch from horror, as Scripture doesn't, yet they reveal God's justice, offering grace to all, but honoring free will's defiance (John 3:36).

So why read this book? Because Hell is not a myth to be dismissed or a dark fairytale to be softened. It's a truth woven into God's Word, a warning that demands our full attention. In that moment when Pan fled, I learned that Jesus' power triumphs over evil, but Hell is where that power is forever out of reach.

Part Two of *A Song of Light and Fire* is not a theological essay, though it is grounded in rigorous study. It is not a novel, though it is written in story form. It is an honest depiction of what Hell is, drawn from the Scriptures, and tracing God's Word to its logical and terrifying conclusion. This is a chilling dose of reality, a warning rooted in love. It's for the skeptic who doubts Hell's existence, the believer who's grown complacent, and the seeker who senses there's more. It's for you, dear friend, standing at the crossroads of eternity. The Scriptures are clear: "The wages of sin is death, but the gift of God is eternal life in Christ Jesus our Lord" (Romans 6:23). Hell is not your destiny unless you choose it.

I present you now with the true story of Hell, uncensored. Join us as we descend, not to despair but to understand. Let Severus' story, and others, show you the cost of a life apart from God. Let Scripture's warnings awaken your heart. And let the triumph of Jesus' victory— seen in that moment when Pan fled—remind you that grace is still within reach. Turn the page, face the abyss, and choose the light.

—Cory Rosenke

CHAPTER I
THE GOD-KING

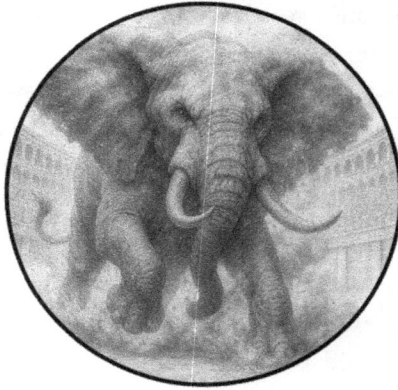

The Carthage amphitheater roared, a cauldron of bloodlust under the searing African sun. Dust swirled in the arena below, kicked up by ten thousand stomping feet, their cheers a thunder that shook the stone tiers. The air reeked of sweat, wine, and the iron tang of fresh gore. Banners of crimson and gold snapped in the breeze, proclaiming Emperor Septimius Severus' birthday, a festival of death to honor his divine reign. From his gilded dais, Severus presided, his purple robes gleaming, a crown of laurel glinting on his brow. At fifty-eight, he was Rome's master—conqueror, lawgiver, and god incarnate. His heart pounded with the spectacle of power unfolding before him.

The arena was a slaughterhouse, sand churned red from the morning's gladiator bouts. Now, a small band of Christians stood in the center, ragged and defiant. The emperor regarded each of them with a bored expression.

There was an old man muttering prayers, his gray hair plastered with sweat. Then a pregnant woman clutching her belly, her face pale but fierce. *This should be interesting.*

Next was a broad-shouldered prisoner. He was trembling, eyes darting, searching for a way of escape. The emperor smiled, savoring his enemy's fear.

Then there were a couple of thin fellows and a wild-haired old woman. A blond prisoner stood out from the rest. He appeared calm, almost casual. *I'll break you and your insolence.*

Lastly, there was a young woman, striking even in her tattered tunic—perhaps especially in her tattered tunic. The emperor smiled wickedly. The woman had long, dark, curly hair, and she glared at the crowd, her chin lifted high.

Severus didn't know their names—he didn't care. They were rebels, spitting on his divinity, and their blood would paint his glory.

A horn blared, sharp as a blade, and a cage screeched open. A lion surged out, its eyes wild with hunger. The crowd howled, a wave of glee crashing over the stands. The elderly prisoner stepped forward, his voice cracking but loud. "The Lord is my strength!" he shouted, fists clenched, his frail frame a twig before the beast.

Severus leaned forward, a grin twisting his lips. "Listen to the fool," he mocked, turning to Senator Cassius Dio, a sweaty heap of toga and jowls seated beside him. "He's shouting to his carpenter god. As if that will stop the claws."

Cassius chuckled, wiping his brow. "He's so old, he's half-dead already, Caesar. The lion's just finishing the job."

The lion pounced, a golden blur, slamming the old man to the sand. Claws ripped his chest—blood spraying like wine from a cracked jug. His scream choked off as his bones snapped under the beast's ferocity. The crowd roared, fists pumping, and Severus clapped, slow and mocking.

"That's one down." He lifted a silver goblet, swirling wine. "To his faith—may it rot with him."

Livia, a golden-haired courtesan lounging on his left, giggled, her silk veil slipping to reveal a neck pale as marble. "Such a quick end to him, Caesar," she purred, her fingers brushing his wrist. "You make death a dance."

Severus glanced at her, his smile sharp. "Death is my art, Livia. And the arena is my canvas."

His hand grazed her thigh, a bold move with Julia Domna, his wife, sitting stiffly to his right. Julia's eyes were ice, fixed on the arena. She said nothing but noticed all, and Severus smirked, relishing her anger.

Drusilla, the other courtesan, leaned in, her ebony skin gleaming under sheer linen, her voice a velvet tease. "You sure know how to please the crowd, Caesar."

"Flatterer." Severus chuckled, his fingers lingering on her arm. "But you're right—it's a fine start."

His gaze returned to the arena, where the lion was dragging the prisoner's corpse, leaving a red smear. The crowd chanted, "Severus! Severus!" and his chest swelled, the sound of their praise sweeter than wine.

A royal guard, Centurion Vitus, approached, his face grim under a dented helm. "Caesar," he said, saluting, "the bear's next, then the leopard. The elephant's ready for the big show." His voice was rough, a soldier's growl, but his expression held a flicker of unease.

Severus nodded, swirling his goblet. "Good, Vitus. But wait—any word from Britannia yet? That worm of a governor has been dodging my dispatches." His tone was light, but his eyes narrowed, like a predator sizing up prey.

Vitus shifted, armor clanking. "A rider came at dawn, Caesar. The governor whines about Pict raids—says Hadrian's wall is crumbling, begs for two more legions. Claims the tribes are uniting, some chieftain stirring them up or something."

Severus' jaw tightened, his smile gone. "Uniting? He's got eight thousand men, and he can't hold a ditch?" He leaned closer, his voice low and venomous. "Send a message, Vitus. Tell that whining fool I want that chieftain's head in a box by spring, or his wife and brats will decorate the wall instead."

Vitus swallowed, nodding. "It'll be done, Caesar."

Severus leaned back, his smile returning, cold as a blade. "And Vitus, make it clear: Failure will result in a one-way trip home—minus his head. Britannia's mine, not some barbarian's playground." He waved a hand, dismissing the centurion, who saluted and hurried off.

Cassius coughed, his voice oily. "Bold, Caesar. The Senate will applaud your grip on the provinces. Britannia has always been a leech, but you'll bleed it dry."

"Or I'll burn it," Severus quipped, his tone casual but edged. "The Senate is to jump when I say jump, Cassius. Don't forget that." He sipped his wine, eyes returning to the arena.

A second gate groaned open, and a brown bear lumbered out, its growl shaking the air. It sniffed the old man's dead body, but the lion snarled, defending its kill. The beasts clashed, claws slashing, dust billowing. The crowd gasped, then cheered as the bear backed off, its gaze focusing on the prisoners. It charged the broad-shouldered man, its heavy paws a blur. The prisoner screamed, his chest crumpling with a wet crack, blood gushing as the bear's jaws clamped his shoulder, dragging him off.

Severus yawned, feigning boredom, though his pulse raced. "Sloppy," he muttered. "The bear's too slow."

Livia's laugh was bright, her hand on his knee. "But the blood, Caesar, it's like a river! You give them such a show."

"They live for it," Severus agreed, proud with indulgence. "And I live for the screams." He glanced at Julia, expecting a reaction, but she stared at the sand, her face a mask. "What's wrong, wife?" he taunted, loud enough for the entire dais to hear. "Too much gore for your delicate stomach?"

Julia's eyes met his, sharp and cool. "It's your day, husband." Her voice was smooth but laced with acid. "Though I'd rather see someone else die today, not just your filthy Christians."

The words were a slap. Severus' smile tightened, irritation flaring, but he waved her off, turning to Drusilla. "See, my sweet?" He cupped her chin in his hand. "Even my wife enjoys a little violence."

Drusilla giggled, her lips brushing his ear, and he laughed, the sound drowning Julia's barb.

A third cage sprang open, and a leopard leapt out, its spotted coat flashing in the sun. It circled the pregnant woman, tail flicking, then it struck, claws tearing her side and jaws crushing her throat. She collapsed, blood pooling, her hand frozen on her belly.

Severus waved dismissively. "Waste of a breeder," he scoffed coldly. "But she'd only have birthed more rebels."

Cassius nodded, swigging wine. "Good riddance, Caesar. Her kind is a plague."

Livia's fingers traced his arm. "You're so decisive," she giggled, her tone dripping admiration. "It's...thrilling."

Severus smirked, his ego successfully stroked, as the courtesan had intended. "Decisions are power, Livia. And power is my birthright."

His eyes flicked to the arena, where a wild-haired woman screamed, "You've forsaken us, God!" and bolted. A guard's spear flew, piercing her back with a thud. She fell, blood blooming, and the crowd cackled, a vicious wave.

Severus clapped, amused. "Run all you want. Rome always catches up."

A roar shook the arena—not a horn, but a raw, earth-rattling bellow. An elephant stormed from a hidden gate, its tusks gleaming like swords. Its trunk thrashed, eyes mad, as its feet pounded the arena floor. The lion and bear scattered, their snarls lost in the beast's fury. The crowd surged to its feet, screaming their delight.

Severus' expression lit up, his goblet forgotten. "Now that's a monster," he leaned forward. "Let's see it crush them."

The elephant charged the two skinny prisoners—a gaunt young man and a scarred rebel. The young man tripped, his face a mask of terror. The elephant's foot smashed down, flattening his chest with a sickening crunch, blood and bone pulping into the sand. The scarred man swung around, hot with defiance, but the beast's trunk whipped, caving his skull with a wet snap. His body flew, tumbling like a broken doll, landing in a twisted heap. The crowd's roar was deafening, a tidal wave of glee. Severus laughed, loud and raw, slamming his fist on the dais. "Glorious!" he shouted. "That's power, Cassius—raw and unstoppable!"

Cassius clapped, his face red with wine. "A beast fit for you, Caesar! They'll sing of this for years!"

Drusilla's voice was a purr. "It's like you sent the beast yourself, Caesar. The crowd is yours."

Severus grinned, his heart racing, the bloodlust a fire in his chest. "They're mine, Drusilla. Every scream, every cheer—it's all for me." He glanced at Julia, expecting her to roll her eyes, but her gaze was locked on the elephant, her expression unreadable. "Speak, wife," he snapped. "Or does the beast scare you silent?"

Julia's lips curved into a faint, dangerous smile. "It's...impressive, husband. A fitting mirror for your strength." Her tone was honey, but the edge cut deep. Severus scowled, but the arena pulled him back.

Vitus returned. "Caesar, we're down to the last two. Gladiators are ready."

Severus waved a hand. "Make it quick, Vitus. Their preaching grates my nerves." His focus turned to the blond man and the young woman, the last standing. A gate opened, and two gladiators strode out, swords flashing, armor glinting.

The blond man faced them, his voice clear. "Christ is my king!" he shouted, loud enough for the dais to hear.

Severus' lip curled, his fingers tightening on Livia's wrist. "His king?" he hissed. "I'm his king—and his god." He leaned forward, voice sharp. "Vitus, kill him. Now!"

The gladiator's sword slashed, slicing through the man's arm and into his side, blood spurting. The prisoner staggered but spoke, his voice steady. "You can know Him too," he called to the gladiator. "God's grace is yours—find it in Jesus."

The blade thrust, piercing his chest. The man fell, blood pooling, and Severus snorted, his face cold. "Grace," he spat. "A weak maggot's plea."

Livia laughed softly. "He thought he'd win with words, Caesar. You showed him."

"Words are nothing," Severus barked. "Death is truth."

The second gladiator turned toward the dark-haired woman, her eyes blazing. "Jesus, I'm coming!" she shouted, her voice ringing through the arena.

Severus' jaw clenched, her defiance a slap in the face. *Why won't these rubbish Christians just die screaming like everybody else?*

"End her!" he growled.

The gladiator's sword flashed, cutting her neck. Blood sprayed, her cry choking as she crumpled, clutching air.

The crowd chanted, "Kill! Kill!" and Severus clapped, his smile thin.

"Finally," he said, though her words stung, a splinter in his pride. "Her god is as dead as she is."

Drusilla's hand rested on his arm. "You've crushed them, Caesar. Rome bows to you."

Severus nodded, his irritation fading, her flattery soothing. The arena quieted, the sand a red ruin. He stood, robes gleaming, and raised a hand.

The crowd exploded, chanting, "Severus! Severus!"

He soaked it in, the adulation a drug. "They worship me," he turned to Cassius, voice low. "And they'll beg for more tomorrow."

Cassius bowed. "A triumph, Caesar. The Senate will carve this day in stone."

"See that they do." Severus' lips tightened. "And remind them that betrayal is a slow death."

He turned to Vitus. "Clear the sand, Centurion. The gladiators are next. Keep the mob fed."

Vitus saluted before rushing off. Severus glanced at Julia, his voice commanding. "Several senators are coming over tonight, wife. Be prepared and don't disappoint me." It was an order he dared her to defy.

Julia rose, face held in a tight smile. "I serve Rome, husband—always."

She glided away, her scent lingering, and Severus watched, a flicker of suspicion in his gut. *She's plotting something*, he thought, but the courtesans' laughter pulled him back.

Livia leaned close. "Come to us tonight, Caesar. The villa's ready for you."

Drusilla's fingers grazed his neck. "We'll make you forget the arena." Her eyes held a promise.

Severus' pulse quickened, his smile wolfish. "If the feast bores me."

He rose swiftly and exited the dais. Livia and Drusilla followed, their silks whispering. The crowd cheered him, a tide of worship, and he drank it deep, his heart cold but alive.

The emperor vanished into the golden halls of his Carthage palace, a shadow fretting within him—not remorse, but a hunger no blood could satisfy.

What makes those Christians so damn tough?

The words of the blond one gnawed at him, faint but stubborn. *God's grace is yours—find it in Jesus.* He crushed the thought, his smile returning. *I'm Rome's heart,* he told himself. *And gods don't kneel.*

Years passed—his life a crown of triumphs. Parthia's kings knelt, Britannia's tribes submitted, Rome's coffers overflowed. Severus' palaces sparkled with marble, his feasts drowned in delicacies, his bed warmed by whomever he desired. The emperor's name was sung like a hymn across the empire. His whims became law, his power a blade no one could dull.

Yet, beneath the glittering triumphs, an emptiness gnawed at his soul, a hollow ache no conquest could fill. The blond Christian's words—"God's grace is yours"—stalked him like a relentless ghost, their quiet truth a whisper he could not silence.

Severus was Rome's god, his empire unyielding, but something pursued him, an unseen force that pricked his soul in the silent watches of the night.

I need no grace, he snarled, clenching his fists, but the hunger grew, and the shadow deepened, chasing him toward a reckoning he could not outrun.

"Pride goes before destruction,
a haughty spirit before a fall."
—Proverbs 16:18

CHAPTER 2
THE TRUTH-TELLER

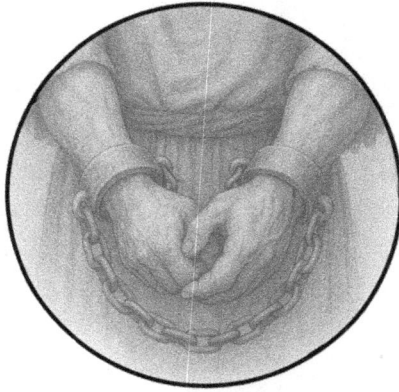

The imperial palace in Rome hummed with decadent energy, its grand hall a dazzling swirl of light and sound. Marble columns glowed under flickering torchlight, warm and golden. Crimson silks hung on the walls, swaying in a gentle breeze scented with jasmine and sweet wine. Tables sagged under heaps of roasted peacock, honey-drenched figs, and oysters shining in their shells. In the center of it all, a fountain sprayed sparkling water, its soft splash lost in the dreamy strum of lyres and flutes. The emperor's guests—senators, diplomats, wives, and courtesans—lounged about the hall on cushioned couches, laughing sharply, whispering their endless secrets. Slaves glided past silently, carrying silver trays piled with delicacies.

Severus lounged on a golden couch, crimson silks spilling around him like a king's cloak. His purple toga, draped low, revealed a proud chest. A laurel crown sat on his oiled, silver-streaked hair, catching the light.

Annia, her red curls tumbling like a wildfire, pressed close on his left, her sheer gown slipping to flaunt her curves. Her lips grazed his ear, whispering flirty words with a soft, teasing voice.

Flavia, blonde and sleek, draped over his right, her fingers caressing the emperor's neck.

Across the hall, Julia Domna sat on an ebony couch, watching the emperor—her husband—publicly lounge with his newest playthings. She burned with a quiet rage, her smile tight, noting every insult.

Clearing his throat, Senator Cassius staggered up, his goblet raised high. "To Emperor Severus, Rome's divine ruler!" he shouted. "You smashed Parthia, tamed Britannia's wild Picts, built our glory! Your legions crush our enemies; your wisdom outshines all!"

The crowd cheered, goblets banging together, their voices loud and rowdy.

Suddenly, the bronze doors slammed open, cutting the senator's big moment short, silencing the hall with an echoing clang. Centurion Vitus stormed in, his armor streaked with blood and dust.

"Emperor!" He dropped to one knee. "We've captured Maximus, the traitor!"

Severus leapt to his feet, surging with excitement. "Maximus," he bellowed, eyes blazing. "Bring him to me!" His voice cracked like a whip.

The hall hummed with intrigue, the guests leaning forward, eager to witness the spectacle.

Guards dragged a chained prisoner to the center of the hall. He stood tall, his blond hair matted with blood and soil, his green eyes fierce and unyielding. Maximus, once a tribune of unmatched renown, had forsaken his legion's glory for a Christian cross, evading capture for years as a shepherd of souls. His arrest was a triumph for Severus, a prize he had hunted across provinces. Now, finally, Maximus stood chained before him.

The guests buzzed, whispering the prisoner's tale—warrior to preacher, honor to treason.

Severus stood, toga swirling, filling the room like a storm. "Maximus," he hissed, his voice smooth but edged like a blade. "You've stirred up my empire with your nonsense. Where's your little flock of Christians hiding now?"

The prisoner stood quietly, with no hint of fear. The crowd murmured, shifting in anticipation.

The emperor's grin tightened, his voice colder. "Who's slipping you coin for this rebellion? Talk, or I'll burn every Christian from here to the sea." He stepped closer, willing Maximus to crack.

The prisoner didn't budge. His silence was loud, like a slap in the face.

Severus moved closer, eye-to-eye. "Why spit on a god, you fool? Speak, or your innards will paint my hall red tomorrow." He stared intensely, waiting for a flinch.

Maximus remained calm, cheeks relaxed, his silence a wall nothing could break.

Julia's lips twitched—maybe curious, maybe amused. Annia and Flavia swapped quick looks, their flirtatious energy gone.

Severus laughed, short and mean, waving a hand as he turned away. "Fine. I'll chop his head off at dawn. Get him out of my sight." His voice was hard, done with games.

"Emperor Severus," the prisoner's voice rang out. "Hear me: I bring you news of Jesus Christ."

The words struck like lightning in the room. The hall gasped, goblets rattled, and senators stared in disbelief, mouths agape. Cassius coughed violently, wine trickling down his plump chin. Julia's goblet paused mid-air, her eyes keen. A flute emitted a squeak, its player taken by surprise.

Severus' grin faded momentarily, then returned with an amused, playful expression.

"Go on, pastor," he invited, reclining beside Annia, her warmth diverting his attention. "Spin your little tale before you start bleeding." His tone was mocking, but his expression showed a spark of intrigue.

Maximus continued, chains rattling. "Severus, God, who is loving and just, created everything, ruling over it—the sky, the sea, the stars, even Rome itself."

The crowd gasped once more, but Severus gestured for silence. Maximus pressed on, undaunted. "This God, our Father, fashioned mankind in His image, to shower them with good gifts—life, love, a world brimming with beauty. He longed to walk with them, His cherished children, to share His boundless joy. But in greed and wickedness, mankind turned away, choosing sin over righteousness, falsehood over truth. They spurned the Creator who loved them, chasing shadows of their own making."

Maximus hesitated briefly, contemplating. "What would you do, Emperor, if your people rejected the gifts you provided, the victories you achieved for them, even renouncing your name and authority?"

Severus grinned like a jackal. "I'd pile their heads like a pyramid," he stated matter-of-factly, lifting a jewel-encrusted goblet high, as if toasting his guest's hypothetical demise.

"I know you would, Emperor." Maximus indicated the room. "We all know you would. But God chose a different path. He sent His Son, Jesus, to bear our punishment. You see, God's love for us is deeper than we can ever imagine—including His love for you."

Maximus looked at Severus thoughtfully. "How many Christians have you crucified, Emperor—hundreds?"

Severus examined his fingernails, as if bored. "Thousands!" he boasted proudly.

"Thousands!" the prisoner sighed. "Those poor souls had no choice, but Jesus willingly died on the cross to pay for our sins. But His death isn't the reason I'm here, Emperor. I'm here because Jesus *rose* from the dead, after being crucified, impaled, and entombed! He conquered death, and because of His resurrection, He has the power to raise us as well. If you repent of your sins and place your trust in Jesus, you will have eternal life in His kingdom."

Maximus paused, waiting for the emperor to respond. Severus sat in silence, as if pondering the words spoken. The hall was still, hushed.

Then the emperor burst out laughing, throwing his head back. "You believe I need to be saved by a carpenter?" He leaned in, lips spitting venom. "Tomorrow, you will die, Maximus. Your fairytale won't save you. My lions are starving."

The crowd erupted, clapping and jeering, but the prisoner's voice sliced through the noise, calm and precise. "I'm not afraid of dying," he replied frankly. "I'll be with Christ in Heaven, while you sit on a throne that's crumbling to ash."

His words hit with force—like a threat.

The centurion's hand shifted to his sword hilt. Julia's eyes flickered, drawn by something in his tone.

"Heaven?" Severus scoffed, his voice laced with sarcasm. "What is this paradise you're so eager to trade your life for? Answer me quickly."

Maximus surveyed the room, observing the many faces anticipating his reply. Taking a deep breath, he released it slowly, closing his eyes, as if envisioning something. The room fell silent, attentive—expectant. "Heaven is eternal joy, where pain, sorrow, and fear vanish forever." The prisoner's lids remained shut. He spoke slowly, as if describing a vision unfolding before him in real time. "Golden streets glisten, crystal rivers sing, trees yield endless fruit, their leaves whispering life. But the true essence of Heaven isn't peaceful forests or shining cities, it's God Himself—our Father, walking with us, His love our eternal dwelling place."

A smile appeared on the prisoner's lips, his eyes still closed. "You'll share laughter with friends from every era, worship in radiant light, forever complete. It's not just a location; it's life with Jesus. It's life...in abundance."

Maximus opened his eyes, turning to the emperor. "Trust Him, Caesar. Embrace His limitless mercy, and you'll discover peace that never diminishes, a joy that fills every moment. Accept His gift of grace to you."

The crowd held silent, wrestling with the prisoner's words.

When Severus finally spoke, his tone was harsh and mocking. "Bow to a carpenter?" he fumed, leaping to his feet. "I am the god of Rome, you fool! You'll face lions, not gleaming avenues!"

Maximus stood tall, his tone gentle yet commanding. "Choose Christ, Emperor. His mercy is available, even to you."

"You're calling me a sinner?" Severus flared with anger. "I'm divine, Maximus. Rome worships me, not your nobody god."

He leaned back on his golden couch, exasperated, glaring at the prisoner who dared enter his hall and summon him, *Caesar*, to repentance. His jaw clenched, a vein pulsing at his temple.

Then, the emperor's expression shifted, his tone becoming sly, condescending, as if baiting a trap. "Your God is said to be good and loving, right? So why's He burning people in Hell? Explain the flames, the screams."

Maximus tilted his head patiently, like a friend preparing to speak truthfully. "Hell is not God's fire, Emperor. It's the natural consequence of existence without Him—dark and chaotic. Hell is you continually destroying yourself and others, over and over again. It's a place where His divine presence, His goodness and love, is absent from human hearts and their surroundings. It's a realm where humanity exists solely in its own godless state. Indeed, Hell *will* be a place of fire, and the gnashing of teeth, but God does not desire any of us to experience it."

The room remained silent, the prisoner's words impacting not only the emperor but the entire imperial hall.

Maximus continued. "We are designed to live in connection with God, but if we decide to live apart from Him—that's our decision, not His. The world we currently live in—this hall, the oxygen we breathe, your beloved arena—this isn't all there is. It's a choosing ground, Emperor. And our choice is light or darkness, Heaven or Hell. God does not choose for you. It's up to you. Choose pride and invent your own truth, or choose humility and follow *the* Truth."

Maximus glanced at the centurion, a smile forming at the corner of his lips. "I was not captured, Emperor. I was sent to share this truth with you; even if it ends my days on this temporal plane." The prisoner turned, his gaze taking in the whole room. "So I say to all of you: Repent now, make Jesus your Savior."

The crowd gasped, more than one senator choking on his drink. Cassius slammed his goblet down, wine splashing on his toga.

Severus roared with contemptuous laughter. "You want me crawling on my knees like a servant?" He stood tall, glowering. "I am Emperor Septimius Severus, the divine! Tomorrow, your head will roll."

Maximus smiled softly, his eyes piercing. "Laugh now, Caesar, but truth doesn't change to suit us—not even you. Jesus is Lord. Repent or be judged." His voice was calm, a final plea for the emperor's soul. "Choose quickly, while you've still got time."

Severus' laughter turned cold, slicing like a knife. He waved a hand. "Take him," he growled. "He can pray to his carpenter in chains. Dawn will shut him up."

Guards seized Maximus, dragging him out, his voice fading, "Repent, Emperor..."

The crowd buzzed with whispers. Julia's gaze was hard, like she was weighing something.

Severus turned back to the party, clapping his hands. "More wine, more music!" he ordered, sinking beside Flavia, pulling her close, her lips brushing his ear. Annia leaned in, her hands roaming, teasing, trying to pull him back to the fun.

The lyres kicked up, louder, the fountain's spray catching the torchlight, sparkling like tiny stars. The guests laughed, their smiles fake, scheming behind every word.

Cassius, still red-faced, grabbed another goblet, yelling, "To Caesar's glory!"

The crowd echoed the words, but it felt hollow, Maximus' presence still lingering like smoke in the room.

Julia watched from her couch, a tight smile on her face. "That was quite a show, husband," she said, a hint of mockery in her tone. "You played the god so well, as always."

Severus smirked, his hand on Annia's waist. "Rome is my heaven, darling, and I'm its deity."

A gray-haired senator stumbled over, drunk, raising his goblet. "To

Severus, who crushes rebels like bugs!" he slurred, spilling wine on the floor, the crowd laughing, clapping.

Cassius joined in—again—shouting even louder, "Maximus will make good lion feed!"

The hall cheered, though with less enthusiasm than earlier. Julia stayed quiet, watching Severus, like she saw something nobody else did.

"Keep the music going!" Severus shouted, waving at the musicians, who scrambled to play faster, their notes wild now, almost desperate. The crowd danced, swaying, their togas and dresses a blur of color, their laughter forced, eyes darting, always watching for a chance to climb higher.

Flavia's lips grazed his jaw, but Severus' mind wandered, the prisoner's words still echoing—*repent, Jesus, Heaven, Hell*—poking holes in his vanity. He pushed Flavia back, just a bit, his grin fading, the party's shine starting to crack.

As the revelry dimmed, Severus stood, swaying a little from the wine. "I'm done," he muttered, heading for his chambers, Annia and Flavia trailing like shadows, their eyes hungry, ready to please. The bed chamber was all soft silk and warm light.

"My emperor," Annia purred, her gown slipping from her shoulders, red curls spilling as she pressed against him. Flavia joined, her lips fierce, blonde hair falling, their touches a fire that tempted him to forget everything. But Maximus' words clung tight—*God made it all, man fell, Jesus saves, repent before it's too late*—souring their seduction.

"Out," Severus snapped, his voice rough, cutting through their giggles. They froze, faces falling, then slipped away, leaving him alone.

He sank onto silk sheets, a dim lamp flickering, its shadows dancing like ghosts on the walls. Maximus' voice wouldn't quit—*God created, man sinned, Jesus died, repent*. He saw Heaven in his mind, streets shining like gold, peace he'd never felt, but mocking his power, his throne. Hell scared him more, and the talk of a choosing ground disturbed him. The idea that he had spent his years in meaningless pursuits, completely missing the purpose of earthly life—it was preposterous. Still, conviction lay heavy upon him.

Nonsense!

He shoved the prisoner's words aside, pride flaring like a torch. "I'm a god," he muttered, fists clenched. "I don't kneel to anybody. I make my own truth."

His heart pounded, thoughts reeling. Maximus' unflappable demeanor irritated him—calm, sure, a man who looked at death with a smile. "I'm Rome," he whispered, voice hoarse, trying to believe it.

The shadows grew darker, sharper, creeping closer, like they had claws.

Suddenly, a crushing pain gripped his chest—a fist closing hard around his heart. Severus gasped, clutching his toga, breath short and ragged. Sweat beaded his brow, nausea churning his gut.

Too much wine, he thought, but the pain surged, radiating to his left arm, a heavy, searing ache. His vision blurred, the room tilting, his pulse erratic. He writhed on the bed, gasping, each heartbeat a labored thud. Then, a strange calm settled over him. He felt weightless, rising above his body. Looking down, he saw himself—pale, still, sprawled on silk sheets, eyes wide, hand frozen on his chest. The pain was gone —peace enveloping him.

I'm free.

Joy surged through him, as if all burdens had melted away.

Abruptly, the putrid reek of sulfur overwhelmed his senses, and a cold blackness yanked at him. He fell into darkness—screaming.

The mortal body of Septimius Severus lay still, eyes wide, hand frozen over a heart gone quiet. The palace slept, blind to its emperor's fall. Whispers of his death would soon echo through the empire. History would record his reforms, purges, and triumphs, but remain silent on his soul—dragged to the place he had chosen—lost forever.

"What good will it be for someone to gain the whole world,
yet forfeit their soul?"
—Matthew 16:26

CHAPTER 3

THE FALL

Darkness swallowed Severus whole. For a moment, he was at peace, free from pain; the next, he was falling. His gut twisted as he dropped through endless black, the air screeching past like a horde of angry ghosts. He flailed, hands grabbing at nothing. No emperor now—just a man, scared and blind.

What's happening? Panic clawed his mind.

The fall dragged on, his bloodcurdling screams lost in shadow. Then, with a bone-crushing thud, he hit the ground, pain ripping through his ribs, his back, his head. It knocked the breath out of him —a burning agony that left him sprawled, gasping on a floor cold as death.

He lay there for what seemed like an eternity, his body screaming, each breath a struggle. His fingers scraped the stone, searching for something solid, but the pain wouldn't quit; throbbing like a relentless war drum.

I'm not dead, he told himself, *but where am I?*

He pushed to his knees, wincing as his joints groaned. His eyes fought the darkness, but a grim fog hung over everything, blurring the world like a bad dream. He squinted, heart sinking as he made out stone tiles—familiar but wrong. This was his courtyard, the heart of his palace in Rome. The columns, the fountain, the benches, they were all there but colorless, wrapped in a haze that stank of rot. Confusion hit him hard, heavier than the fog.

This can't be real, he reasoned, stomach knotting. *A trick? Some cruel jest?*

He was Septimius Severus, emperor, conqueror. This gray, empty place wasn't his, and yet it felt too real, too heavy on his chest.

His legs shook as he pushed himself upright, pain stabbing his hips.

"Caracalla!" he yelled, expecting his son's sharp reply. The silence hit him like a slap, cold and final. "Geta!" he tried, calling for his younger boy, but the sound just echoed, fading into nothing.

Anger surged, hot and familiar, but it couldn't hide the panic creeping in. *Where are they?* His heart raced. *My sons, my blood—they should be here.*

He stumbled across the courtyard, each step a fight against the quiet that pressed in. *They wouldn't leave me,* he told himself, but doubt gnawed like a rat. *Caracalla's too ambitious, Geta too weak—did they turn on me?*

The palace felt wrong, empty, like a grave. He pushed into the main hall, and it struck him—too quiet, too still. The ceiling was lost in fog, the walls, once bright with paintings, were now cracked and bare.

This isn't right. Unease crawled up his spine. *My palace was alive, full of power.*

The dining room, where he'd laughed with senators over wine, was a shell of itself. Tables were flipped, chairs broken. His once impressive throne now loomed like a tombstone, its gold faded to dust. It hit him hard. *My throne, reduced to this?*

"Guards!" he shouted, voice breaking. "Slaves! Get out here!"

The words came back, mocking, and a chill sank into him. *This isn't my Rome. What's happening?*

He stood frozen, chest tight, picturing his sons' faces—Caracalla's smirk, Geta's nervous eyes. *They can't have betrayed me, not after all I've given them.* But the silence screamed otherwise, and fear dug deeper, a blade in his heart.

Confusion gnawed at him, a beast in his head. *I felt it—the end.* But now he was in this strange place, a palace that felt like his but wasn't.

Did Caracalla do this? he wondered, fists tight. *Lock me away to steal the throne?* His mind spun—poison, betrayal? He thought of Carthage—the arena where he'd sent countless Christians to die, their prayers loud in his memory. *Has their God cursed me?*

Vanity shoved the horrifying thought down. *I don't kneel to gods.* Still, fear grew, a cold knot he couldn't shake. *What is this place?* He hated how it made him feel—small, lost, like a weak, frail boy. He kept moving, shouting for his sons, voice raw.

I built an empire. This isn't how it ends.

Fear tightened, a cold weight chilling his gut. Rome was alive, loud, powerful—but this was dead, and it scared him more than he'd ever admit.

Thirst struck like a knife, his throat so dry it hurt, his tongue heavy.

I need water.

He stumbled to the courtyard fountain, its stone figures twisted and ugly in the fog. He leaned in, desperate for a sip, but the basin was cracked, dry as death.

"No," he growled, smacking the edge in frustration, pain coursing through his hand. *I'm an emperor, not some street rat.*

He headed for the storerooms, searching for jars that held wine and oil. He tore into the first one, but found only broken clay shards that sliced his hands. *There's got to be something.* He ripped through shelves, dust choking him. Blood dripped from his cuts, but he didn't care, driven by a need that burned. *My throat's killing me. This can't be my palace.*

He ransacked another storeroom, then another, desperation clawing at him. *Where's my wine, my water?* He kicked a shattered jar, pain flaring, and dropped to his knees. *Is this a punishment?*

He remembered Maximus, who begged him to trust in Jesus. *I laughed him off. Should I have listened?* The thought stung, but pride snapped back. *No. I'm Severus. I don't bow.*

The thirst wouldn't stop, becoming a fire in his throat. *Where has everything gone?*

He crawled to one last storeroom, hands scraping stone, finding more shards, more dust. *This isn't right. I ruled Rome. I deserve better.*

His mind churned—every victory, every enemy crushed, and now this? The fog seemed to laugh, pressing closer, and he slumped against a wall, beaten but stubborn.

I'll find water. I'll find answers.

Thirst owned him, and he hated how it made him feel—small, weak, human. He shut his eyes, begging for rest, just a moment to breathe. *Let me sleep,* he thought, but his head wouldn't stop—memories of battles, betrayals, his own iron will. No rest came, no peace. *Why can't I just close my eyes?*

Exhaustion dragged at him, but this place, whatever it was, gave no mercy. *I'm still emperor,* he told himself, but doubt crept in. *Or am I nothing now?*

As thirst consumed him, a ragged scraping sound cut through the heavy air. Severus' body tensed, his heart jumping.

In a doorway across the courtyard, a shadow lurked, darker than the fog, human-like—but wrong. Fear hit him hard, raw, making him feel like a boy again, and he hated it.

He froze, his breath short. The shadow crouched, motionless. *Is it a guard? Something worse?* His hand reached for a sword he didn't have, ego yelling at him to stand and fight. But his legs felt like stone, his voice stuck.

The figure moved a little, releasing a low, venomous chuckle, like a snake ready to strike.

It knows me, he thought, skin crawling. *It's here for me.*

Panic squeezed his chest, and he despised himself for it.

The shadow rose slowly, still veiled in darkness.

"Severus," it hissed, voice smooth but sharp, "I wondered when you'd join us."

"Who's there?" Severus forced out, voice shaky. "Show your face, or I'll make you regret it."

The figure laughed, a sound that stung like a whip. It stepped into the dim light, fog parting, and Severus' breath caught.

It was Senator Didius Julianus, a rival from his early days as emperor, a man whose cunning had nearly toppled him. Severus had ordered his death, watched his blood pool on the palace floor. Now, Didius stood, his face a wreck—a gash across his cheek showed his jawbone, shining sickly in the haze. His eyes smoldered, sharp and alive.

"No warm welcome, Emperor?" Didius asked, his smile crooked, the gash twitching. "You look like you've seen a ghost."

Severus' head spun, fear piercing like a blade. *Didius, back from the dead?*

"This isn't real," he growled, though his voice wavered. "I'm Septimius Severus, ruler of Rome. I don't belong in this place."

Didius' expression flickered, like a wolf spotting weakness. "This place?" he laughed, waving at the gray courtyard, voice dripping with scorn. "This is Hades, Severus, where your crown is dust."

He stepped closer, voice low, cutting. "You built your empire on blood—mine and countless others. Now you're one of us."

Hades. The word landed like a stone, and terror flooded him, unstoppable. *No way! I'm bigger than this.* Pride fought back, but his heart was racing with dread he couldn't hide.

"You're lying," he spat, voice cracking. "This is some kind of trick, a bad dream."

Didius laughed, eating up his fear. "A trick? Open your eyes, Severus. No sons, no army. Just you, stuck with us."

He leaned in, gash gaping, his voice a snarl. "You're not dreaming. You're damned."

Severus' mind scrambled, pride wrestling with terror. He saw a nameless woman's face, defiant in the arena, her prayers ringing out. *Is her god doing this?* Terror dug in, but he pushed it away.

"If this is Hades," he retorted, "what are you doing here, Senator? Still plotting, even while dead?"

Didius' smile broadened, sly and dangerous. "Plotting? Maybe. You always thought you were smarter, Severus. Thought you'd buried me for good, didn't you? But look at us now, side by side." His voice was thick with contempt. "You cut me down to keep your throne, but what did it get you? A grave, your sons fighting like rats over scraps?"

Severus' hatred raged, pushing his fear aside. "I saved Rome," he snapped. "You were a traitor, Didius. You would have burned it all down."

"Traitor?" Didius sneered. "You called anyone a traitor who got too close to your power. Half the Senate...anyone with a spine. You drowned us in blood, and for what? To die gasping, your empire crumbling?"

He stepped closer. "You're no emperor here, Severus. You're nothing."

Panic squeezed Severus' chest, but vanity wouldn't let go. *Nothing? Me?*

"You're less than nothing," he cursed. "A dead man whining about old fights. If this is Hades, I'll get out."

Didius' laugh was mocking. "Big talk. But you feel it, don't you? The quiet, the weight. This place breaks you down."

He stopped, surveying his former emperor like a prize, then softened his voice with calculated flattery. "You were sharp once, Severus. Cruel, sure, but sharp. That's why I'm here, talking to you, and not with one of those countless fools out there digging in the dirt."

Severus squinted, suspicion curling tight. *He's after something.*

"Get to the point, Didius," he snapped impatiently. "What's your angle?"

Didius shrugged, his gash shifting, ugly in the light. "No angle. Just trying to get by. You're new here, Severus, but you'll see: Hades is a cage, and you either work with others or you don't."

He leaned in, voice low. "I know things, Emperor. Things you'll want to hear."

"Like what?" Severus shot back. *He's playing me.*

Didius' eyes flicked to the fog, then back, voice dropping to a hush.

"Talk, that's all. Whispers about a sacred scroll, buried somewhere in these ruins. Word is, it's got power—maybe even a way of escape. A door out of this pit."

Hope sparked, wild and rabid, a rope thrown into this gray hell. *A way out?* Severus grabbed at the thought, but doubt held him back. *A scroll? Sounds like a trap.*

"If it exists, why haven't you found it?"

Didius smirked, a thin layer of warmth poorly draped over his blatant disdain. "I've looked, but it's tricky. Two heads are better, especially one like yours. You beat me before, didn't you?" His tone was half-praise, half-mockery.

Severus hated him, hated the truth in his stare, hated this place. *He's full of it, but what else do I have?* The scroll, if it was real, was his shot.

"We look for it, together," he commanded, his contempt obvious. "But if you double-cross me, Didius, you'll wish you'd stayed dead.

Didius' smirk grew, and he turned to the gates. "Double-cross? We'll see who makes their move first, Emperor."

They stepped out of the crumbling palace and into the streets, now a wasteland. Rome's glory was gone. Buildings stood broken, their roofs collapsed. The fog ate the light, making everything flat, like a dead man's dream.

Shadows moved out there—thin figures, eyes sharp, digging through the rubble. Some tore at walls, others fought, growling like dogs.

"The scroll," Didius whispered, nodding at them. "They're all after it, ready to slit throats for it."

Severus watched, fear and suspicion twisting inside him. These people were scum, nothing like him, but their desperation felt familiar.

The city went on, empty and splintered, and he knew one thing for certain: Trust was a lie, but that scroll was his only way out.

"Such is the destiny of all who forget God;
so perishes the hope of the godless."
—Job 8:13

CHAPTER 4

THE SCROLL

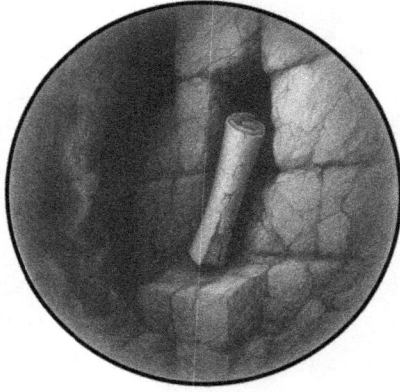

Severus stepped from the gray haze of the broken palace into the wasteland of Hades, Senator Didius Julianus a shadowed presence at his side. The city was no longer the eternal empire but a festering wound, its stones slick with a rancid, oily film that glistened like the hide of some diseased beast. Buildings stood broken, spilling splintered beams and rusted iron into streets choked with ash and debris. A thick fog coiled through the air, strangling what little light dared penetrate the void above, casting the world in a nauseous gray pallor that stung Severus' eyes and coated his tongue with a bitter tang. *This is no Rome I know.* His heart was a tight knot of unease. *This is a grave, and I'm buried in it.*

Didius turned toward him, sharp with calculation. "You're not like the rabble out there, Severus," he said, his voice low and probing. "You know things—plots, secrets, the kind that kept you on the throne. That's why I'm with you."

His words were honeyed, but the smirk twisting his ruined face betrayed a deeper game.

He's using me, Severus thought, his own cunning flaring. *But I'll use him first.*

"If this scroll exists," Severus reasoned, "it's in the archives. Hidden, no doubt, but I've unraveled tighter snares than this."

Didius' smirk widened, a flicker of respect warring with suspicion. "Your move, Emperor. Lead the way."

They ventured deeper into the hellscape, the air heavy with the stench of rot, a metallic bite that clawed at their throats. The streets were a labyrinth of ruin, each corner hiding jagged remnants of Rome's past: toppled statues, their faces eroded to blank stares; fountains cracked and dry, their basins filled with an ugly black sludge. *I ruled this city,* he fumed. *How dare it turn on me.*

A pile of rubble blocked their path, and as he climbed over, his fingers brushed something sharp—a dagger, half-buried under a broken slab, its blade dulled but heavy, crusted with dried blood. He pried it free, the metal cold against his palm, and tested its balance. *A small gift from this pit.* He grinned, tucking it into his belt, its weight a spark of control in this chaotic abyss.

Didius' gaze lingered on the blade, but he said nothing.

The wasteland was not empty. Shadows clung to every ruin—ragged figures, their bodies gaunt, eyes glinting with hunger. They crouched in doorways, perched on crumbling ledges, or leaned against walls, their eyes tracking Severus and Didius like wolves circling prey.

A man, his tunic torn to ribbons, stood motionless in an alley, his fingers twitching as if clutching an unseen weapon. A woman, her face a map of scars, watched from a shattered balcony, her lips parted in a silent snarl. Others melted into the fog, their breaths rasping, their forms taut, poised to spring. *They're waiting for a mistake.*

Severus gripped the dagger tightly, his pulse a steady drum of caution.

"Vermin," he muttered, contempt masking the chill creeping up his spine.

Didius cackled, an amusement that quickly morphed into a venomous hiss. "Vermin? No, Severus, they're us, stripped to bone and truth. This is Hades, were your crown is ash."

He gestured to a figure sharpening a splintered bone against a flattened stone, its gaze locked on them. "Look at them. They rape, they kill, they tear each other apart, and no death to end it. You rise, broken, bleeding, violated, and fight again, clawing to be stronger, to crush before you're crushed. Man, woman, young, or old—it doesn't matter. Everyone falls." His voice dropped. "You'll fall, too, Emperor. You'll learn what it means to be prey."

Severus' stomach twisted, the words a poison seeping into his spirit. He saw it in the watchers' eyes—a need beyond survival, a lust to dominate, to destroy. *I'm not them!* His pride flared like a shield. *I'm Septimius Severus, conqueror, emperor. I bow to no one.* But Didius' face savored his unease, and Severus hated the doubt it stirred.

"You speak like a man who's tasted it," Severus barked, mocking.

Didius chuckled grimly, unashamed. "I have. And I'll taste it again. So will you. You will feel the pain, Emperor, and the humiliation. And if you're thinking that killing and raping might bring you pleasure, do not be fooled. There's no pleasure here. There's only the impulse to hide, to run, or to dominate."

The senator's words hung heavy, but Severus forced himself to focus. *The scroll is my way out,* he thought, clinging to the spark of hope Didius had dangled.

"The archives," he stated, voice like iron. "Move."

They pressed through streets thick with debris, the watchers trailing at a distance, their footsteps a soft, menacing rhythm. Some emerged closer, their forms more distinct—a young woman, barely eighteen, eyes hollow, clutched a rusted nail; an old man, his back bent, dragged a club fashioned from a chair leg. Their silence was worse than screams, a promise of violence held in check, waiting for a flinch, a stumble. *They smell weakness.*

Severus' hand never strayed from the dagger. He met their hungry looks with his own, cold and unyielding, but the strain of tension pressed against him—like a vice tightening around his ribs.

A dryness seized Severus' throat, a throbbing ache that gnawed at his focus. *I need water!* He turned to Didius, his voice desperate. "Where can we find water in this cursed place?"

Didius laughed, a dry, choking rasp, scraping the air like shattered glass. "Water? There's no water!" His expression distorted in harsh amusement. "The only way to keep the madness of thirst at bay is to distract yourself with action—keep moving." Didius licked his cracked lips, a slow, involuntary motion, as if the words had roused his unending thirst.

Severus stared, disgust and unease warring within him. *No water?* The realization became a knot in his gut. *This hell takes everything.*

The archives loomed, a crumbled monument of stone and mold, its columns fractured, its doorway a yawning wound. The fog thickened here, curling like fingers around the entrance, the stench of mildew and decay choking him. Inside, the air was a suffocating blend of dust and rot, the floor littered with shredded scrolls and broken shelves, a slaughterhouse of knowledge. Severus' hope flickered, a fragile flame in the darkness. *If the scroll is here, it's buried deep,* he thought, scanning the chaos.

"It's been torn apart," he pointed, his voice flat, masking the frustration devouring him. He moved to a shadowed wall, fingers tracing a seam he'd known in life—a hidden compartment, carved for imperial secrets.

"There's a chamber here, I think."

Didius' eyes widened, a flicker of greed, but he nodded, silent.

Severus pressed the seam, and with a groan, the stone shifted, revealing a narrow recess. A scroll, brittle and yellowed, tumbled out, landing in his hands. His heart leapt, a wild surge of hope mirrored in Didius' quick intake of breath.

Is this it?

Severus' fingers trembled as he carefully unrolled the parchment, its edges crumbling under his touch. The words stared back, and horror gripped him—not the sacred scroll, but his last will and testament, decreeing the division of power between Caracalla and Geta.

Didius read the words, countenance falling, his hope curdling to anger. "Worthless," he spat, but before Severus could respond, a shriek tore through the silence. Scavengers, a dozen strong, burst from the shadows, their faces twisted with madness, seeing the parchment in his hand.

"The scroll!" one screamed.

A woman with a half-burned face lunged at Severus. He sidestepped, slashing his dagger across her arm. Didius grappled with a man wielding a broken pipe, but the attackers swarmed, their howls a chorus of greed and despair. Crude weapons—jagged stones, splintered boards, and rusted iron spikes—flashing in the dimness. Severus drove his blade into an assailant's shoulder—the man's scream piercing the gloom. He bolted for the door, a horde of screeching marauders at his heels. *Didius can rot,* he thought, not sparing a glance as the senator's shout was cut off—a pipe cracking against his skull, his form lost in the chaos.

Severus ran, heart hammering, the hellscape a blur of fog and ruin. Footsteps pounded behind, the scavengers baying like wolves on the hunt. He veered into an alley, scrambling over a pile of rubble, hands torn by sharp stone, blood slicking his fingers. A rusted ladder clung to a crumbling wall, its rungs groaning under his weight as he climbed frantically. An attacker's fingers grasped his ankle, nails digging in. He kicked free—pain flaring—and hauled himself onto a rooftop, tiles sliding underfoot, some plummeting to the street below.

Keep moving, he screamed at himself, leaping to the next building, then another, navigating a maze of collapsed peaks and yawning gaps. The fog cloaked his path—a treacherous ally—but a stone whizzed past, clipping his temple, blood trickling down his cheek. He didn't stop, lungs wheezing, muscles screaming, until the scavengers' cries faded into the haze.

He dropped to the ground, collapsing behind a fallen chimney, gasping for air. The city's pulse—screams, crashes, the distant snarl of violence—throbbed in his ears, unrelenting. *I have to get out of this place,* he raged wildly, desperation choking him. *I hate this!*

He wanted to scream in frustration but held silent for fear of being discovered. Blood dripped from his temple, stinging his eye, but the scroll's promise now burned brighter than the pain. *It's real—it has to be,* he promised himself, clinging to the hope Didius had planted.

The wasteland stretched around him, a vast sea of ruin that offered no mercy. He wiped the blood from his face, hand trembling, and forced himself to stand.

I'm not done! Pride flamed in his chest. *Not now, not ever.*

A soft crunch broke his thoughts. Severus twisted, raising his dagger, every sense alert.

Out of the fog, a figure emerged, its form hauntingly familiar, stepping from the haze like a ghost from his past. *Livia.*

Her beauty, once a flame he'd consumed until it guttered out, was barely recognizable. Scars laced her cheeks and forehead, jagged and raw. Rags clung to her bony frame, soiled and torn. Her eyes, though, smoldered with a fire that stole his breath, a hatred veiled by a trembling smile. *She's weaker than I remember*, he mused, mistrust stirring.

Born in a stinking shack to a washerwoman and a drunk, Livia had clawed her way out of Rome's gutter. As a girl, she escaped to the tavern stables, a rare gift with horses her only advantage. She would calm wild stallions with a soft hum, braid their manes by moonlight, and steal rides on merchants' mounts, racing with joy through dark alleys. At twelve, she tamed a trader's unruly colt, earning a coin and a dream of breaking free from her grim world.

By sixteen, Livia's golden hair and radiant beauty became her sharper tool. She mastered manipulation—her charm a malevolent snare. She'd flash smiles to swindle bread from bakers, then spy on others for a merchant's gold, discarding their trust with a cold smirk. Livia assured herself that *they* were corrupt and she righteous—her delusion justifying ever bolder and more malicious acts.

At eighteen, a palace official, captivated by her allure, brought her to the emperor's court as a courtesan. Livia excelled, her sly flattery and calculated touches enchanting Severus, her equestrian skill briefly dazzling him in royal displays. She played palace men against each other, spreading rumors to ruin reputations, relishing in their downfall, all to cling to power and influence. But Severus grew bored, tossing her aside at twenty, her beauty faded and used.

Banished, Livia sold herself on Rome's streets, her heart a stone, manipulating clients with the same cruel cunning. At twenty-four, staggering drunk in a crowded market, she stumbled into a wagon's path. Its wheels crushed her—a fleeting scream lost in the chaos—her body left broken in the dust, a forgotten star extinguished.

"Severus?" she queried. Her voice was soft, quivering, as if on the edge of tears. "You're here, at long last. I've been waiting—praying you'd come to this wretched place."

She stepped toward him hesitantly, scarred hands outstretched, her eyes wide with feigned relief. "I knew you'd find me, my emperor, you always did."

She's lying.

His grip on the dagger tightened, the warmth of her words clashing with the tight press of bitter lips. He remembered Livia's youth, her body offered freely until he tired of it, discarding her like a worn cloak. Now, she was a shadow of that woman, yet something in her trembling form felt too perfect, too practiced. *She plays the victim, but she's a blade.* His pulse quickened.

"You've heard of the scroll?" he asked, probing, but keeping his distance.

Her smile flickered with a practiced meekness. "Of course," she answered, voice laced with a fragile lilt. "Everyone whispers of it. A sacred scroll, they say, hidden in this hell, with the power to escape the pit. I've heard the rumors since I fell here, scraps of hope passed among the damned."

She stepped closer, rags swaying, her eyes never leaving his.

"It began with a shadow, a dark figure no one could name, speaking of a relic buried in the ruins. Some say it's in the temples, others in the catacombs. I've chased the tales, gathered clues, but I'm too weak alone." Her voice broke, a calculated quiver, and she lowered her gaze, as if ashamed.

She's baiting me, he thought, suspicion a reflex, but her words roused a hunger for the scroll's promise.

"Where might it be?" he pressed coldly, testing her.

Livia's lips curved, a smile too sweet for the scars marring her face. "I have ideas. The Senate chambers, perhaps—places of power, where secrets were always kept. And there are tales of mysterious catacombs hidden far out in the wasteland. I've watched, listened...but this place breaks the weak. I need you, Severus—your strength, your mind... your body."

She reached out, fingers brushing his arm, her touch light but deliberate. "I've waited for you, my emperor, to lead me, to claim what's yours." Her eyes gleamed, a mockery of devotion, and she leaned closer, breath warm against his cheek. "The scroll could be my gift to you, a token of loyalty, to restore you to glory."

Every word is poison.

His skin prickled where she touched him. He studied her, the scars mapping her face, the rags that barely concealed her form, and saw the lie in her. *She hates me.* He read the truth in the way her fingers lingered too long, too close to his throat.

"You'd gift me the scroll?" he asked, his voice a low challenge, his cold smile matching hers. "After all these years?"

Livia's laugh was soft, almost tender. "Time means nothing here."

Her eyes locked on his, a predator's gaze beneath a mask of weakness. "I've always known your worth, Severus. Let me prove it. We'll find it together, you and I, as it should be."

Her hand slid to his chest, her touch a calculated lure, and she pressed against him, lips grazing his jaw, sending a shiver through him. *She's a trap, honed by this hell.* Yet her cunning—her knowledge of this place, was a tool he could wield.

"You know the paths," he admitted, hiding the wariness coiling in his gut. "Show me."

Livia's smile widened, a venomous charm. She nodded, "Follow me, my emperor." Her breath was hot against his skin, her stare burning with a flame that promised more than alliance.

I'll play her game, he thought, his own cunning rising to meet hers, knowing she was no true ally.

In her mind, unspoken, a vow took shape: She'd play his guide—

lead him through this gray abyss, and when the right moment came, she'd plunge a blade into his heart, savoring his fall, her vengeance a fire that would simmer for eternity.

"Do not be deceived: God cannot be mocked.
A man reaps what he sows."
—Galatians 6:7

CHAPTER 5
THE JUDGMENT

Time in Hades was a ghost that slipped through Severus'
fingers like mist, its relentless gray fog smothering any sense
of passage or measure. Had months drifted by? Centuries?
Millennia? The wasteland of Hades offered no answer, only an eternal
twilight that gnawed at his sanity. *I was emperor, the god of empires.* But
here, time mocked his existence with its suffocating haze. The fog
coiled like a living thing, whispering despair, while the ruins stood as
silent sentinels, their jagged edges slicing the air.

His throat throbbed with unquenchable thirst. *There's no
water.* Didius had informed him of that ages ago, but was it true?
Perhaps his old rival was hoarding a secret stash somewhere? Desperation, suspicion, and hatred drove him. When Severus wasn't
searching for the scroll, he was looking for water, convinced that a
stream, a fountain, or even a jar must exist somewhere. Scars laced his
sullied flesh, wounds that throbbed without healing. *How long will this
torment stretch on?* The thought was a cold blade in his soul—sharper
than the dagger at his belt.

Severus kept Livia near, her gaunt frame a tool he wielded with ruthless precision. *She's a viper*, he thought, catching the glint of malice in her expression.

His paranoia proved true in a blocked alley as he heaved debris to clear a path. When his back was turned, she spotted an iron rod jutting from the rubble. Without a moment's hesitation, she yanked the rod from the debris and plunged it into his back in one swift movement, attempting to skewer him to the ground like a pinned insect. White-hot agony dropped Severus to his knees, warm blood spilling down his spine. *Traitor!* Pain seared his vision, but his dagger flashed, sinking deep into her chest. She gasped, a choking gurgle.

They fell, panting, blood pooling on cracked stone, their wounds pulsing in Hades' undying cycle. Severus stirred first, rage exploding within him. "I'll break you," he shouted, binding her with ropes scavenged from the ruins. He used her body violently, cruelly, without mercy, though it rendered him no pleasure—only the bitter thrill of dominance, a fleeting shield against the void. *She's mine to crush*, he fumed, forcing her to kneel, to serve, her scars a canvas for his wrath.

His vile acts against her were empty, a ritual of false supremacy that left him colder, her eyes blazing with a defiance he couldn't snuff out. *She'll never bend*, he seethed, hate swelling like a tide that consumed him.

Livia's escape came during an ambush. A band of scavengers, their eyes wild with greed, coveted his dagger. Severus was leading Livia through a burned-out forest when the attackers leapt from behind dead tree stumps, their clubs smashing his skull and splintering his ribs like dry twigs. Pain engulfed him, a black tide, his vision fading as blows rained down.

After the scavengers had collected their prize and left, he rose, battered yet undying. Livia had vanished into the fog. *She'll pay*, he vowed, his hate a thorn that pressed deeper with each betrayal.

The endless wasteland fueled Severus' descent into an ever-deepening darkness, each encounter inflaming his will to dominate. A long trail of alliances—forged in desperation and shattered by treachery—marked the relentless passage of time, each one crumbling under mistrust. In his wanderings, he increasingly met souls speaking strange, foreign tongues, their jumbled words a barrier that stoked bitter frustration. For survival and intel, he gleaned fragments of their speech, a galling necessity for an emperor.

Whispers of a mysterious orb supplanted tales of the lost scroll—a fresh promise of escape that kindled hope amid gnawing doubt.

Across the vast hellscape, the damned searched with frenzied obsession—for water, for the orb, for tattered garments and ragged footwear—coveted attire rapidly torn to shreds by the unforgiving expanse. Vicious clashes flared as souls hunted one another, preying on the weak for worn boots or frayed cloaks—a murderous, predatory cycle that stripped away all imagined dignity.

Severus was captured and enslaved by a band of ruthless cutthroats, but eventually broke free, fleeing across a dry seabed, its barren shores littered with the twisted remains of wrecked ships and forsaken harbors.

He formed a brief alliance with a scavenger named Jackson, a lean man with shadowed eyes who claimed to have died in a "Vietnam"—a distant war of roaring machines and fiery jungles, far removed from Severus' ancient era. Jackson's words were fragmented, laced with a sly edge, his broken speech veiling intent that Severus strained to unravel. *He's luring me*, Severus suspected, mistrust deepened by Jackson's fleeting smirks and evasive glances.

Jackson pointed toward a ravaged citadel across a serrated canyon, his voice urgent yet slippery. "The orb's there, buried in the rubble—trust me." But Severus sensed a trap and turned on him, shoving his companion against the canyon wall, a shard of glass pressed to his throat.

"Tell me where it truly lies," Severus growled, infuriated by Jackson's garbled reply. The man's eyes darted, betraying his deceit. Rage surged through Severus, and he slammed Jackson to the ground, crushing his chest beneath a heavy stone slab. *Death is too fleeting here*, he mused, leaving Jackson gasping, pinned under terrible weight, his curses swallowed by the timeless fog.

The orb's promise kept Severus moving, each failure feeling like a lash on his soul. His hate, vanity, and paranoia stoked an anger that swelled with every step, his feet now torn and bleeding, soles shredded by the wasteland's merciless grit.

He climbed a ruined tower, chasing a whisper of an orb hidden in its spire, only to find dust and emptiness. *This place mocks me,* he ranted, but pride and desperation fueled his manic hunt. Each betrayal, each false lead, hardened him further, his soul forged into a seething crucible of fury and domination. The orb was his only tether to sanity.

I won't break, he boiled, hate driving him. He interrogated a madman, his screams yielding nothing but lies, so Severus cut him down, stripping the man's frayed shirt before moving on, his dominance a hollow victory. *They're all against me.*

———

The cycle of Hades continued for long ages, until a great shift shook its foundations. A sacred countdown had reached its end. A clock—ruled not by time but by God's sovereign will—struck the appointed hour. The Day of Judgment had come.

Severus was creeping through a darkened alley toward a rumored orb cache when a faint tremor rippled through the gray stone beneath his bloodied feet, a shudder that seemed to rise from the depths of Hades itself. He froze, his ragged breathing loud in the oppressive silence, the air thick with the stench of decay.

Then, a sound—a distant, anguished wail—burst like a thousand voices crying out in unison, echoing from some unseen chasm. The screams clawed at his ears, raw and terrifying, a chorus of torment that sent chills racing down his spine.

The fog shifted, and a wave of heat brushed against his fouled skin, faint at first but growing, as if the wasteland itself were exhaling a fiery breath. Severus' heart pounded, his gaze darting through the haze. For a moment, the shadows parted, and he glimpsed a vision—a cavernous abyss where molten rivers churned, crimson and amber, their glow casting writhing shapes against jagged walls. Flames flick-ered, hungry and relentless, consuming all in their path.

The vision vanished as quickly as it came, swallowed by the fog, but the heat lingered, a searing promise that clawed at his mind. A low, guttural roar rumbled from the depths, shaking the ground a second time. Fear squeezed his chest as the air grew hotter still.

Then, a blinding light flashed from out of nowhere—from every-where—searing his eyes and lancing his skull in pain. The brilliance was unbearable after Hades' eternal gloom. His hands clawed at air as he staggered, blind, the world dissolving into a white void. *What sorcery is this?* he stormed, panic rising.

Shapes emerged—a vast throng of the damned, their faces hollow, eyes wide with dread, their rags fluttering in an unfelt breeze. He stood among them, no longer in Hades but before a towering throne. Its radiance stole his breath away. *This is no earthly realm*, he gasped, awe gripping him, his heart beating like a frantic drum.

The throne pulsed with majesty, surrounded by creatures of inde-scribable power and splendor. Their wings were as molten gold, and their voices cried out in a thunderous hymn of "Holy, holy, holy." Their eyes shone like stars, piercing his soul. At the throne's center was a Presence—unseen yet all-consuming, radiating glory, a holiness that laid bare every shadow within him.

Severus quaked in the throne's light. *This is beyond my empire.* His breath was shallow, the majesty an indomitable force that staggered him. The angelic creatures roared, a chorus of eternity that shook his bones, their golden wings shimmering like a sea of fire.

No mortal could stand here. He whimpered, fear threading through his reverence, his heart trembling under the gaze of He who saw all—every sin, every lie. The damned around him mirrored his awe, eyes wide, their groans softening to whispers as the throne's glory held them in thrall.

They feel it too. He saw their trembling hands, their bowed heads—a shared submission before the divine. The Presence pulsed, its holiness an inferno that burned away all pretense, and Severus felt small, a speck against the infinite. *I was a god.* But the thought crumbled like ash before this truth.

The crowd groaned, and Severus looked up, following their gaze. There in the vastness above them, their lives spread unfurled before the throne. Severus saw his life—the bloodied sands of Carthage, where Christians fell to beasts and swords; Livia suffering under his cruelty; Maximus' plea for repentance, which he scorned with a laugh. *I was divine,* he reasoned, but the images seared—his lust with Annia, his betrayal of allies, his rejection of Christ's mercy. No blood of Jesus covered him, no grace shielded his depravity.

Regret surged, a tide that drowned his pride. *I chose this path,* he realized, conviction piercing him, his heart fracturing under divine gaze. *Could I have knelt?* Maximus' words echoed in his mind—*repent, and live.*

The song of the glowing creatures reverberated through him, and he felt unworthy before the Creator's majesty. *I was blind.* He trembled; the weight of regret harder to bear than Hades' torments.

Then, pride stirred—a vile serpent uncoiling in his chest. *God dares to judge me?* he fumed, offense devouring his brief conviction, his awe twisting into anger. *I am Septimius Severus, Rome's heart!*

He glared at the throne, fists clenched, his defiance a storm against the Light. *I crushed kings, forged an empire—He has no right!*

The damned shifted, their groans turning to murmurs, faces hardening as spite and bitterness reignited. *They resist, too,* he relished, seeing a man spit, a woman sneer, their submission replaced by scorn. *I am no sinner like them.* Severus was appalled, self-worship blinding him to his own corruption.

The heavenly creatures' song thundered on—"Holy, holy, holy"—unrelenting, but the crowd's insolence grew, their voices rising in an anger that mirrored his own.

"We are gods, not worms!"

Rage flared, the throne's judgment an insult to their vanity.

Hatred consumed Severus, a whirlwind that blew away regret. *I'll not kneel to this!* He raised his fist to the throne, hot with rebellion. The damned erupted, their murmurs swelling to shouts, vile and obscene.

"Curse you, tyrant!" a man roared.

"You're no god!" a woman shrieked, spitting blasphemies.

They hate as I hate. Severus joined the chorus, his voice raw: "I am Emperor Septimius Severus. The world is as I say it is!"

The crowd chanted a rhythm of vile curses, a shared fury against the Presence.

"We'll not bow!" The voices of the damned peaked, obscene, a sweeping tide of insurrection, their pride making a final stand before judgment.

A voice from the throne thundered, not with spoken words, but with truth clearly discerned within each reprobate heart, a verdict that shook the heavens: *You chose self over Me, conceit over mercy. Your names are not written in the Book of Life. Depart from Me, I never knew you.*

Each syllable was a gavel, shattering their pride, its authority crushing all defiance. *To the fire, where your will reigns eternal.*

As the verdict echoed, radiant figures descended from the throne's light—angels, heavenly forms blazing with divine authority, wings shimmering in cascading hues like living flames. Eyes that once kindled hope now burned with righteous judgment—twin embers of wisdom and terror.

With swift, unerring precision, the angels seized the condemned, hoisting the rebellious throng into the air. Severus thrashed against them, but the angels' strength was absolute, their purpose unwavering. Mighty voices that had sung "Holy, holy, holy" now resounded with the finality of divine justice, a chilling decree that shook the heavens, sealing the fate of the unrepentant.

Severus screamed as he was hurled into a gaping abyss. "Noooooooooo!"

Terror swallowed him as he plummeted through a void hotter than Hades, a sulfurous stench stinging his nostrils as the heat intensified with each passing moment. The light of the throne faded from view, its glory a mocking memory. *I was a god.* But the truth stung—his empire was dust, his soul damned by his own defiant will.

Severus crashed onto black stone, his body wracked with agony from the fall. Blood oozed from gashes on his arms, his ribs screaming with each breath. Slowly, he forced himself to stand, legs trembling, white-hot pain lashing across his spine. He surveyed the scene around him with unbelieving eyes.

He stood in an enormous cavern, its vaulted ceiling lost in darkness. The walls were jagged with volcanic glass, hinting at a labyrinth of caverns sprawling across countless levels. To his left was a boiling pool of lava, its smelted surface churning crimson and gold, spitting sulfurous fumes that clawed at his lungs.

As he stared, shapes emerged in the molten tide—glittering coins, warped crowns, and gilded chains, the selfish and unjust gains of the world, charred and melted into ruin. Each bubbled and sank, a testament to greed's fleeting glory, devoured by the seething pool's unyielding hunger. Flames flickered, casting grotesque, writhing shapes against the walls.

Suddenly, a cry of anguish pierced the air, then another. The hair on the back of his neck stood on end as heat blistered his skin. Then, a scraping sound—like claws across stone.

Out of the shadows emerged a monstrous figure—a towering inferno from ancient tales. Its form burst forth in roaring flame, wings of fire billowing wide, pulsing like the heart of a furnace. No armor clad its molten body, only searing heat. Its eyes blazed like hot coals, radiating cruelty.

The beast spoke, slowly, a voice that crackled like flame devouring bone. "I will savor every morsel of you, god-king."

Severus gaped, his heart frozen with fear. The beast advanced toward him, the cavern floor trembling under the repugnant weight of its approach. Severus' mouth opened in terror, but no scream escaped his cracked lips. Horror consumed him—teeth gnashing—his soul laid bare before the abyss.

"Anyone whose name was not found written in the book of life was thrown into the lake of fire."
—Revelation 20:15

150

CHAPTER 6
THE HUNTED

S everus staggered through fiery catacombs, desperate to escape his tormentor's merciless cruelty. He fled in panic, skin scorched, wounds oozing from tortures that flayed his soul and whispers that tore his mind. The cavern walls glowed crimson, dripping like hot wax, and the air was thick with sulfur and ash that inflamed his throat. *This is worse than Hades.* The fresh memory of glowing fangs haunted his thoughts, driving him like a lash. He'd escaped the monster's flame-like clutches by slipping through a narrow crevice as the beast fed on a lesser creature.

There has to be a way out of this place.

The catacombs twisted through the underworld, a maze of scalding stone with steaming cracks that plunged to unseen depths. His feet blistered on smoldering ground, each step a spike of agony, his body prickling with fresh burns. *Escape is all I have left.* He was unarmed—vulnerable and directionless in a burning labyrinth.

Unlike Hades' earthlike wasteland in which humans were the primary threat, this abyss was completely alien—teeming with terrifying predators that hunted relentlessly. Severus was frantic, his eyes darting like a caged animal. Caverns stretched endlessly around him, laced with lava flows that twisted like snakes through the suffocating darkness.

His mind unraveled—regret and rage colliding like blades. The offer of grace extended by Maximus flashed through his mind: *Repent, and live.* And the last words of that blond fool in the arena, *God's grace is yours—find it in Jesus.* No chance for that now, for the opportunity had passed. Regret gnawed at him for rejecting their message, for choosing pride over grace. His sanity frayed, each scream from the darkness a reminder of his fall. *I was divine!* he seethed, fists clenched, his hatred for God clashing with his lament at not honoring Him.

He crept through a tunnel, its walls slick with molten veins, heat squeezing his lungs. *I need a weapon.* He scanned the shadows wildly. A shard of obsidian gleamed, its edge sharp as glass. *This will do.* He snatched it up triumphantly, testing its weight. Using another stone as a chisel, he shaped it into a crude yet effective dagger.

Paranoia coursed through him as he maniacally probed the darkness. Black, mangled clumps loomed—gnarled growths with huge thorns, glinting like poison needles. *Hell's cruel cactus garden,* he thought, dodging their spikes.

A growl echoed, and he froze, spotting a creature—beastly, yet human-like—with glowing eyes. Its claws scraped the stone menacingly. *What's that?* He watched in horror as it skulked, then bowed in abject reverence.

A colossal figure emerged, its form a nightmare of power. Its hide was black as charred bone, split with jagged fissures that pulsed with inner fire, as if molten fury seethed within it. A cluster of eyes—six, eight, more—gleamed across its face, each a pit of searing malice. When it moved, embers trailed in its wake. Grotesque, bat-like wings clung to its twisted spine, quivering with latent menace.

It's unkillable!

Gripped with panic, Severus leaned tighter into the shadow, recognizing the creature to be of a similar form as his recent tormentor. His heart raced, knowing that one spark of wrath could ignite the beast into a roaring inferno.

The smaller creature groveled before this blazing sovereign, its submission absolute. *It's a slave to that giant,* he realized, Hell's cruel hierarchy snapping into focus. Severus crept into a crevice, escaping their notice.

Time stretched, unmeasurable, each moment an eternity. Several times, he slipped off slimy rocks into scorching lava pools. The agony was unimaginable as he scampered back onto hot stones, his body a map of ruin. As in Hades, there was no reprieve of death in this place, only ceaseless agony. Solitude weighed heavily upon him—a soul-crushing force.

Once, he fell through a gaping chasm not visible in the blackness, plummeting wildly before smashing onto rocks far below. Severus picked himself up and kept on going, each torturous step blurring into countless others. Ages ground by in the unchanging dark, his torment an infinite echo in the void.

He witnessed horrors—relentless, soul-searing horrors, like a man, flesh shredded by demonic claws, writhed on scalding stone, his blood sizzling as it pooled.

"Mercy!" he screamed, eyes wild with terror.

There's no mercy here.

Severus' stomach churned at the stench of charred skin. Demonic whispers, inaudible yet palpable, seemed to mock the man's pleas, a twisted presence in the air.

He passed a chamber where a fiery monster was flaying one of its worshipers, viciously tearing its writhing form in a fierce act of rage. *They torment each other!*

Severus found grim comfort in their mutual destruction. The beast roared—a thunderous wail of frustration that shook the walls, scattering embers like cursed stars. The ex-emperor crept past, heart pounding, heat searing his lungs.

Another passage carried a woman's anguished wails. "Save me!" she begged, her futile cries echoing off bleak stone, intertwined with the sinister hiss of demonic laughter. Harrowing shapes writhed along the cavern walls, rising and falling with her screams. The air quivered with every shriek, gasp, and gurgle—the bloodcurdling chorus of total unraveling.

Severus turned away, survival his only creed, the residue of her despair clinging to him like soot. *No one helps.*

The most effective strategy to combat maddening thirst was to keep moving. Corridors opened in every direction—a maze of peril, each crack a threat, each mysterious silhouette a predator. His mind reeled, regret for his sins warring with his anger at God's verdict. *I ruled the world!* he ranted, his feet screaming, his body wracked with pain. *How long can I endure?*

The tunnel widened, and Severus froze, senses thrumming.

Something's out there. He gripped his dagger, its blade glinting faintly, poised for attack. Shadows stirred, revealing three figures crouched in the gloom, their eyes flashing with wary malice.

Humans. His pulse quickened, torn between apprehension and necessity. *They're no allies—but monsters stalk me.* In this moment, the alien threat outweighed his fear of human betrayal.

He edged forward, dagger lowered yet ready, his voice a low snarl. "Who are you?"

The figures stiffened, their forms half-lit by the cave's crimson glow. Confusion and caution etched their brows.

They don't understand me. Rage simmered deep within Severus. In Hades, unfamiliar tongues had mocked his self-importance, forcing him to scavenge fragments of strange languages for survival. *An emperor, reduced to this.*

He tried again, spitting out a phrase from another tongue, his voice sharp and impatient. "Name yourselves!"

Still nothing.

Their faces, haggard and taut, bore the same torment as his own. A gray-haired man, his eyes burning with haughty defiance, clutched a spear fashioned from the prickly spines of the cavern's cactus-like growths. Behind him, a woman hovered, her body angled as if seeking shelter in their presence. To the right stood a lean man with matted brown hair, his lips twitching in a ceaseless murmur of incoherent curses, each word a spark of venom that tainted the air.

They're broken.

The gray-haired man spoke, his voice commanding. "Drop that dagger stranger, or we'll spill your guts."

Severus caught the words, jagged and foreign, piecing them together. *English*—one of the tongues he'd grudgingly learned in Hades. Bitterness gnawed at him—he, an emperor, stooping to their lesser speech. But his eyes drifted to their feet. Black boots—spiked, gnarled, shielding them from the searing stones. *Those could save me,* he gawked, agony throbbing through his blistered soles.

Scowling, he forced out their tongue. "Your boots." He pointed, voice steady despite the fire in his feet. "I need them."

They stood silent, regarding each other suspiciously. Finally, the woman tossed him a pair—ragged but tough.

A trick?

Severus snatched them up. The material was coarse—black and thorned, like the growths he'd seen. He slid them on, relief surging as the throbbing eased.

"Scab cactus," the woman said, answering his unspoken question. "They belonged to someone who..."

Her voice trailed off. She glanced at the gray-haired man, her tongue darting nervously across dry lips. "Well...that person isn't with us anymore. The cactus hide is the only thing that holds up against the serrated stones."

They work! Severus exhaled in sharp reprieve, grimly considering the fate of their previous wearer. "Why help me?" he pressed, studying their faces for deceit.

"We need numbers," the gray-haired spoke carefully, his tone cold but calculated. "Demons hunt us. Alone, we have no chance."

The man's arrogance grated, but Severus saw truth in his words. *Survival requires allies.*

"What do you know about this place?" he demanded, eyes flicking over them, seeking any sign of weakness or treachery. His English, rough and halting, reached them, though it stung his vanity.

The gray-haired man and the woman traded glances, then nodded toward the cursing man.

"Ask the preacher," the woman said. "He's the expert."

Preacher? Praedicator! Severus turned to the lean man, whose rage boiled as hot as his own.

The preacher's lips tightened into a thin line, bitter as the ash dusting his face. Severus studied his scowl. *This is a dangerous man.*

The man had once been a preacher, raised in America's heartland, where faith ran deep. Straight from high school, he entered seminary, earning his MDiv through a rigorous four-year program. His gift for preaching shone early—a rare blend of inherited charisma and keen intellect. Smooth, engaging, and quick-witted, he wove sermons that captivated his congregants' hearts and minds.

God had anointed him to spread the hope and truth of His Word to lost souls, yet pride took root, and discontentment festered. He scoffed at "rigid, outdated" interpretations of Scripture, craving a broader stage.

As his church's attendance surged, he veered from God's will, skillfully tailoring sermons that catered to a godless world's desires. He twisted sacred texts to indulge his ambitions—wealth, acclaim, fleshly pleasures—while softening sin's sting to keep pews filled. Few seasoned pastors challenged his warped teachings, granting him free rein to mold a flock that professed love for Jesus yet lived in defiance of His commands.

The Holy Spirit relentlessly stirred his conscience, urging repentance, but the roar of applause and the world's adulation drowned out the call.

Demonic forces, powerless to physically harm on The Choosing Ground, wove subtle snares. They whispered lies of self-justification—*You're enlightened; you deserve this*—stoking his arrogance with visions of grandeur. He drank deeply of their deceit, blind to the abyss he courted. In the end, he led countless souls astray, his betrayal of God's Word sealing their fate and his own.

His shock at hearing Jesus say, "Depart from me, I never knew you," ignited a consuming rage. Now, he cursed the God whose truth he had forsaken.

Severus knew none of this, but the preacher's face—etched with vanity and seething fury—betrayed his story.

"This is the Lake of Fire," the preacher spat, his voice heavy with bitter knowledge. "Named for a vast lake of lava at its heart, a cavernous expanse that stretches without end."

Severus leaned closer, brow arched attentively. "Those flaming giants—tell me more," he pressed, probing for any edge.

The preacher spat again, a curse slipping through his lips. "The giants are fallen angels, now alpha demons, cast out for rebellion." His words flowed with grim certainty. "Indestructible to us, their flames burn with the glory they lost."

He paused, nostrils flaring. "The smaller ones—slave demons—are their hounds. Gangly, with, claws, fangs, and glowing eyes. They serve, but hate drives them to feed on us—or each other when they're desperate." As he spoke, the preacher's hands carved vivid shapes in the air, bridging the foreign tongue to better pierce Severus' understanding.

His voice darkened. "Beware of the rakers—humans turned spies, serving alphas for survival. Trust no one in this pit."

He knows too much, Severus thought, but the preacher's knowledge was a lifeline in Hell's chaos.

"Where do we go?" Suspicion lingered, his hand resting on his dagger.

"Upper regions," the preacher motioned with his chin. "Less demon activity...maybe. Staying here is a death sentence."

The gray-haired man nodded, his arrogant eyes glinting in the lava's glow. "The upper chamber is our best shot."

Severus considered their words, annoyed at playing the follower but recognizing the security in numbers.

"We can't stay here." The woman spoke quietly.

They're desperate, like me. But their plan aligned with his survival instincts. *Allies!—for now,* he decided.

They crept from the cave into catacombs that wound through

scalding stone, across lava flows that dimly lit their path. The stale air echoed with the unending sound of agony, but they moved on, taking no notice.

Since arriving, Severus had wandered—not lost, but with no conscious direction other than away. Now they had a destination: the upper chambers.

They trudged onward, sweat cutting rivers through the dust on their tormented faces, their lips cracked and dry with thirst. There were no days to count, no sunrises or sunsets, just relentless drudgery.

They edged silently past a lava pool filled with dozens of souls screaming in agony. Slave demons surrounded the pool, laughing, cracking whips, blocking any chance of escape or reprieve.

Hell's law is indifference.

The group pressed forward, apathetic—stealth and shadow their only protection.

Further on, they crouched on a scorched ledge, watching with dread and amazement as two alpha demons clashed in the ultimate battle of titans. As the monsters fought, flames erupted from cracks in their charred skin, igniting their malevolent forms into blazing infernos that lit the cavern with hellish fury.

Diabolical eyes gleamed through the fire, unyielding in their wrath, as guttural roars rattled the cave walls. Fiery green whips lashed with venomous cracks, countered by the deafening clang of enormous black swords. Silver blood sprayed from gaping wounds, hissing as it seared jagged stone.

Sparks rained down from the weight of their blows, forcing the watchers to retreat, coughing on ash, unable to glimpse the battle's end as flames consumed the ledge.

Onward they trudged, ever onward, relentless. They reached a vast, sinister plain, its surface scarred by rivers of lava. The cavern arched high overhead—a somber black sky. Garnet gemstones studded the unseen ceiling above, sparkling like blood-red stars as wisps of acrid smoke drifted past like poison clouds. Scabbed cacti loomed about—gnarled sentinels, their needle-sharp spines glinting in the dim light.

Huddled in shadow, they scanned the exposed expanse, pulses racing as they assessed the peril of crossing this raw wound in Hell's crust. Every rustle, real or imagined, tightened their grips on their makeshift weapons.

The preacher's voice broke the silence, bitter as the dust on his lips. "This plain's a graveyard." His face was tight with apprehension. "Rakers hide among these thorns, waiting to betray. You watch—we'll come across some lone soul begging to join us, only to report our location back to their master."

They surveyed the crossing silently, then the woman spoke. "What do you think, Doc?"

Doc? Severus turned to the gray-haired man. "You're a doctor?"

The man smirked, self-importance flaring in his eyes. "A brain surgeon, from New York." His tone carried the memory of his past. "Best in my field. Worked in the finest hospitals."

Doc had fought his way to the top, driven by an obsession for worldly reputation and social status, his ego growing with each accolade. He had been a brilliant, hard-working surgeon, but pride in his success proved to be his undoing, flooding his heart with self-righteousness.

Doc's younger sister had often shared her faith with him, only to face his ridicule. He derided her lack of education, dismissing her beliefs as outdated, prejudiced, and unintelligent. He was his own god—a deity of science and self-reliance. Once engrossed in X-rays and brain scans, he now pondered how best to traverse this fiery plain.

"If you're a doctor, can you help my burns?" Severus watched him, hopeful.

Doc's laugh was cold, his words grim. "Hell has no cure," he scoffed bitterly. "The anguish is eternal. There's no salve for these torments."

After agreeing on a route, the group pressed forward, their shared desperation a brittle chain that held them together. Surprisingly, with the exceptions of ravenous thirst and blistered skin, they crossed the plain without incident.

The path led them to a narrow stone bridge spanning a black, bottomless abyss, the air thick with stench and choking fumes.

One misstep...

Severus hesitated, remembering his last fall. His heart raced, tense at the thought of crossing such a thin gauntlet. Doc led the way, an arrogant sneer masking the apprehension that consumed him. The preacher followed, cursing under his breath. The woman trailed, her steps cautious but bold.

Severus studied her face. *Who are you?*

The woman had been born Elizabeth Elaine Montgomery. Raised in a Christian family, she went to church every Sunday and youth group on most Friday nights. She prayed the prayers of her parents, even singing their songs, but she left home determined to forge her own path—to develop her own truth.

Attracted to the excitement of independence and the allure of sex, she distanced herself from those who might advise restraint. Eventually, she married a Buddhist man, preferring the thought of a godless eternity.

Still, even in marriage, Elizabeth was restless, eager to experience all the pleasures the world had to offer. Her discontentment resulted in repeated acts of infidelity—ultimately, divorce. She moved seamlessly from one relationship to the next, blaming others for her failed connections.

Elizabeth was considering reconciliation with her parents when she tragically drowned off the coast of California while kayaking. Now she was here, entombed in the eternity she had scoffed.

She crossed the narrow bridge and Severus followed, his boots trembling on a stone arch no wider than his hips, its edges crumbling into the yawning chasm below.

The abyss seethed with a foreboding darkness that writhed like a living thing. Tendrils of shadow clawed at his balance—a whispering malice threatening to drag him into oblivion. A rancid stench—rotting flesh laced with a putrid, festering reek—struck him, triggering a flashing vision: abominations of unimaginable terror, chained in blackness, seething with rage, watching from the depths below—willing him to fall into their gaping jaws.

His heart pounded, each step a battle against the ravenous void. He grasped futilely at the air for support, the bridge groaning under his weight, teetering on the edge of collapse. Finally, he stumbled to the far side, panting heavily, a wave of relief crashing over him. His eyes met Elizabeth's—shared terror passing between them.

"Let's keep moving," she said with a shudder, anxious to distance herself from the bottomless crevice and whatever lurked within it.

After much twisting and winding, they finally reached the upper catacombs. The air was colder—but no less corrupted.

"Stop!" Severus rasped urgently. "Do you hear that?"

The group halted, listening intently, eyes scanning the shadows.

"It's quiet."

An eerie stillness clung to the air, contrasting the usual hiss of lava, crackle of flames, and screams of agony. They proceeded cautiously, their breathing loud in the unexpected hush.

The preacher glanced at Severus' dagger—a look that Severus didn't miss. Though united by a common goal, suspicion lingered in their fragile alliance.

The group crept onward toward a great chamber looming ahead in the darkness. It opened before them—a wide cavern of serrated obsidian, its edges glistening like the teeth of some primordial beast. The vaulted ceiling was swallowed by shadow—an oppressive void that seemed to reverberate with ancient curses. Within the walls, faint lava veins pulsed erratically, their molten glow casting sickly, blood-red hues across the uneven surfaces. A tingle ran up Severus' spine, morphing into a visceral alarm that clawed at his instincts.

This is a false haven!

He gripped his dagger tightly, the air thick with dust and dread. The group fanned out, their scab cactus boots crunching on blackened stone, scanning the darkness for threats.

We're exposed, Severus seethed, paranoia churning his gut.

A low growl cut the chamber, and three slave demons lunged

through the gloom—gangly, human-like, each a grotesque variation of affliction.

The first was tall, its claws curved like scythes, its glowing eyes rabid with hunger. The second, squat and hunched, had yellowed fangs that jutted unevenly, its breath foul and diseased. The third, wiry and sinewy, bore claws tipped with cruel barbs, its lidless eyes pulsing like dying stars.

Hell's hounds, Severus thought, their tormented wails echoing as they attacked, a chorus of hatred that chilled his bones.

Severus leapt forward, his dagger slashing the first demon's throat, black blood spraying, its gargled scream a raw cry of despair. Doc drove his spear into the second's chest, its fangs snapping inches from his face. The preacher's bone shard plunged into the third's temple, its barbed claws raking the air, fangs bared in agony. Elizabeth stabbed a demon in its flank, her spike sinking deep, black blood gushing onto her hand—scalding like acid.

She's no coward.

The demons collapsed, their bodies twitching on the bedrock floor, but a deeper roar shook the chamber. An alpha demon that had cloaked itself in shadow suddenly blazed forth, its fiery wings billowing, molten eyes blazing with the misery of lost glory.

A fallen angel. Severus gaped in horror.

Before the alpha could strike, a figure burst from the shadows—a human, wielding a sharpened bone shard. "This way!" he shouted, waving to a narrow crevice.

A stranger was not to be trusted, but they stood no chance against the alpha—and the slave demons they'd cut down would soon revive.

We can't fight this!

Severus signaled the group to flee.

Following the stranger, they sprinted toward the shelter of the crevice—the alpha's flames scorching the air behind them, its roar a deafening promise of pursuit. Through twisting catacombs they fled, boots pounding the cave floor as darkness devoured their path. Blackest blackness enveloped them, their fingers groping along the cavern walls for guidance, hearts pounding in fear of an unseen chasm yawning before them. Each step risked oblivion, their ragged gasps echoing in the void, but the alpha's shrieks drove them recklessly on.

Halting in a narrow tunnel, they panted, bent in exhaustion. They strained to hear, but the demon's roar had faded in the distance. Pale, luminescent veins cast an eerie glow again, illuminating their weary forms.

Blood dripped from a gash on Severus' arm, his burns pulsing with unrelenting fire. Doc's face was grim, his pride masking his pain. The preacher's curses faltered, though rage still simmered. Elizabeth clutched her spike tightly, the demon's acid-like blood blistering her hand.

We survived, but the tension among them was a living thing.

The stranger stood apart, back turned, his tattered cloak swaying in the tunnel's faint draft.

There's something familiar about him.

The newcomer stepped forward, the faint light revealing harsh features etched with Hell's typical torments—sunken cheeks, scarred skin, heat blisters, eyes hollow with despair.

Severus gasped, shock striking him like a blade.

The man's gaze met his, recognition flickering across his haunted face.

Father!

"...the smoke of their torment will rise for ever and ever."
—Revelation 14:11

CHAPTER 7
THE CROWN

The tunnel walls pulsed with faint lava veins, casting mournful silhouettes that danced like specters across the burning stone. Severus stood, blood dripping from a tear on his arm, his scab cactus boots muddied with char and sweat. His burns screamed, a relentless fire beneath blistered skin, but his gaze was fixed on the stranger before him: his father, Publius Septimius Geta. The man's sunken cheeks, scars, and blistered skin bore the marks of unending torment. His hollow eyes held recognition but no warmth, only suspicion, as if sizing up a rival predator. The air was thick with ash, sulfur—and strained silence.

"Who are you now, boy?" Publius rasped, his voice coarse, like stone grinding against stone. He stepped closer, bone shard glinting in the dim light, his cloak swaying like a tattered shroud. "What life did you carve out before this pit?"

Severus' lips curled into a sneer, arrogance flaring despite the agony pulsing through his body.

"I was emperor of Rome," he answered curtly. "I ruled the world,

Publius. Kings knelt, armies quaked, and my name was a god's. And you?" He scanned his father's ragged form, contempt flashing across his face. "A failure, forgotten, scraping by in obscurity."

Publius' posture stiffened. "Emperor or beggar, you're here, same as me." His tone was cold, probing. "What sins dragged you to this abyss?"

Severus' jaw tightened, memories of blood-soaked arenas and his defiance of grace clawing at him.

"I was divine," he spat. "I bowed to no one—not anyone."

The words tasted foul, regret gnawing at him, but he crushed it beneath his pride. Publius' gaze lingered, haughty with judgment. The weight of shared damnation hung heavy between them.

The group shifted uneasily. Severus and his father were speaking Latin—a language the rest didn't understand. They stood tense and uncertain, sensing the friction. Doc gripped his spear, eyes darting between father and son, calculating. Elizabeth's face was taut with anxiety. The preacher muttered curses, his rage a constant, unnerving force that scorched the air. They were allies by necessity alone, bound by the threat of demons, not friendship or loyalty.

"We're exposed here," Doc warned, his voice cutting through the tension like a scalpel. "That alpha is still hunting, and the slave demons have revived by now. We need to move."

Severus nodded. "The alphas are unkillable. We barely escaped one. What hope do we have?"

Publius' lips curled into a harsh smile that seemed to hide something sinister—knowledge, or deceit. "There's a way," he said, surprising the group by speaking English, though his tone carried the low hiss of a snake. "A way to end the torment and rule this hell."

The group froze, staring at Publius. Severus' heart quickened, apprehension coiling in his gut like a viper. "Speak," he demanded, dagger twitching, ready to strike.

Publius stepped closer, his voice hushed like a conspirator. "The Crown of Ash," he whispered, words heavy with promise and peril. "Whoever finds it and wears it becomes the Prince of Demons, the ruler of Hell. No more running, no more agony. You command the alphas, the slaves, all of this pit."

The words struck like a match, igniting greed and doubt. Severus' thoughts raced, memories of the sacred scroll and the orb—false hopes that had led to ruin—flashing through his mind. *Another lie*, he cautioned himself, but desperation clawed at him. *I was emperor*, he reasoned, ego surging. *Who better to reign here?* His eyes narrowed, studying his father's face for deceit. "How do you know this?"

Publius' expression soured, his voice grim as he recounted his tale. "I trapped a slave demon, weak from hunger, and pinned it to the stone with a spike through its chest. It screamed and begged, but I carved its flesh, flayed it strip by strip, until it spilled its secrets. It spoke of the Crown, lost when Lucifer, the first Prince of Demons, was cast into the Lake of Fire. The demon swore it's real, hidden in the deep caverns where even alphas fear to tread. They torture souls for its location, desperate to claim it."

Severus considered Publius soberly. He saw the hunger in his father—ambition, not truth—and his mistrust deepened. The others exchanged glances, expressions etched with doubt and greed.

"A myth," the preacher spat, but his voice wavered, betraying his desire.

"It's our only chance." Publius shrugged. "The alphas hunt us. The Crown is the only way to turn the hunted into the hunters."

Elizabeth glanced nervously about, her voice cautious. "If it's real, why hasn't an alpha found it already?"

"Because it's buried where their courage fails," Publius answered sharply. "The deep caverns, where the darkest angels were chained before the Judgment. A place of serpents and shadows even they avoid."

Doc's sneer was cold. "You trust a demon's word? You're a fool, Publius."

Publius' gaze didn't waver. "I trust its terror. It spoke to save its wretched hide. The Crown is real."

Severus' mind churned, torn between skepticism and ambition. The Crown felt like another trap, like the scroll or the orb, but the misery of Hell—the burns, the demons, the endless agony—pushed him toward it. *I'll rule again*, he schemed, pushing doubt aside.

"We find it together," he commanded, voice hard and unyielding. "No one moves alone. We share the Crown, or we die."

The group nodded, their agreement fragile, laced with distrust. Publius' lips twisted into a sly grin, and Severus felt a chill slither down his spine. *He's hiding something*. But survival demanded they act.

"Tell us more, Publius. Where do we start?" Severus' gaze pierced his father like a spear.

The newcomer smiled, thin and unreadable—a predator's grin. "The deep caverns. A path through the lower lava plain, past the scab cacti, then descending where the light dies. I know the way."

Severus gripped his dagger, blisters pulsing with unrelenting fire. *A trap*, he thought, but the Crown's promise was a beacon in his mind, drowning his doubts.

They would hunt it together, five damned souls, each ready to betray the others for a taste of power. They headed out, creeping through the catacombs, their boots crunching on blackened stone. Severus led, his dagger gleaming in the faint lava light. Publius followed, his eyes scanning the shadows with a confidence that set Severus' nerves on edge. Together, they were a pack of vipers, united only by the hunt for the Crown of Ash, each poised to strike the other at the first sign of weakness. Severus watched Publius closely. His father's calm demeanor displayed a stark contrast to the chaos of Hell.

He's too certain. Severus squirmed internally, but his paranoia was spread evenly among his companions. Doc's arrogance grated on him like sandpaper; the preacher's rage was unnerving, and Elizabeth's silence seemed to hide a schemer's heart. *They're all playing their own game.*

His hand never strayed from his dagger, its weight a cold comfort.

Screams pierced the air as they passed a grotesque sight: souls hanging upside down over boiling lava, their flesh sizzling, their wails a dark symphony of anguish. Some begged for mercy, voices raw, but the group pressed on, jaws firmly set.

168

"No salvation here," Doc muttered under his breath, but his posture betrayed a shudder of dread, a crack in his proud facade.

"Keep moving," Publius ordered, leading them past the tortured souls with a slithering ease.

Severus' gaze lingered on the victims, their agony a mirror of his own torment. *The Crown is my only escape.*

The plain stretched far, a graveyard of soot and bone. *Where do all the bones come from?* he wondered. But that was a mystery to unravel at another time.

The group moved in tense silence, their boots leaving faint trails in the dust. Further on, they spotted a lone figure stumbling through the shadows, clutching a jagged stone, his eyes wild with terror.

"A straggler," the preacher snarled, his voice low, edged with beastly hunger. "He might know something."

Severus nodded. "Take him."

They closed in, surrounding the man like wolves. The straggler was gaunt, skeletal, his blistered skin scarred and peeling. His breath rasped as he clutched his meager weapon in futile defense. He spoke rapidly, voice trembling with desperate pleas, but his words—a jumbled torrent—were alien to their ears.

The preacher's eyes narrowed, frustration flaring at the incomprehensible speech. "Does anyone understand this gibberish?" he snapped.

The members of the group shook their heads, irritation mounting.

The preacher stepped forward, bone shard gleaming. "The Crown of Ash," he growled. "Where is it?"

They crowded the straggler toward the edge of a high cliff rimming a river of molten lava. The man's eyes widened, panic seizing him as he faced their harsh, bewildered glares. He cried out again, voice cracking with fear, hands trembling, but his strange tongue only deepened their confusion.

"Speak sense, man!" the preacher spat, anger boiling at the unintelligible cries. He drove his shard into the man's shoulder, twisting it with savage precision. The captive screamed, his body convulsing.

Severus watched without mercy, for survival demanded answers, and the straggler's foreign tongue fueled his own vexation. *Is there no end to the languages these wretched fools babble?*

The preacher carved deeper, each cut a calculated act of cruelty. "Speak, or I'll peel you to the bone!" he roared.

The man sobbed, his desperate cries rising—struggling to answer a question he couldn't fully grasp. His words, unintelligible to them, pulsed with a frantic rhythm, pleading for understanding. The preacher lurched forward, catching fragments of "caverns" and "angels" amid the babble.

"Deep caverns...dark angels?" he muttered, rage briefly sedated. "We already know that."

Then, with callous contempt, he shoved their captive over the cliff's edge, screams echoing as the man plummeted into a lava river far below, his body consumed in a burst of flame.

Severus' jaw tightened, eyes gleaming, but he said nothing. *Hell's law is indifference.*

The group turned away, their expressions flat and unreadable.

"The deep caverns," Publius asserted, pleased, as if the man's agony meant nothing. "Just like I told you."

The group pressed on, descending a winding path into dense shadow. The air grew heavier, the stench of decay and sulfur thickening—like a poison clinging to their skin. The lava flows faded, replaced by an oppressive blackness that swallowed their vision. The only light came from a torch Publius had fashioned from scab cactus and ignited with lava. Its flickering glow cast eerie silhouettes, turning the catacomb walls into a nightmare of shifting forms.

"Stay close," Publius warned, leading the way, his torch a beacon in the void, though its light barely pierced the gloom. Severus followed—dagger ready. The others trailed in apprehensive silence, their breaths loud in the stillness, their footsteps echoing like bitter accusations.

The path twisted downward, slick and treacherous. The air was cooler here, but no less suffocating, a harsh force that pressed against their chests. Rumors of the deep caverns swirled in Severus' mind—serpents that swallowed souls whole, digesting them for millennia; angels of unfathomable violence, chained in darkness, their wrath a storm of destruction. He shuddered, recalling the soul-chilling vision he'd seen when crossing the narrow gauntlet. *The Crown is worth it,* he promised himself, his ambition a fire that burned away doubt. But the gloom seemed to whisper otherwise, a premonition of dread that crept closer with every step.

Severus glanced at Elizabeth, her silhouette trembling in the dim light. Her eyes, once fierce and defiant, now glistened with sorrow. In that moment, Elizabeth's mind had drifted to a memory she'd long buried beneath years of rebellion—a sunlit afternoon with her father, a man whose gentle love had never wavered despite her scorn. They'd sat by a quiet stream, and he'd spoken softly of Christ's goodness, a love that offered peace beyond the world's fleeting pleasures. She'd laughed then, her heart set on tasting every carnal delight the world could offer, rejecting the faith she deemed too restrictive. Now, in this forsaken abyss, the memory of that gentle stream and her father's tender gaze pierced her with unbearable regret. She'd traded eternal joy for empty thrills, and the cost was ceaseless torment, where the warmth of her father's embrace and Christ's mercy were forever out of reach. A sob caught in her throat, not for the horrors around her, but for the love she'd spurned—a love that had once been hers, now a distant star in Hell's unyielding night. Severus did not know her memory, but he could see the grief trailing down her cheeks.

The descent was grueling, the path narrowing, the walls closing in like a tomb. The air grew colder and the stench stronger—a rancid blend of rot and oppression. The shadows seemed to pulse, alive with unseen threats. Publius moved confidently, his torch casting long silhouettes that danced like demons. Severus' apprehension deepened with each step, his eyes locked on his father's back. *He's leading us somewhere, but to what?*

The others felt it too. They were a pack of jackals, each sensing a trap but too desperate to turn back, the Crown's lure a chain that enslaved them to their lusts.

The path opened into a vast chamber, its walls jagged with dark crystal, the air sharp with an unnatural chill that seeped into their bones. The darkness was heavier here—the torchlight struggling to pierce it. Severus felt a prickle of dread—a tingle running up his spine, his instincts screaming of danger.

Then, a heavy stone door slammed shut behind them with a deafening clang that echoed like a death knell, sealing them in.

Severus' heart raced. He raised his dagger, his voice a snarl. "A trap!" he shouted, glancing at Publius. But before they could react, slave demons lunged from every direction—their glowing eyes burning with hunger, claws and fangs gleaming like cursed blades. There were dozens of them, a pack of hellhounds, their wails filling the chamber.

The ensuing battle was chaos—a torrent of anguished shrieks, the air thick with the stench of blood and dust. Severus fought with desperate precision, his dagger a blur, his body pushed beyond its limits. He ducked a claw, slashed a demon's arm, and kicked another back. Doc fought beside him with grim efficiency, his spear a whirlwind, teeth bared in a mask of defiance—but his eyes betrayed his fear.

As the heat of battle raged and defeat seemed certain, a memory flashed through Doc's mind—stark and unbidden—cutting through the chaos like a beacon from a life long lost. He saw himself standing in a sunlit auditorium, his hands trembling with pride as he received his medical diploma, the culmination of years spent learning to heal the sick and ease suffering. The applause had been a symphony of hope, his heart bright with the dream of saving lives—yet now, in this infernal pit, he could help no one. His worldly achievements faded to nothing, meaningless in the eternal void.

He fought wildly, hands stained with the blood of endless battle, his life's purpose reduced to dust. Another memory followed: his sister's face, radiant with faith, her voice soft as she read from a worn Bible by candlelight on Christmas Eve, sharing Christ's promise of peace. He had mocked her then, his academic pride dismissing her words as childish myths, his heart hardened by accolades, lust, and ambition. She'd wept, pleading for him to see the truth, but he'd turned away, chasing status over salvation. Now, as the demons closed in, Doc's chest tightened with regret—the weight of his scorn a heavier burden than any claw. He had gained the whole world but damned his soul.

The preacher fought beside them like a hailstorm of rage, his curses blending with the demons' wails. Slashing and hacking, he saw his life flash before him—a cruel montage of choices that had led him to this infernal abyss. A vivid memory surfaced: one quiet afternoon in his office, Timothy, an old friend from Bible school, had approached him with gentle concern. Timothy's eyes had been kind, his voice steady as he spoke of God's grace—a boundless gift that forgave but could not be twisted into an excuse for sin. He'd warned the preacher about his distorted teachings, his lifestyle that flouted Scripture while cloaked in holy rhetoric. The preacher had nodded politely, his smile a mask, but as Timothy walked away, an ardent contempt flared in his heart. He despised anyone who dared question his choices, his self-righteousness a fortress against correction. Now, in the searing heat of Hell, that memory burned hotter than the battle around him. Timothy's words, once dismissed as meddling, now echoed with a truth he had refused to heed—a truth that might have saved him from this torment. Regret clawed at him, sharper than any demon's talon, for he'd traded grace for power, and paid the eternal price. Now, his bone shard carved through demon flesh like a butcher's knife, but his movements grew sluggish, his strength waning.

Elizabeth fought fiercely beside them—a dancer of death, her movements quick and lethal. Her own memories surged, bitter as ash. She saw herself swaying under neon city lights, drunk on wine, tangled in a lover's arms, chasing nights of reckless abandon. She'd forged her own path, scorning faith for fleeting ecstasy. Now, in Hell's unyielding gloom, those pleasures crumbled to dust—her soul yearning for the Savior whose love she'd mocked, His grace forever sealed beyond the cruel grasp of the abyss.

The demons pressed harder, their numbers overwhelming. Severus' chest bled from a fresh gash, his vision blurring. *We can't hold them!*

Suddenly, the group was struck by a shockwave of soul-scorching heat—a harbinger of doom. A blazing nightmare leapt from the void—

a dark alpha, its sinister form wreathed in black and silver flame—like shadow on fire. Countless eyes, a swarm of glowing orbs, burned with hate and fury. Jagged horns curled like grim scythes, dripping molten slag that hissed upon the stone.

The demon's seething malice sucked the air from the chamber. Its roar—a torrent of blood-curdling screams fused with the savage bellow of a thousand ravenous beasts—shook the ground with bone-rattling force. The alpha towered above them—monstrous, unkillable—its diseased hide cracked with fissures that pulsed with an infernal gray ichor.

Severus froze, horror gripping him like a vise, his stone dagger useless against this unstoppable titan.

Publius stepped back, his torch falling to the ground, its flame sputtering. His expression was calm—too calm, a mask of triumph.

"You led us here," Severus growled, his voice thick with betrayal. "You're a raker!"

Publius' smile was cold and unrepentant, a victor's triumph. His lips twisted with cruel amusement.

"Survival, boy," he retorted, devoid of all shame. "The alphas reward their spies, and I choose to live."

The alpha's roar drowned out Severus' curse, a sound that shattered thought. The slave demons swarmed, their claws and fangs overwhelming the group like a tide. Severus fought wildly, his dagger flashing, acid blood coating his hands. He lashed out, cutting only air, but a claw raked his side, pain searing through him like lightning. He stumbled, vision dimming, strength failing. The last thing he saw was his father's smirk, a traitor's grin, as blackness claimed him, a void deeper than the caverns themselves.

———

"Seek the Lord while he may be found; call on
him while he is near."
—Isaiah 55:6

CHAPTER 8
RUN

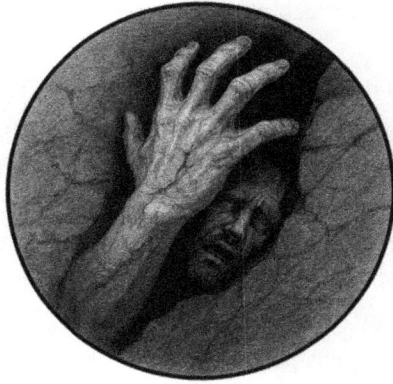

Severus awoke to unimaginable agony. He lay chained to a scalding stone slab that seared his flesh—an incomprehensible torment that burrowed into his bones. The dark alpha loomed over him, its snarl warped with sadistic glee—a towering inferno of wrath and malice. Its fiery whip cracked against his skin, each lash an explosion of pain that tore screams from his throat—raw and guttural, echoing in the chamber. The air was thick with the stench of charred flesh, the walls pulsing with molten veins that illuminated the horror of his plight.

Doc hung nearby, suspended from a barbed hook, his proud eyes dulled by suffering, his arrogance shattered into a hollow shell. Elizabeth dangled beside him, her face a mask of misery, her body bloodied and broken. The preacher's curses had faded to whimpers, his rage extinguished by the alpha's cruelty. Publius Septimius Geta—the traitor—was nowhere to be seen, either rewarded by his demonic masters or devoured, Severus didn't know, and didn't care. His hatred for his father burned hotter than his wounds, a fire that fueled his will to endure.

The torture stretched into eternity, each moment a lifetime of anguish—time unmeasurable in this pit where no sun rose or set. The alpha's whip flayed his skin, peeling it in strips, exposing raw muscle that sizzled on the scalding slab. Its claws tore at his flesh, raking deep furrows that bled black and red, the pain a white-hot blade that severed thought.

The alpha's fiery gaze bore into his soul, seeking answers he didn't have. Through long ages of luring souls on The Choosing Ground, demons now wielded every tongue, warping each syllable to inspire utter despair. "Where is it? Where's the Crown?" the demon roared, its voice a growl that shook the stone—a thunder that rattled his bones.

Severus could only scream, his mind fraying under the onslaught, his body a ruin of desolation. Slave demons joined the assault, their gangly forms circling like vultures, grotesque lips glistening with hunger.

The chamber was a crucible of suffering, the air heavy with the screams of the damned. Severus' vision blurred, blood pooling beneath him, mixing with the ash to form a grotesque, boiling paste. The alpha's whip struck again, splitting his shoulder, and he convulsed, chains rattling, his screams hoarse and raw. Severus yearned for death's embrace, but in Hell's merciless grip, even death was denied him, for the dead cannot die.

The slave demons hissed, their breath hot with anticipation. One leaned close, its yellow eyes smoldering, and Severus saw his anguish reflected in its glossy gaze—a soul stripped of hope, reduced to meat.

The alpha's voice crackled again, "The Crown, maggot! Where is it?"

Wild desperation coursed through him, a flicker of defiance in his shattered soul. He searched for any chance—any weakness in this pit. Two slave demons released his bonds with the intent to flip him over, face down on the scalding stone pan.

Severus seized the moment. With a surge of strength born of

desperation, he tore free and leapt to the floor. Amazingly, his dagger lay there, discarded as trash. He picked it up and slashed the closest demon's throat. Black blood spurted like a geyser, its wail fading to a gurgle as it collapsed. The alpha roared, whip cracking, but Severus was already moving, his frayed boots pounding the chamber floor, blood dripping from his wounds.

He ran—breath ragged, vision blurred—his body a boiling pot of pain that screamed with every step. Claws scraped behind him—a pack of slave demons giving chase, their wails a chorus that spurred him onward.

The catacombs twisted around him—a labyrinth of molten stone and shadow. The walls were slick with slime, the floor littered with volcanic glass that tore at his boots. He stumbled, but terror drove him—a whip more devastating than the alpha's. The demons were close, claws scraping, eyes sparking through the gloom.

Severus turned a corner, his shoulder slamming into a wall, the impact jarring his wounds. He bit back a scream, gnashing his teeth.

He scrambled up a jagged wall, fingers slipping, blisters scraping against rock. Each movement triggered a jolt of fresh agony that threatened to break him. His fingernails tore as he climbed, driven by the wails behind him. He reached a narrow crevice—its mouth barely wide enough—and squeezed inside. The walls closed about him like a coffin, the air thin and foul, his chest heaving.

I'm suffocating!

Panic clawed at him, his burns flaming even hotter in the confined space. The demons dug fiercely at the mouth of the crevice, their wails echoing, but the space was too tight for their gangly forms to follow.

Severus fought his way forward, body trembling, his mind fracturing under the crush of pain and horror. The crevice closed about him even tighter—stone pressing his chest, breath shallow, each inhale a struggle. Desperation was all he had, a bitter fuel that pushed him onward. His fingers dug into the stone, scraping, ripping, his body inching forward through the suffocating gloom.

As he struggled to breathe, he saw flashes of his life—memories surging, sharp as claws, dragging him back.

Suddenly, he was ten years old, standing in the sunlit stables of Leptis Magna. His father, Publius, brought out a striking chestnut colt from a stall.

"For you, boy," Publius said with a warm smile, ruffling Severus' hair.

The colt nuzzled him, and he laughed, his heart soaring, as he mounted it bareback. Publius clapped proudly, his kindness a happy glow that lit Severus' world. That man was gone now, a traitor in Hell, his betrayal a knife that twisted deep.

Why, Father?

The memory turned rancid as his trapped body trembled with exhaustion and deprivation. He kept crawling, clawing, desperate.

Another flash shook him. He was fifteen, in a dusty courtyard, towering over a scrawny boy whose face was tense with fear. Severus grinned cruelly, shoving him toward the dark mouth of a well. The boy begged, voice cracking, but Severus laughed, kicking him in. The boy tumbled, screaming, splashing into shallow water, his cries echoing. Severus leaned over, cackling, tossing pebbles that plinked off the boy's head. Publius watched from the house but turned away—no punishment, no chastisement for his son. His silence fueled Severus' sense of entitlement—a spark that grew into a fire.

I was strong, he thought, yet the boy's screams haunted him now, a reflection of his own trapped panic.

More flashes came—a parade of cruelties he'd inflicted and truth he'd rejected. Christians in arenas, torn by lions or crucified by the roadsides. He had clapped as their blood was spilled. Women he had used and discarded, their tears ignored—Livia's scarred face in Hades, her hatred for him justified. Julia Domna, his wife—her eyes cold as he taunted her with his courtesans. Servants whipped for spilled wine, their whimpers a game, their pain his right as emperor.

I was a god! But the memories choked him, each face a brand of shame—their suffering now his, reflected in the demons' jaws. Regret churned his gut, but arrogance battled it back. *I ruled Rome,* he snarled inwardly, but the faces of his victims flashed brighter, their torment a truth he couldn't outrun.

Maximus' voice pierced the haze—close, as if he were in the crevice beside him: *The Choosing Ground, Emperor—this world is but a fleeting stage to pick light or shadow.*

In Rome's gilded hall, Severus had laughed, deeming the pastor's words to be a fool's babble. *Choose Jesus,* Maximus had pleaded, *Hell is real, but God doesn't want it for you.* Severus had scoffed, trusting in his own strength and wisdom. Now, trapped in this suffocating tomb, those words burned like lava.

The Choosing Ground—Earth, where every soul was granted the opportunity to determine their own fate. He'd cast his lot with vanity, spurning the cross for pleasure and power.

Could I have knelt?

The question twisted like a dagger in his soul. Maximus' honest eyes haunted him—a mirror of the grace he'd mocked. *God's grace is yours,* the blond Christian had echoed in the arena—words Severus had crushed beneath his heel.

He'd been offered life and light but chose death, darkness, and fire. Not a singular, freeing death, but a relentless cycle of undying demise. Pride surged, a persistent ember—*I am Severus, Rome's heart!*—but regret drowned it, a tide of anguish for The Choosing Ground he'd squandered. Hell's jaws gaped wide to claim him.

Finally, the crevice widened, and he tumbled out—collapsing into a tunnel, gasping for air. Staggering to his feet, Severus pressed on. The demons' pursuit faded into the distance, their ugly wails swallowed by the catacombs' depths. His body was a wreck—a shredded tapestry of gore and gashes. As he stumbled forward, his blood left a grisly trail in the ash underfoot.

The Crown is a lie! The realization cut like a knife in his gut.

He lurched through the dark, the air thick with the stench of dust and decay. *I'm so thirsty!*

The tunnels twisted, each turn a gamble, every shadow a threat. He passed a cavern where a lone soul screamed—its body impaled on scab cactus spikes, pleading for mercy that would never come. Severus turned away, his heart cold—survival the only law.

Further on, he glimpsed a slave demon devouring a corpse of some kind, its fangs tearing flesh, its eyes bright with rabid hunger. He crept past, dagger ready. The catacombs seemed to mock him—their endless maze a map of his misery, their silence a taunt that whispered of his failure.

Then, a sound stopped him—music, dreamlike and haunting, like a memory from a world long lost—a melody of impossible grace that tugged at his soul. The sound drifted from a side tunnel, its notes weaving a spell that soothed his tormented mind. Mesmerized, Severus crept toward it, his dagger ready.

Am I hallucinating?

The tunnel narrowed, molten veins threading through the walls— their glow a faint guide in the gloom. His heart ached, the melody stirring memories of Rome's grandeur—of the moments before his fall, of a life where beauty had once existed.

The tunnel opened into a chamber where a soft radiance bathed the walls, a stark contrast to the catacombs' mournful dim. This fresh, soothing brilliance throbbed with life—a beacon of hope in the blackness of despair.

The chamber was vast, its floor clean and smooth, polished by some unnatural force. The walls were carved with faint swirling patterns that seemed to shift and shimmer. The music swelled—a cascade of peace, each note a brushstroke on the canvas of long silence, a melody that wrapped around his heart, easing the pain of centuries.

A man sat at the chamber's center, his form like polished marble— translucent and breathtaking. His features glistened, as if carved by a divine hand, his presence a vision of goodness that seemed impossible in this pit. He wore a flowing robe, its fabric glimmering like liquid starlight, its edges fading into the glow around him. He played an instrument Severus couldn't name—strings glinting like spun silver, runes pulsing with rhythm upon its body, each note a symphony of light woven through shadow.

The man's eyes were closed, his face serene, his movements fluid. Each chord was a deliberate act of creation, a bold defiance against the chaos around them.

Severus stepped closer, enchanted. His soul had secretly yearned for this moment of respite—this fleeting taste of salvation, a peace he'd never known. He stood, transfixed, the music washing over him —a world of life, of laughter, of pleasure. His burns faded to a dull ache, his mind quieting, the storm of pain and regret stilled by the melody.

The man's fingers danced across the strings, the instrument singing—its voice a choir of angels. Severus' breath caught, his heart longing for the grace he'd spurned. He had been an emperor, yet here he was reduced to a broken soul, captivated by a wonder he could scarcely comprehend.

The man's eyes opened, meeting Severus' gaze. He smiled—a spark of angelic warmth, a promise of redemption, a light in the darkness that reached into his soul. Severus froze, heart pounding, their shared smile a tether to a world he'd forgotten—a world of beauty, mercy, and hope. The man's face was tender, his eyes a deep, endless blue—like the skies of a Rome long lost. Severus felt a pang, a longing for something he couldn't name. The music softened, the notes lingering—a gentle caress that held him in place, a prisoner of its welcoming embrace.

Suddenly, the smile twisted—distorting into a smirk of pure malevolence, a chasm of evil that chilled Severus' blood—a black void that swallowed the light, the music, the hope.

The man stood, his form swelling, his magnificence warping into something hideous—colossal, with eyes like dying suns, their glow a sickly yellow that flared with hatred. Wings of shadow billowed behind him, their edges frayed, dripping with ash, their span filling the chamber. His skin was a patchwork of decay and splendor—fragments of marble beauty marred by rotting flesh. His claws gleamed like cursed blades, each one etched with runes that pulsed with malice. His grin was a mockery of the grace he'd feigned—a predator revealed, his presence a force that bent reality itself.

Severus' heart stopped, blood running cold, body trembling. One word escaped his lips in a whisper of dread: "Lucifer."

The Devil spoke, his voice a velvet blade—smooth and lethal, cutting through the silence like a knife. "Hello, god-king." Lucifer's lips twisted with cruel amusement—a hunter savoring its prey, a god toying with a mortal. "I hear you want my crown."

Severus turned to run.

"The Lord is not willing that any should perish,
but that all should come to repentance."
—2 Peter 3:9

ANOTHER LETTER ADDRESSED TO YOU

Dear friends,

I write to you now, not from a podium or a study, but from a quiet place of my heart—as your brother, a fellow struggler who has stared into the abyss and longed to pull others back. My heart aches to have shared these disturbing details with you, to awaken you to the grim reality of Hell and our desperate need for salvation. This book has traced Severus' descent—from Rome's gilded halls to Hades' crushing despair; from judgment's gavel to the Lake of Fire's unending torment.

Writing about Hell was a dreadful experience, far removed from the joy of envisioning Heaven. Sleepless nights haunted me, my mind scorched by premonitions of affliction. Friends questioned why I'd dwell on such horror, their unease mirroring my own.

Heaven's challenge was unveiling a world without villain or struggle, a realm too perfect to grasp—too marvelous for words. Hell's challenge was bleaker: no hope or reprieve, only pain and desperation.

I chose to present these realities in story form to better communicate the raw truth about eternity, immersing us in the stark contrast between Heaven's glory and Hell's despair through the lived experiences of Perpetua and Severus. I ended with Severus fleeing Lucifer, leaving you to ponder his fate. Unfortunately, I can tell you his fate plainly: more suffering, regret, and agony—with no escape. He's there now, in Hades, raging with pride. I confess, I loathe Part Two of this book. Yet I wrote it because Hell is real, and its truth demands our attention.

Life offers us two paths: Heaven or Hell. We might grumble at the binary selection, wishing for alternatives or loopholes, but that's like railing against gravity or our need to breathe oxygen. We can protest, but the truth remains unshaken.

Heaven is eternal communion with God, a place of joy beyond imagination. Hell is eternal separation from God, a realm of torment born of our choices. These are not opinions but realities, as fixed as the stars—even more so. God sets before us life and death, blessing and curse, and pleads with us to choose life. This decision is yours alone.

Throughout these pages, I've repeatedly emphasized that Hell is not God's desire for you. He takes no pleasure in sending anyone to its flames. It's not a punishment for being "bad" but the natural consequence of rejecting the Source of all goodness, the One who made you. God's love is so fierce, so relentless, that He left Heaven's throne —a splendor we can scarcely fathom—to walk Earth's dust. He faced betrayal, agony, and a brutal cross to carve a path to Heaven. He paid the price for our sins, offering salvation as a gift. Yet He doesn't force it upon you. His love respects your choice, though it breaks His heart when you turn away.

So who ends up in Hell, and why? Chances are you've never met anyone as evil as Severus, but we each know a Doc, an Elizabeth, and potentially even a Preacher. Do "normal people" really deserve torment? What about the "nice" people—your kind aunt or your generous friend? Why would they face Hell?

In seeking an honest answer to an admittedly difficult question, we must first clarify humanity's position in the universe. Of all the wonders God has made, we alone are formed in His image. This identity is both a profound privilege and a sacred responsibility. Still, don't let this divine imprint deceive you into imagining we are comparable to God. Our Maker is infinitely beyond us in every way—power, wisdom, beauty, virtue, love. The gap between His nature and ours is immeasurable, like comparing a wisp of dust to a burning star.

To understand who ends up in Hell—and why—we need to step back and look at things from a fresh vantage point.

Picture this: You spend hours crafting a glass mug—blowing the glass, shaping the handle, polishing its curves. It's more than functional; you make it beautiful. It gleams in the light, perfectly formed to hold warmth, to serve others, to reflect your craftsmanship with every use.

Now imagine—purely for the sake of metaphor—that the mug could think, speak, and choose. It's no longer just an object, but a character in a story. Instead of showing gratitude, it resents you—persuaded by its own pride that it has no need for its creator or the purpose for which it was made. Foolishly, the mug leaps from the cupboard, imagining it can fly. Unsurprisingly, it crashes to the ground, shattering into jagged pieces. And there it lies—defiant, dangerous, bleeding beauty onto the floor. This is the ongoing state of the human race since the fall in the Garden of Eden: self-righteous, combative, broken.

But what if the story didn't end there? Suppose the mug, fractured and rebellious, was still cherished by you, the glassblower. Despite its razor edges and proud obstinance, you make an offer: "Let me remake you." You don't discard the shards. You stoop low, carefully gathering them up, and offer to place them in the forge again—not to punish, but to redeem; not to destroy, but to reform. But the broken mug, still imagining itself to be a vibrant masterpiece, scoffs, rejecting your merciful invitation. "I will not be reformed. I am perfect as I am."

And so, heartbroken, you honor its choice. The mug—now just a shattered tangle of glass—cannot serve its purpose. It won't be placed on the table. It can't hold water. Its beauty has turned to menace. It's sharp to the touch, laced with pride and resentment. Eventually, you place it in a separate bin in an out-of-the-way corner. This is Hades—a temporary space, cold and dim, where broken things wait, still stubborn, still proud, still refusing the forge of redemption.

Yet in time, the mug must enter its final forever—just as we must enter ours.

The day comes when the forge is extinguished, the workshop dismantled, and the shelves cleared. The beautiful glassware, the ones that welcomed restoration, are carried to the banquet, gleaming in the light, fulfilling the purpose for which they were created. But the jagged pieces are taken to the trash heap, where no further invitations will be made. There, long removed from their intended shape, they are ground into dust, lost forever. This is Hell—not a tantrum from you, the creator, nor a cruel outburst of vengeance, but the final consequence of a soul's decision to remain unrestored.

It is not the breaking that damns the mug; it is the refusal to be remade.

We are all broken in some way. Every person wrestles with sin. But redemption is offered to all. The forge is not the punishment. It is the rescue.

Hell, then, is not for the broken. It is for the proud.

This metaphor may sound unusual, but it pales in comparison to the real betrayal. Think of it: God sculpted you—your every breath a whisper of His artistry, your laughter a melody He composed, your soul a canvas painted with His divine intent. He lovingly sustains every heartbeat, each pulse a testament to His ceaseless care, knitting you together with purpose and glory. To reject Him is to scorn the Source of all that is righteous and true, to choose darkness over light, to turn from the radiant dawn and embrace a starless abyss.

You may not consciously intend this betrayal, cloaking your heart —even from yourself—in kind deeds or a charming smile, but even the gentlest exterior can veil a profound deceit: a heart curled inward, enthroning itself as god. At the deepest level of reality, this is the rebellion you commit—a treacherous betrayal that severs the sacred bond of existence, turning from the One who breathes life into you.

This is why, despite the outward kindness of a generous friend or beloved relative, they might still be lost. Their good deeds, though admirable, are not fully their own, for all true virtue flows from the heart of God. As Scripture declares, "all our righteousness acts are as filthy rags" (Isaiah 64:6), and again, "there is none who does good, not even one" (Romans 3:12). These words are not poetic exaggeration, but a factual diagnosis of the human condition—echoed by Christ Himself, who said, "No one is good except God alone" (Mark 10:18). Therefore, every glimmer of goodness we display is but borrowed light—reflections of His grace that reveal His image in us, yet cannot bridge the chasm of a heart that exalts itself above its Maker.

To refuse God's invitation to be remade is not merely to resist His authority but to turn away from the very goodness that gives life meaning. Hell, then, is not a consequence for failing to be kind—it is the desolate reality of what remains outside our Heavenly Father's eternal embrace.

For God is light, and without Him, there is only darkness (1 John 1:5; John 3:19); God is love, and without Him, there is only fear (1 John 4:8, 18); God is mercy, and without Him, there is only judgment (James 2:13; Lamentations 3:22–23); God is life, and apart from Him, there is only death (John 14:6; Ephesians 2:1). In other words, Hell is not a vindictively constructed torture chamber, but the desolate void left in God's absence.

The gospel, though, is the hope-filled answer to this darkness, a story so vivid it pierces the heart. Picture a world resounding with sin and self-worship, its people chained to guilt and death, their rebellion scorning their Creator's love. Into this ruin steps Jesus—God Himself, clothed in human flesh. He walks among the broken, healing the sick, feeding the hungry, speaking words bright with hope and restoration.

Yet the world rejects Him. He's betrayed by a friend, mocked by crowds, tortured until His back is torn to ribbons. On a rugged cross, He hangs, nails driven through His hands, a crown of thorns pressed mercilessly into His brow. He gasps for breath, bearing the weight of every failure, betrayal, depravity, and proud heart—yours, mine, the world's—taking our place in a wondrous act of mercy. "Father, forgive them," He prays, even as He dies. The sky darkens, the earth quakes, and death swallows Him, sending the spotless Lamb of God to Hades in our place.

But three days later, Jesus rises from the grave, victorious over death and Hell. His wounds pulse as badges of glory, His resurrection a joyous promise of eternal life. He offers forgiveness, life, and a place in His kingdom to all who believe—all who turn from self-idolization, praising the God who made them. This is the gospel: God's love, poured out in blood, to rescue you from Hell and draw you to Heaven.

It's a gift—not earned, but received through faith—trusting Jesus as Savior and Lord.

If you have not turned to Christ, I encourage you—my dear friend —do it now. Don't wait. The invitation still stands. And if you have, then let your heart burn with love for the lost. Carry this message with gentleness and conviction, and speak while there is time.

Such a gift cannot lie dormant. It stirs the soul to act with urgency and grace. So go tell others, not with judgment, but with a love that reflects the cross. That friend you laugh with over coffee might be completely unaware of the chasm awaiting. Speak of God's grace, the cross, the choice between life and death. Be tactful—listen, love, share your own struggles—but don't delay. Time is fleeting, and eternity looms. Tell your family, your neighbor, the stranger on the bus. Some will scoff, others will listen, but your words might be the seed that leads them to salvation. Don't fear rejection; trust God to work through your faltering voice. The gospel is a fire in your bones. Let it burn brightly for those lost in darkness.

Finally, trust God's heart. We don't know what passed in the final moments of those we love—their private encounters with God at death's door. Did they cry out to Him? Did His mercy meet them? That's not ours to judge. Our task is to share the gospel and rest in God's character. He is flawless in goodness, weaving grace through every story. He is impeccable in justice, ensuring no evil goes unanswered. He is perfect in love, forging a path for all to come to Him. Whatever the fate of those we've lost, we can trust His wisdom and compassion. Hold fast to this hope: God's love is greater than our fears, His plan more beautiful than our doubts.

In the end, we are all glass—broken by sin, yet longed for by the Artist. The forge is still open. The call still stands. Let Him remake you.

With hope and love,
Your brother, Cory

CONCLUSION
YOU WILL EXIST FOREVER

∞

As we near the end of this journey, I want to offer one final encouragement—perhaps the most important of all. In this book, I've presented two contrasting realities: Heaven, a realm of unending joy where every heart finds its home, and Hell, a place of relentless torment where hope withers. These dueling realities are as opposite as fresh air and jagged stone, yet they share one sacred bond: The Choosing Ground, this world you currently inhabit.

Look around you. What do you see? A tree swaying in the breeze? A lamp casting soft light? A window looking out into a community or landscape? For long ages, we've called this place "Earth," a name born in ancient tongues, meaning "soil"—a hollow label, like naming a cathedral "stone" or a symphony "sound." It misses the divine pulse and purpose of this world.

I call it The Choosing Ground, a name that sings of God's design. It's a sacred stage where you, an eternal soul clothed in mortal flesh, choose your forever. This power to choose does not challenge God's sovereignty. It's actually the evidence of it. God, in sovereign love, granted you this responsibility. He made you free, not so you could wander, but so you could willingly return to Him.

You may feel a twinge of weariness today, a quiet ache—or a loud one; the weight of life's cares. You might even be tempted to believe that your best days are behind you, but I assure you, dear reader, that is untrue—unless you've chosen poorly.

Humanity is not a fleeting creation. Regardless of your age or health, you are not reaching the end, for we are eternal beings, fashioned by the hands of a Creator who breathed His own life into us (Genesis 2:7), marking us with His image (Genesis 1:27). This divine imprint ensures our souls will endure beyond the decay of our mortal bodies, beyond the joys and sorrows of this world, into a boundless eternity.

Jesus Himself affirmed this truth, declaring, "I am the resurrection and the life. Whoever believes in Me, though he die, yet shall he live, and everyone who lives and believes in Me shall never die" (John 11:25–26).

The question is not *whether* you will exist forever—that is a certainty—but *where* that eternity will be spent. Will it be in Heaven's radiant joy, fulfilled in the presence of the Lamb, or in the torment of Hell, where the absence of God's goodness leaves only despair?

This world is not your final home. It isn't a place to obsess over empires, wealth, fame, or pleasures that will crumble to dust. It's a temporary stage, designed by God for one purpose: to offer every soul the opportunity to choose their eternal destiny.

The Choosing Ground, as the angel Neriah revealed in chapter 3, pulses with sacred purpose. Neriah's words reveal divine truth: "The Choosing Ground is a fleeting season, brief enough to spare you mortality's endless toil, yet long enough for hearts to make their choice." These words encapsulate the nature of our earthly life—a season mercifully short yet eternally significant.

The brevity of The Choosing Ground is a deliberate act of divine mercy, revealed in Scripture. In Genesis 6:3, God declares, "My Spirit will not contend with humans forever, for they are mortal; their days will be a hundred and twenty years." This passage marks a moment when God shortened the mortal aspect of human lifespans, which once endured through centuries.

Why did God limit our days? Because the more time humanity had, the more we trended toward evil rather than good, entrenching ourselves in sin while growing in vanity—performing deeds to glorify ourselves rather than God, a covert rebellion that blinds us to His grace (Ephesians 2:8–9).

In the ancient world, before the flood, prolonged lifespans led to deeper corruption, as Genesis 6:5 laments, "The Lord saw how great the wickedness of the human race had become on the earth, and that every inclination of the thoughts of the human heart was only evil all the time." More time gave humanity greater opportunity to commit evil deeds and amplify self-righteousness—distancing their hearts from God's call. In other words, the more time we had, the more danger we placed ourselves in.

It's like walking across a frozen lake in early winter: a quick crossing might get you safely to the other side, but the longer you linger, the greater the risk of the ice cracking beneath your feet, plunging you into frigid disaster. This is especially true of those obsessed with building kingdoms on the ice. By shortening our days, God ensured our season on The Choosing Ground would be long enough to choose, but not so long that our hearts would calcify in apathy or self-exaltation.

Consider the mercy in this brevity. A human lifespan, whether a mere thirty years or a full century, is but a breath compared to eternity (Psalm 39:5). If life stretched on indefinitely, the weight of sin's curse —sickness, violence, betrayal, death—would become a relentless burden, a cycle of suffering without hope, compounded by a growing conceit that blinds us to our need for grace.

But God has mercifully limited our days, ensuring earthly toil does not stretch into eternity. As Job 14:5 declares, "Man's days are determined; You have decreed the number of his months and have set limits he cannot exceed." This limitation is a grace, a boundary protecting us from endless struggle in a broken world, and from the peril of a heart sealed against redemption. A single lifetime, however brief, provides ample opportunity to hear God's call, to see His hand in creation, to encounter His love through the gospel.

Scripture assures us that God has made Himself known to all: "For since the creation of the world God's invisible qualities—His eternal power and divine nature—have been clearly seen, being understood from what has been made, so that people are without excuse" (Romans 1:20). Mountains, oceans, stars, conscience—all testify of Him; His moral law stirring each soul with a sense of right and wrong (Romans 2:14–15).

And for those who hear the gospel, the choice is even clearer: "For God so loved the world that He gave His one and only Son, that whoever believes in Him shall not perish but have eternal life" (John 3:16). This season is your moment to decide. Will you embrace the light of Christ, or walk the path of self-glorification?

The Choosing Ground is not a neutral stage; it's a battleground where eternity is at stake, its very fabric hinting at the two destinies that wait beyond the veil of mortality. These hints are subtle yet profound, woven into the daily experiences of our earthly existence, pointing us toward the realities of Heaven and Hell.

On one hand, The Choosing Ground offers glimpses of Paradise: the laughter of a child, the breathtaking beauty of a sunset, the kindness of a stranger. These are divine signposts, whispers of the Heaven that is coming. On the other hand, The Choosing Ground also bears shadows of Hell: sickness, violence, betrayal, brutality. These are not merely hardships but warnings of the Hell that is coming, a place where God's common grace is utterly withdrawn, leaving only despair and self-torment.

These experiences are not random—they are divine signposts. The beauty calls us to come home. The suffering urges us to flee what lies ahead. Heaven and Hell cast shadows here, not to overwhelm us, but to awaken us.

This book has unveiled these contrary destinies in vivid detail. Our journey began in the darkness of a Roman dungeon—Perpetua and her companions torn mercilessly by beasts and blades. But faith in Christ carried them to a home where every longing is fulfilled.

In contrast, Severus' path began bathed in lavish praise, his every whim catered to, surrounded by rich decadence. But pride, and his rejection of Christ, led him to the gray desolation of Hades, and the torment of the Lake of Fire. He endured (endures) the lash of demonic whips, the betrayal of allies, and the crushing weight of eternal separation from the God who longed to save him.

These are the true outcomes of the choices made during this fleeting season—outcomes that Scripture affirms with unyielding clarity: "The wages of sin is death, but the gift of God is eternal life in Christ Jesus our Lord" (Romans 6:23). Like Perpetua and Severus, your choice here shapes your eternal path, a decision that echoes through time, as it did for God's people long ago.

Centuries before Christ's light pierced the world, God's call to choose resounded through His servants. Moses stood before Israel, his voice thundering with divine urgency: "This day I call the heavens and earth as witnesses against you that I have set before you life and death, blessings and curses. Now choose life..." (Deuteronomy 30:19). His words were no mere counsel but a cosmic summons, the Creator Himself laying bare the paths of eternity.

Life—rooted in obedience to God—promised blessing and communion with Him, the Source of all love and goodness. Death, born of rebellion, led to ruin, an existence devoid of all love and goodness. Moses pleaded for life, not for God's sake, but for the people's, that they might thrive in His presence.

Some twenty-six years later, Joshua echoed this charge, standing resolute before a new generation: "Now fear the Lord and serve Him with all faithfulness. Throw away the gods your ancestors worshiped beyond the Euphrates River and in Egypt, and serve the Lord. But if serving the Lord seems undesirable to you, then choose for yourselves this day whom you will serve...But as for me and my household, we will serve the Lord" (Joshua 24:14–15).

Joshua challenged the people to reject the hollow idols of the past and present, to cast aside every false allegiance, and to embrace the one true God. His bold declaration—"we will serve the Lord"—was a stake in the ground, a testament to unwavering fidelity.

This ancient summons speaks to you today. Will you embrace the gospel's truth, where Christ's sacrifice opens the way to Heaven's radiant joy? Or will you turn to the fleeting gods of this world—self, wealth, pleasure—doomed to crumble into Hell's despair?

Moses and Joshua spoke to their time, yet their words echo through eternity, urging you to follow Christ, the only path to life.

To fully grasp the immensity of this choice, you must see life and death anew. Too often, we think of death as the end. But it isn't. When we die, it is not the end of life; it is merely the end of choice. Our decision to align with God's authority and goodness—or remain in misalignment, rejecting His Lordship—is finalized at that moment. As Hebrews 9:27 warns, "It is appointed for man to die once, and after that comes judgment." Death is not the cessation of existence but the sealing of our eternal destiny, a far graver ending than a mere stoppage of life.

Whether a life ends swiftly in a car accident or slowly in the grip of disease, the true significance lies not in the stilling of breath but in the finality of the choice made. Will that soul stand before the throne of the Lamb, welcomed into eternal joy, or will they face the judgment of separation, cast into the torment of Hell? That is the ending that matters most, the one that echoes forever.

This truth should also reshape how we perceive "premature" deaths, particularly among children. Is it unfair for God to allow their season of decision to be shortened? Here, an understanding of timelessness and God's foreknowledge comes into play.

Early death, while a tragedy for us, can be a mercy from God. Perhaps God sees goodness in a young soul and moves them forward as a reward, like skipping grades in school, ushering them into His presence. Or perhaps God, in His omniscience, sees a future trend downward—a path toward rebellion—and pulls them to Himself before it's too late, preserving their eternal destiny. We cannot know the answer, but we can trust the God who does, the One who sees the end from the beginning (Isaiah 46:10).

In closing, The Choosing Ground is not a place to be distracted by the fleeting pleasures of this world—laughter fades, sunsets give way to night, and kindness is but a moment. Nor is it a place to be hardened by life's struggles—sickness passes, violence subsides, and nature's brutality is temporary. These are mere shadows compared to the eternity that awaits.

Jesus Himself warned, "What good will it be for someone to gain the whole world, yet forfeit their soul?" (Matthew 16:26). The treasures of this world—wealth, fame, pleasure—are chaff in the wind of eternity, but the soul is eternal, and the choice made here will echo forever.

The conclusion is clear: choose life. Walk the path that leads to the New Jerusalem, where the River of Life flows, the Tree of Life bears fruit, and the Throne of the Lamb radiates with glory. Choose the road that leads to worship that shakes the heavens, to a home prepared by the One who knows each heart intimately (Psalm 139:1–4).

Beware the enemy of your soul, who weaves lies to lure you toward fleeting pleasures. Resist him, and he will flee (James 4:7). Do not let the world's deceits or its struggles harden your heart.

Your choice rests on this gospel truth: "If you declare with your mouth, 'Jesus is Lord,' and believe in your heart that God raised Him from the dead, you will be saved" (Romans 10:9). Make that declaration today, not with mere words, but with a truly surrendered heart, embracing an eternity in the presence of the Lamb.

Finally, I encourage you to see The Choosing Ground for what it is —a brief season to decide your forever. To that end, redefine this world in your mind.

It is my prayer that you choose Christ, the Gatekeeper to eternal life, so that one day we can stand together in Heaven's light. For those who choose quickly and wisely, we are tasked with helping others embrace life, sharing the hope of the gospel with a world in desperate need of salvation.

We are also gifted with the opportunity to begin living the Kingdom life now—a life marked by a peace that surpasses understanding, the joy of walking in God's presence, and a love that reflects His heart to those around us. This is a foretaste of Heaven's glory, a vibrant promise that transforms our fleeting time on The Choosing Ground into a celebration of what's to come.

You will exist forever, so step boldly into that forever with Christ, and let your light shine as a radiant testament to His eternal love!

You have reached the end of this book, yet eternity's anthem still resounds—from Eden's dawn to Babel's ruin, from the empty tomb to the final Judgment—a song of light and fire. Its chilling, glorious refrain echoes around and within you. Heed its solemn warning, embrace its radiant promise, and with me, join your voice to the everlasting chorus.

THANKS & DEDICATION

To the hard times—those stern companions who bent my knees and lifted my gaze heavenward. What I've oft thought to be my final ending has, again and again, become a dazzling new beginning. From that grace, these pages were formed.

To my Savior—the Lamb who has gone ahead, preparing a home more wondrous than words can hold. Every line herein beats with anticipation of the day when I shall see with glorified clarity what I can now only imagine.

To my soulmate—my best friend—you are the echo of encouragement, the quiet flame of inspiration, the hand that steadied me when doubt pressed close. This book carries your fingerprints.

To my children and grandchildren—each of you a reflection of Heaven's light, a living glimpse of the joy to come. Thank you for believing in me, even when my failures were plain to see.

To my friends and colleagues—you bore the weight of my many rough manuscripts, patiently reading, wisely refining, and teaching me that fellowship is the chisel that shapes the stone into something enduring.

To my father, who first encouraged me to dream big, and to my mother, who taught me that hearty laughter is as much the soundtrack of Heaven as the singing of angels.

To Perpetua, her companions, and all who clung to the promise of hope in their darkest hours—your witness is a lantern still burning, reminding us that light overcomes the final shadow.

This work is not mine alone. It is ours—a song born of light and fire, woven with faith, offered in humility, and dedicated to the One from whom all light flows and to whom every song returns.

POST-CREDIT SCENE
UP, AROUND, AND THROUGH

Perpetua clung tightly to the cliff face, thousands of feet up, her amber eyes scanning the massive stone wall for a ledge or crack—any hold she could grasp. A warm updraft danced around her, teasing the dark curls that framed her brow, now etched with fierce determination. On Earth, this climb would've been suicide. One slip—a scream—and she'd plummet through desperate air to a shattering end. But here in Heaven, it was pure adrenaline, a rush thrumming in her veins like a wild song.

The cliff itself was a marvel beyond words, a towering edifice of celestite—its grand surface shimmering with the radiant hue of God's own eye, interwoven with outcroppings of coarse dawnstone and sparkling skygem. Perpetua gripped a jagged edge, hauling herself up, leg kicking to a foothold, the stone's welcoming surface spurring her ascent. The dizzying height was a thrill—a jolt of exhilaration.

She paused on a ledge, twisting her body to gaze in wonderment at the vast ocean sparkling like diamonds behind her. Tall islands rose in the distance, their shores bright with golden haze, as if lit by an inner fire. Far below, near the cliff's base, her boat—a tiny speck of white wood—bobbed at anchor, its sails fluttering in the breeze. The horizon stretched endlessly, a breathtaking expanse that made her heart soar— its beauty a heavenly echo of Earth's, magnified beyond imagination.

Suddenly, Mago's cheerful voice cut through her reverie, playful and bright. "You know, Perpetua, technically we could just glide up this cliff with no problems!"

He pulled himself up beside her—panting, smiling—his blond hair swirling in the breeze.

She laughed, tightening her grip on the stone wall. "And miss this thrill? No way!"

They surged upward together, muscles singing with effort—not strain, just the electric joy of the climb. Perpetua reached for a higher hold, while Mago arched, wiggling his toe into a small crag, their laughter bouncing off the cliff.

A shadow swept across the stone wall as a massive eagle, its wing-span rivaling Neriah's, soared past, eyes flashing with amusement at their gravity-defying adventure. The great raptor banked sharply, circling back for a second look, its presence a joyful companion on their ascent, free from all earthly fear.

Mago grinned, stretching for another jagged ridge. "I wonder what the eagle is thinking."

Perpetua grunted, willing herself higher, sensing the summit's nearness. "Maybe it's here to cheer us on!"

As they searched for another hold, fingers clawing into the celestite, a snow-white mountain goat bounded onto a nearby ledge. Its regal, translucent horns glinted like prisms in the heavenly light. The creature moved with effortless grace, hooves dancing on the rock as if woven from the cliff itself—a living embodiment of the moun-tain's spirit. Its deep, soulful eyes locked onto them with a mischie-vous glint, as if inviting them to share its fearless elation.

"Well, hello there!" Perpetua chirped playfully, her face flushed with the glow of joyful exertion. "I shall call you Billy."

The goat blinked, letting out a comical bleat that echoed off the cliff. Perpetua stifled a laugh, her nose wrinkling in delight.

Their final ascent was a burst of energy, Perpetua lunging for a higher crevice, her body suspended in mid-air before catching the stone with dexterous fingertips. Mago scrambled beside her, his hands gripping the rock with fierce determination. With one final tug, they summited, rolling onto a wide blue ledge, their seals of light pulsing together in syncopated harmony.

They lay there for a moment, breathing heavily, souls tingling with the thrill of the ascent. Mago rose first, helping Perpetua to her feet. They turned—breath catching—as the scenic expanse unfolded around them.

Behind and below them, the uncharted ocean extended beyond sight, an aquatic wonder waiting—calling—to be explored. Above them, the sky blazed with the delicate blush of sunset interwoven with the fiery brilliance of sunrise, a celestial tapestry of bliss and glory. Impossibly white clouds, thick and plush as heavenly pillows, drifted overhead. Mago grinned, certain he could leap atop them if he tried.

Before them, massive, untamed peaks thrust into the heavens—jagged blue mountains, sculpted by holy winds and abounding grace, their chiseled slopes dusted with a glowing mist that blazed like snow on fire. At the mountains' base, a crystal-clear lake gleamed like a vast mirror, its surface a kaleidoscope of color reflecting the sky's radiant hues. A waterfall thundered from what seemed to be a floating cliff, cloaked in a silvery vapor that swirled like a living veil. Whatever its source, the water roared, a ribbon of liquid light that shimmered with ethereal splendor. The entire scene defied logic, a testament to Heaven's boundless wonder.

Between the lake and the rapturous overlook where Mago and Perpetua stood, a tall forest swayed in a gentle breeze. Its canopy stretched into the distance—a tangled expanse of emerald leaves, vibrant blossoms, and golden needles—the woodland depths whispering of adventures yet to come.

The companions stood together, staring, mesmerized, a tide of worship rising from united hearts.

"Wow," Perpetua breathed.

Mago knelt to open a small backpack, gently lifting out Pippa—a tiny miulume no larger than his hand, its soft fur shimmering like starlight. He passed it to Perpetua along with a piece of bread. Pippa scampered onto her shoulder, its pink nose twitching as it caught scent of the loaf. It leaned forward, sniffing curiously, and Perpetua smiled, breaking off a small crumb.

"Here you go, little one," she murmured, offering it to Pippa, who nibbled delicately, its tail flicking with delight. Perpetua inspected the bread closely, eyes softening. "Thank You, Lord, for Your limitless provision, and for our dear brother Marcus—and his delicious bakery."

Mago nodded, adding a quiet, "Amen," their giggles mingling as they munched. The bread burst with warm flavor as a soft breeze wrapped around them, imparting energy for the journey ahead.

"You know," Mago said, swallowing, "Thomas almost came with us, but he's busy overseeing the construction of that new wharf. He said he'll come next time."

"Next time," Perpetua echoed, eyes closed, savoring the bread's taste, drinking in its scent, as Pippa nuzzled her cheek with a contented chirp.

The air beat with a rhythmic swoosh as the great eagle swept past again, soaring toward the gleaming lake. As they traced its elegant movements, their eyes dropped to the forest below. That was their route—up, around, and through that mysterious wood. There was no path to follow, no schedule to keep. They were free. Perfectly free.

Gazing at the forest, they wondered what heavenly surprises awaited them. What tales would they share upon their return? What book might Mago pen to capture it all?

The breeze swirled again, and a voice broke through—a happy, playful voice Perpetua recognized immediately to be her Heavenly Father's, His tone brimming with love and laughter.

"Come and see, My children," He called, His words echoing

through the mountains, the waterfall, the very air they breathed. "It's waiting for you."

Perpetua's eyes flared wide, meeting Mago's. "Did you hear that?"

"I heard it," he grinned.

"What do you think He wants to show us?"

Her mind raced. *A singing river? A crystal cavern? A heavenly creature? A whole new dimension?* She knew one thing for certain: whatever "it" was, it would reveal the ever-deepening goodness of their Father's heart.

The breeze pulsed warmer, urging them onward.

Perpetua gently set Pippa down, and the tiny creature bounced forward excitedly, its shimmering fur catching the light as it darted ahead.

Mago took Perpetua's hand. "There's only one way to find out. Let's go see."

They stepped forward together, hearts pounding with anticipation, into the thrilling expanse of Heaven's infinite unknown.

PART 3
THE LIGHT BEHIND THE FLAME
(INTERPRETIVE APPENDICES AND FOUNDATIONAL RESOURCES)

COMPLETE APPENDIX
TABLE OF CONTENTS

BIBLIOGRAPHY (SOURCES AND RESOURCES)

- • Bible Translations, Books, and Articles, Cited, Referenced, or Paraphrased in *A Song of Light and Fire: An Uncensored Journey Through Heaven and Hell*

APPENDIX A
CRAFTING HEAVEN'S VISION

INTRODUCTION

As I penned *A Song of Light and Fire: An Uncensored Journey Through Heaven*, my heart trembled with awe, seeking to unveil a Heaven that stirs your soul—not a distant dream, but a truth that reshapes today. You may wonder how I crafted my vision of a realm "no eye has seen, nor ear heard" (1 Corinthians 2:9). The task was humbling, yet anchored in conviction. Heaven is God's masterpiece, prepared for those who love Him (John 14:2–3). Here, I provide historical information regarding chapters 1 and 2, and detail the interpretive methods behind chapters 3 through 9, weaving Scripture, God's character, and Eden's continuity to honor diverse theological perspectives while uncovering unifying insights. My aim has not been to define Heaven's every facet but to invite you into its glory, trusting that reality will surpass these pages.

INTERPRETIVE FRAMEWORK

My approach to depicting Heaven is guided by four main principles, ensuring fidelity to biblical revelation while embracing its transcendent wonder:

1. **Scripture as Bedrock:** A vision of Heaven demands an unyielding commitment to Scripture as its foundation, ensuring every depiction aligns with divine revelation. In crafting this book, I meticulously studied and cross-referenced over 270 distinct passages, from Genesis's

creation narrative to Revelation's eternal city, to uphold theological fidelity. This rigorous adherence to the Bible's authority guards against speculative distortion, grounding core elements in texts like John's promise of eternal life and Ezekiel's celestial visions.

2. **God's Character as Lens:** Interpreting Heaven through God's attributes—love, joy, creativity—is crucial for reflecting the Creator's essence as revealed in His works, from galaxies to sunsets. This lens ensures imaginative details resonate with His boundless generosity and delight in His children. Neglecting God's character would yield a sterile vision, devoid of the relational warmth and splendor that define His eternal Kingdom. By prioritizing His nature, the portrayal invites theological reflection on a Heaven shaped by divine affection and artistry.

3. **Eden's Continuity as Blueprint:** An accurate interpretation of Heaven necessitates viewing it as the fulfillment of Eden's original design, where humanity enjoyed perfect communion with God. Elements like rivers, trees, and fellowship, present in Genesis's garden, must persist in Heaven—magnified beyond earthly limits—as Revelation's restored creation affirms. This blueprint ensures theological coherence, anchoring Heaven in God's redemptive plan to renew His first paradise.

4. **Otherworldly Description:** Biblical fidelity requires honoring Heaven's otherworldly nature, as depicted in Revelation's jeweled city, Ezekiel's radiant throne, and Isaiah's awe-inspiring angels. These surreal, transcendent images demand a portrayal that transcends earthly constraints, embracing fantastic imagery to reflect Scripture's vision. An easily perceptible depiction would betray the text's call for imagination beyond human

comprehension, diminishing the awe of God's eternal realm. By upholding this principle, the vision remains true to the Bible's pattern of unearthly description.

As I crafted this narrative, I sought to honor diverse theological interpretations—debates over timing, judgments, or Heaven's nature —embracing a broad spectrum of evangelical perspectives to weave a richer tapestry. This openness birthed fresh insights, such as balancing immediate entry into paradise (Luke 23:43) with views of time in Sheol (1 Samuel 28:11–15), or Paul's concept of "sleep" (1 Thessalonians 4:13–14), reconciling varied interpretations to deepen the narrative's resonance. At my vision's core lies a guiding rule: Heaven will be infinitely better than Earth (The Choosing Ground), so glorious it transcends our frail minds (Ephesians 3:20). This book, shaped by earthly imagination, is but a shadow of true Paradise, which outshines every word herein. With confidence in Scripture's truth and humility before its mystery, I offer these chapters as an invitation to dream of a home beyond imagining, as Wayne Grudem affirms that Scripture's revelation of Heaven invites our trust in its radiant promises (*Systematic Theology*, Zondervan, 1994, p. 1159). Timothy Keller likewise emphasizes that Heaven's beauty is God's lavish gift, rooted in His unchanging Word (*The Prodigal God*, Dutton, 2008).

HERMENEUTICAL APPROACH

Hermeneutics is the disciplined practice of interpreting Scripture to discern its intended meaning, guided by rigorous attention to context. In crafting *A Song of Light & Fire*, I anchored every depiction of Heaven in the biblical text, ensuring fidelity through analysis of each passage's literary, historical, and theological setting. For example, the Shekinah glory in Chapter 3 draws from Exodus 24:16–17, understood as God's radiant presence in its Old Testament context. My approach remains rooted in historic Christian conviction yet intentionally draws insight from across the Christian spectrum—embracing Baptist focus on the promises of salvation (Luke 23:43), Pentecostal emphasis on worship and spiritual vitality (Revelation 5:11–14), and Reformed devotion to the majesty and sovereignty of God (Revelation 4:2–3). By integrating these perspectives, I sought to present a vivid, Scripture-faithful, and cross-denominational vision that welcomes seekers from every Bible-believing tradition. As D. A. Carson notes regarding Scripture, "We are dealing with God's thoughts: we are obligated to take the greatest pains to understand them truly and to explain them clearly" (*Exegetical Fallacies*).

IMAGINATIVE ELEMENTS

The narrative weaves imaginative elements—seals, lumora fruit, miulumes, dappled stags, and Mago's visions of cloud kingdoms, fire kingdoms, and realms of light and shadow—to evoke Heaven's transcendent glory. These creations are not mere fantasies, but carefully analyzed for their theological grounding, continuity with Eden, and role in portraying a paradise that surpasses its original design. They reflect God's character—His love, provision, creativity, redemption, and boundless generosity, giving gifts "far more than we can ask or imagine" (Ephesians 3:20). While Heaven may or may not hold fruit that "tastes like light" or tiny cats purring in trees, these elements serve a vital purpose: to draw readers from the sterile "known" into the beautiful, awe-inspiring unknown of God's masterpiece.

Heaven is not merely Eden restored but Eden glorified, a truth best conveyed through creatures, sounds, and environments beyond earthly limits. Our mortal minds cannot fully grasp this splendor, but God-given imagination bridges the gap, inviting us to envision a paradise that exceeds Eden's beauty. To imagine Heaven as anything less than utterly brilliant—shattering every boundary of earthbound logic—would diminish God's infinite creativity, bordering on theological heresy. Scripture offers vivid glimpses, not exhaustive details, of Heaven's glory (Revelation 21:11–22:5). Philosophically, imagination may be God's gift to help us "read between the lines," enabling us to anticipate His eternal home in ways consistent with His generous, limitless nature (Psalm 104:24).

J. I. Packer explains in *Knowing God* (InterVarsity Press, 1973) that Scripture's glimpses of Heaven are genuine revelations of divine glory, intended to fill believers with unending joy. Wayne Grudem notes in *Systematic Theology* (Zondervan, 1994) that the Bible's descriptions of Heaven awaken in God's people a longing for its surpassing reality. John Piper writes in *Desiring God* (Multnomah, 1986) that Heaven restores the joy first known in Eden, where creation delighted in God's unhindered presence. Together, these perspectives present Heaven as the culmination of God's creativity (Psalm 104:24) and creation's worship (Psalm 148:3–10), echoing Eden's harmony when humanity walked with God (Genesis 3:8). Timothy Keller affirms in *The Reason for God* (Dutton, 2008) that Heaven fulfills all of God's redemptive purposes, surpassing every earthly hope. John Walvoord declares in *The Revelation of Jesus Christ* (Moody, 1966) that the new creation completes God's promise beyond human imagination. Donald Bloesch concludes in *The Last Things* (InterVarsity Press, 2004) that Heaven's eternal glory will outshine even the beauty of Eden itself.

On this foundation, I imagine. Through *A Song of Light and Fire*, I've invited you to imagine with me—a Heaven so radiant, so vibrant, it stirs your soul to worship the God who prepares it for you (John 14:2–3).

AN ARGUMENT FOR TIMELESSNESS IN ETERNITY

The concept of timelessness in eternity is not merely a theological abstraction but a profound reality that reshapes our understanding of God, Heaven, and our ultimate destiny. Eternity, as depicted in Scripture and supported by respected philosophers and theologians, transcends the linear constraints of human time, existing as a singular, boundless present where past, present, and future converge in the radiant presence of God. This argument draws on biblical evidence, particularly Scriptures like Psalm 90:4 and 2 Peter 3:8, alongside the doctrine of God's foreknowledge, and integrates compelling insights from respected Christian scholars such as Augustine, Boethius, and C. S. Lewis, as well as modern scientific perspectives that align with metaphysical reflections on time. Together, these sources weave a tapestry of timelessness that is both biblically grounded and intellectually captivating, inviting believers to marvel at the eternal nature of God's Kingdom.

BIBLICAL FOUNDATIONS: TIME IN GOD'S PERSPECTIVE

Scripture provides a clear foundation for timelessness in eternity through passages that contrast human temporality with divine eternity. Psalm 90:4 declares, "For a thousand years in Your sight are but as yesterday when it is past, or as a watch in the night." Similarly, 2 Peter 3:8 states, "With the Lord one day is as a thousand years, and a thousand years as one day." These verses suggest that God's experience of time is fundamentally different from ours, unbound by the sequential march of days, years, or centuries. They point to a divine perspective where vast spans of human history are compressed into a moment, implying that God exists outside the constraints of linear time.

This biblical insight is further illuminated by the doctrine of God's foreknowledge, which underscores His timeless nature. Psalm 139:1–4 reveals God's intimate knowledge of all things before they unfold: "O Lord, You have searched me and known me...Even before a word is on my tongue, behold, O Lord, You know it altogether." Acts 2:23 speaks of Jesus' crucifixion as part of God's "definite plan and foreknowledge," and Revelation 13:8 describes the Lamb as "slain from the foundation of the world." These passages portray God as seeing and knowing all events—past, present, and future—simultaneously. His foreknowledge is not a mere prediction but a comprehensive vision of all moments in a single, eternal "now." This aligns with the concept of timelessness, where eternity is not an endless succession of moments but a unified present in which all of God's purposes coexist.

APPENDIX A

THEOLOGICAL AND PHILOSOPHICAL SUPPORT: AUGUSTINE AND BOETHIUS

Christian thinkers have long grappled with the nature of God's eternity, offering arguments that resonate with Scripture and appeal to reason. Augustine of Hippo, one of Christianity's most revered theologians, articulates a profound vision of timelessness in his *Confessions*. He writes, "Your years are one today, and all Your tomorrows are contained in Your today, for You are eternal...Your years neither come nor go; our years come and go, that they all may come." For Augustine, God's eternity is not an infinite extension of time but a state of being where all moments are present at once, unchanging and complete. This perspective elevates eternity above the fleeting nature of human experience, suggesting that Heaven, as God's dwelling place, shares this timeless quality where believers will dwell in a perpetual "today" with Him.

Boethius, a sixth-century Christian philosopher, further refines this idea in *The Consolation of Philosophy*. He defines eternity as "the simultaneous and perfect possession of infinite life," contrasting it with time, which is fragmented into past, present, and future. Boethius argues that God, existing in an eternal present, perceives all events as a single, unified moment: "God sees all things in His eternal present, not as future or past, but as now." Apologists like Thomas Aquinas echo this, asserting that God must exist outside time and space to be God, for a deity bound by temporal or spatial limits would be contingent, not the uncaused cause of all existence. This view, deeply influential in Christian theology, supports the notion that Heaven transcends linear time, allowing figures like Perpetua from 203 AD and Ramona from a futuristic Alberta to meet in a shared, joyous moment, as if all eras converge in God's radiant presence.

MODERN INSIGHTS: C. S. LEWIS AND SCIENTIFIC PERSPECTIVES

C. S. Lewis, a beloved Christian apologist, offers a vivid and accessible reflection on timelessness in *Mere Christianity*. He likens God's relationship with time to an author's relationship with a book: "God is not hurried along in the time-stream of this universe...He has infinite attention to spare for each one of us...You are as much alone with Him as if you were the only being He had ever created" (Harper, 2001 edition). Lewis suggests that God's timelessness allows Him to engage with every moment and every soul simultaneously, a concept that mirrors the biblical portrayal of Heaven as a place where all the redeemed—from every tribe, nation, and era—stand together before the throne (Revelation 7:9). This imagery of timeless unity, where Miriam from a desert and Ezra from ancient Jerusalem laugh as kin, captures the essence of eternity as a singular, all-encompassing present.

Modern science, while not explicitly theological, provides complementary insights that Christians can appreciate. Physicist Albert Einstein, respected for his groundbreaking work on relativity, demonstrated that time is not absolute but relative, affected by gravity and speed. His theory suggests that time can dilate or contract, challenging the notion of a universal, linear progression. Christian physicist John Polkinghorne, reflecting on relativity, notes that the physical world hints at a flexibility in time that aligns in spirit with theological ideas of God's transcendence over it. While science cannot fully grasp eternity, these findings resonate with the biblical idea that God's reality—and by extension, Heaven—operates beyond our temporal framework, where a "day" can be as a "thousand years."

METAPHYSICAL AND THEOLOGICAL IMPLICATIONS

The concept of timelessness has profound implications for theology, particularly in understanding God's foreknowledge and the nature of Heaven. Many theological debates, such as those surrounding predestination or eschatology, could be enriched by embracing God's time-less perspective. For instance, the tension between free will and divine foreknowledge dissolves when we consider that God sees all choices and outcomes in His eternal "now," not as a sequence of events He predicts or controls. As Boethius argues, God's foreknowledge does not impose necessity on human actions, for He sees them as present, not as future. This perspective preserves human agency while affirming God's omniscience, rooted in His timeless nature.

In Heaven, this timelessness manifests as a joyous convergence of all moments. The biblical promise of a "new Heaven and new Earth" (Revelation 21:1) is not merely a future event but an eternal reality where all God's redeemed—from Adam to the last believer—stand united. The imagery of travelers from different eras meeting in a shared, radiant moment reflects this truth. As Lewis writes in *The Great Divorce*, "All moments that have been or shall be were, or are, present in the moment of eternity" (HarperOne, 2009). This vision of Heaven as a place where time's boundaries dissolve invites believers to anticipate a reality where every story, every sacrifice, every prayer is woven into a single, glorious tapestry of worship.

A COMPELLING VISION FOR BELIEVERS

The timelessness of eternity is not just a theological concept but a source of profound hope. It assures us that God's Kingdom is not bound by the fleeting nature of earthly time, where loss and separa-tion dominate. Instead, Heaven is a place where all moments are redeemed, where Perpetua's courage in 203 AD and a modern believ-er's quiet faith in 2025 are celebrated together before the throne. As Augustine reminds us, in God's eternity there is no before or after, but only a present. This truth invites Christians to live with an eternal perspective, trusting that every trial, every act of love, is already part of God's timeless glory.

For Christians, the arguments of Augustine, Boethius, Lewis, and even the scientific echoes of Einstein and Polkinghorne converge with Scripture to paint a compelling picture: Eternity is not an endless timeline but a vibrant, singular moment where God's presence encompasses all. Psalm 90:4 and 2 Peter 3:8 are not mere metaphors but invitations to glimpse God's reality, where a thousand years are as a day because He holds all time in His hand. The doctrine of foreknowledge, seen in Psalm 139 and Revelation 13:8, affirms that God's vision is not sequential but eternal, seeing all at once. This timelessness transforms our hope, assuring us that Heaven is a place where every heart is known, every story complete, and every soul united in the Lamb's eternal "now."

Yet even here, Scripture preserves a mysterious tension. Eternity is indeed God's timeless dwelling, but it is also portrayed as a realm where redeemed souls experience waiting and anticipation. In Revelation 6:10, the martyrs beneath the altar cry out, "How long, Sovereign Lord, holy and true, until you judge the inhabitants of the earth and avenge our blood?" Their plea suggests that, while Heaven transcends earthly time, there remains some form of sequence—an unfolding of God's purposes that those before His throne perceive. Far from contradicting timelessness, this contrast deepens its mystery, reminding us that Heaven holds both God's eternal "now" and a rhythm of expectation known only to Him.

Let us, then, embrace this vision with awe and anticipation, knowing that in eternity, we will step into a reality where time's chains are broken, and all moments sing together in the presence of the Alpha and Omega.

HISTORICAL ANALYSIS: CHAPTERS 1 AND 2

This section grounds chapters 1 and 2 in a historical context, focusing on Perpetua's martyrdom and the Roman games, drawing on primary sources (e.g., *Passion of Perpetua and Felicity*, c. 203 AD), Tertullian's writings, and scholarly analyses, critically evaluated for accuracy.

APPENDIX A

CHAPTER 1: THE MARTYRS

Name Changes for Perpetua's Friends: Chapter 1 introduces Perpetua, a twenty-two-year-old Christian noblewoman martyred in Carthage in 203 AD, alongside her companions, whose names I adjusted for modern pronounceability while preserving their historical reality, as documented in *The Passion of Perpetua and Felicity*. The historical figures include:

- Revocatus, a slave, renamed Marcus to enhance accessibility.
- Saturninus and Secundulus, free men, renamed Mago and Lucius, respectively, for readability.

These changes ensure contemporary audiences can engage with the narrative without distorting the identities of these figures, whose martyrdom is confirmed by the *Passion* and a basilica inscription in Carthage honoring Perpetua and Felicity.

Christian Persecution (64–313 AD): Christian persecution began under Emperor Nero in 64 AD, when he scapegoated Christians for Rome's Great Fire, as recorded by Tacitus (*Annals*, Book XV, chapter 44). This initiated intermittent persecution, varying by emperor and region, until the Edict of Milan in 313 AD, when Constantine and Licinius legalized Christianity. Key periods include:

- Nero (64–68 AD): Blamed Christians for the fire, initiating mass executions.
- Domitian (81–96 AD): Exiled Christians like John (Revelation 1:9) for refusing emperor worship.
- Trajan (98–117 AD): Required sacrifices to Roman gods, with death for refusal (Pliny the Younger, *Letters*, Book X, 96–97).
- Septimius Severus (193–211 AD): Banned conversions in 202 AD, leading to Perpetua's arrest.

- Decius (249–251 AD): Mandated universal sacrifices, intensifying persecution.
- Diocletian (284–305 AD): Launched the Great Persecution (303–313 AD), targeting churches and scriptures.

These persecutions, intended to crush the Christian faith through violence and terror, ultimately backfired on Rome. As Tertullian famously summarized, the blood of martyrs served as seed for the church (*Apologeticus*, c. 197 AD).

CHAPTER 2: VIOLENCE OF THE ROMAN GAMES

Purpose and Violence of Roman Games: Chapter 2 depicts the martyrdom of Perpetua's group on March 7, 203 AD, during games celebrating Caesar's birthday, as confirmed by *The Passion of Perpetua and Felicity*. Roman games (*ludi*) were multifaceted spectacles honoring gods, emperors, or events like imperial birthdays. They served cultural, political, and social purposes: to reinforce Roman identity, entertain the masses, and showcase imperial power through displays of dominance over enemies, including Christians, viewed as threats to Roman piety. The games included chariot races, theatrical performances, and executions, with violence as a central draw. Christians faced brutal execution methods, as noted by Tertullian (*De Spectaculis*, c. 200 AD) and Eusebius (*Ecclesiastical History*, Book VIII), designed to deter defiance and entertain crowds.

- Beast Attacks: Exposure to lions, bears, leopards, or other predators in arenas.
- Gladiatorial Fights: Pitted against trained fighters, often without weapons.
- Burning Alive: Coated in pitch and set ablaze to light Nero's gardens or city streets (Tacitus, *Annals*, XV.44).
- Crucifixion: Mimicked Jesus' death for public humiliation.

- Beheading or Sword: A common execution, as with Perpetua, Mago, and the apostle Paul, often following other torments.

These acts were choreographed for maximum spectacle, turning executions into pageantry that both terrorized Christians and amused spectators, yet often strengthened believers' resolve.

Attendance at Carthage's Amphitheater: The narrative estimates ten thousand attendees at Carthage's amphitheater for Severus' birthday games. While no primary source specifies the exact number, Carthage's amphitheater, smaller than Rome's Colosseum (fifty to eighty thousand capacity), is estimated to have held twenty to thirty thousand, based on archaeological comparisons with North African arenas like El Jem. Given Carthage's population of two hundred to three hundred thousand and the significance of an imperial birthday, a crowd of ten thousand is historically plausible. The *Passion* implies a large audience, noting the crowd's reaction, which supports this estimate as reasonable, enhancing the scene's dramatic impact without contradicting evidence. Additionally, I included predators not specified in Perpetua's account to vividly reflect the broader reality of Christian persecution, as such beasts were commonly used to execute believers under Roman rule (Tertullian, *Apologeticus*, c. 197 AD).

INTERPRETIVE ANALYSIS: CHAPTERS 3 THROUGH 9

Below, I provide a detailed analysis of chapters 3 through 8, outlining the interpretive process, scriptural foundations, and theological considerations for each.

CHAPTER 3: THE GLORY

OVERVIEW

Perpetua's emergence into radiant light portrays the believer's immediate awakening beyond death—the soul's entrance into the manifest
presence of God (the Shekinah). This interpretation draws from Scripture, historical testimony across cultures, and classical theology, all of
which affirm that death is not a pause but a passage: to be away from
the body is to be at home with the Lord (2 Corinthians 5:8).

INTERPRETIVE PROCESS

1. **Human Experience and the Moment of Passing**: I
   concluded Chapter 2 and began Chapter 3 with Perpetua's
   death and immediate transition into eternal life—a moment
   designed to reflect the authority of Scripture while being
   illuminated by the collective witness of human experience.
   Across centuries and cultures, those near death have
   described overwhelming light, peace, angelic presence, and a
   sense of ascent. Such testimonies are not doctrinal, but they
   are directional—echoes that resonate with the verities
   revealed in Scripture: Stephen, "full of the Holy Spirit, gazed
   into heaven and saw the glory of God" (Acts 7:55–56); Jesus
   assured the thief, "Today you will be with Me in paradise"
   (Luke 23:43); and John confirmed that the believer "has
   passed from death to life" (John 5:24). Thus, I allowed these
   accounts to serve as reflective parallels, shaping how
   Perpetua's final breath gives way to first light—the
   beginning of life unending.

2. **Balancing Theological Views through the Shekinah
   Glory**: My interpretive process confronted Scripture's
   apparent tension concerning the timing of Heaven. Paul

describes believers who "sleep" until the resurrection (1 Thessalonians 4:13–14), yet Jesus promises immediate fellowship: "Today you will be with me in paradise" (Luke 23:43), and Paul elsewhere affirms that to be "away from the body" is to be "at home with the Lord" (2 Corinthians 5:8). These passages are complementary, not contradictory. I interpret Perpetua's spirit as entering Christ's Shekinah at death—fully present with Him, yet awakening progressively into greater understanding. Louis Berkhof writes, "The souls of believers immediately after death enter upon the glories of heaven." Thus, the *when* of Heaven is not an either–or but a sacred harmony: immediate communion yet ever-deepening perception—the eternal dawn of endless day.

3. **The Nature of Divine Glory**: In portraying Perpetua's arrival, I followed Scripture's own sensory realism rather than speculative invention. Ezekiel saw brightness "like the appearance of the bow... on the day of rain" (Ezekiel 1:28), and Moses witnessed glory "like a devouring fire" on Sinai (Exodus 24:17). Such descriptions are theophanies perceived through human faculties—light that resounds, warmth that can be tasted, color that sings. I drew on this biblical pattern to represent divine revelation as overwhelming yet tangible. Millard Erickson defines the Shekinah as "the immediate self-manifestation of God's presence among His people" (*Christian Theology*, 1998), and my interpretation seeks that immediacy: the moment when holiness ceases to be merely observed or imagined and instead becomes lived and experienced.

4. **Angelic Guidance and Transition**: In shaping this moment, I drew from the biblical assurance that no believer dies unattended. Scripture records that "the poor man died and was carried by the angels to Abraham's side" (Luke

16:22), and affirms that angels are "ministering spirits sent out to serve for the sake of those who are to inherit salvation" (Hebrews 1:14). Within my interpretive process, I portrayed Neriah—the luminous guide—as the visible embodiment of that heavenly ministry. The scene is not invention but revelation of God's personal care at the threshold of eternity. Psalm 91:11 declares that He "will command His angels concerning you to guard you in all your ways," revealing a Father who does not leave His children to cross alone. Sinclair Ferguson observes that angelic ministry "reflects the Father's tenderness in bringing His children safely home" (*The Holy Spirit*, IVP, 1996). Thus, the angelic presence in Perpetua's passage is both theologically grounded and tenderly personal—heavenly order meeting human frailty in the gentlest possible form.

5. **The River and the Completion of Choice**: The "river of the water of life, bright as crystal," flows "from the throne of God and of the Lamb" (Revelation 22:1), signifying purification, welcome, and unending joy. It typologically echoes Israel's crossing of the Jordan into inheritance (Joshua 3:15–17), the moment when wilderness wandering gave way to promise. In my interpretive process, I sought to mirror that continuity: as Israel passed from wilderness into rest, so Perpetua crosses from mortality into eternal life. In this scene, the river is not merely symbolic—it is the living movement of grace itself. Its current carries the redeemed into perfect belonging, washing away the last remnants of sorrow, fear, and separation. In Heaven, water does not erode or destroy; it renews. Flowing from the very throne of God, it is both the source and the summons of life—the eternal expression of divine generosity. Perpetua's passage through the river completes what The Choosing Ground began: she who chose Christ's light now belongs wholly to it. The radiant water envelops her as she rises, the burdens

of earth dissolving into brightness. "He will wipe away every tear from their eyes" (Revelation 21:4). Thus, the river becomes the final threshold between all that was broken and all that is whole—the boundary where time yields to eternity and joy begins without end.

THEOLOGICAL/LOGICAL CONCLUSION

Together these interpretations reveal death for the believer not as fading into shadow but as awakening into light. The scriptural, historical, and experiential evidence together affirm a conscious, personal passage into Christ's presence. The testimonies of light and ascent echo Stephen's vision (Acts 7:55–56); the "today" of paradise (Luke 23:43) harmonizes with the "sleep" of resurrection (1 Thessalonians 4:13–14); and the sensory imagery of Ezekiel and Moses reminds us that divine glory is tangible. Perpetua's transition marks faith becoming sight—her spirit entering the radiance of the Shekinah, attended by angels, and carried across the river of life. Each element —light, sound, motion, and touch—exists to show that Heaven is not a distant ideal but a realized promise. Grace, then, does more than save from death; it transforms dying itself into the first act of eternal life.

CHAPTER 4: THE GATE

OVERVIEW

Perpetua's crossing of the River of Life and approach to Heaven's golden gate portrays the culmination of redemption—the moment when the soul, fully glorified, enters the immediate presence of Christ. This analysis explains how resurrection, judgment, and worship converge to depict Heaven's entry not as an end but as the beginning of eternal communion.

INTERPRETIVE PROCESS

1. **The Trumpet and Resurrection**: The trumpet that sounds as Perpetua rises from the river is not intended to suggest the rapture or the second coming of Christ, but rather the renewal of creation—the restoration of God's original design. In Scripture, the trumpet announces transformation, not departure: "What is sown perishable is raised imperishable" (1 Corinthians 15:42), and again, "At the last trumpet... the dead will be raised imperishable, and we shall be changed" (1 Corinthians 15:52). Its call signifies the reunion of spirit and body into the "spiritual body" (1 Corinthians 15:44), conformed to Christ's "glorious body" (Philippians 3:21). Thus, the trumpet becomes Heaven's proclamation that the old has passed away and the new has come—the mortal exchanged for immortality, the corruptible redeemed into incorruption—fulfilling the mystery that "death has been swallowed up in victory" (1 Corinthians 15:54).

2. **Seals of Light and Heavenly Identity**: The seals of light adorning the redeemed represent restored innocence—the reversal of Eden's shame. Before sin, humanity was "naked and not ashamed" (Genesis 2:25); after the Fall, coverings became symbols of alienation (Genesis 3:7). In Heaven, that estrangement is undone. The redeemed are "clothed in fine linen, bright and pure—for the fine linen is the righteous acts of the saints" (Revelation 19:8). These garments shine not to conceal but to reveal holiness itself. Each robe becomes the visible form of invisible grace—its colors expressing the unique testimony of a life redeemed. These seals signify not uniformity but divine artistry, each pattern reflecting the story God has written in mercy. John Piper affirmed that the saints will not merely wear garments but

the brilliance of holiness itself (*Desiring God*, 1986): "They
shall walk with Me in white, for they are worthy"
(Revelation 3:4).

3. **Language and Unity of Worship**: Perpetua's effortless
   comprehension of every tongue reflects not a single
   universal language but the restoration of perfect
   understanding. This unity mirrors Pentecost (Acts 2:6) and
   fulfills Revelation 7:9, where every nation and tribe joins in
   one voice of praise. My interpretation emphasizes that
   heavenly communication does not erase diversity but
   perfects it—each voice distinct yet harmonized in love.
   This unity embodies the relational nature of Heaven:
   knowledge made perfect through affection, communion
   unbroken by sin. Perpetua's dialogue with Miriam thus
   symbolizes the Spirit's unifying power, perfecting
   fellowship without conformity. As J. I. Packer observed,
   perfected knowledge joined to perfected love will make
   fellowship "as natural as breathing" (*Knowing God*, 1973):
   "For we know in part and we prophesy in part, but when
   the perfect comes, the partial will pass away" (1
   Corinthians 13:9–10).

4. **The Harvest of God**: The multitude gathered before
   Heaven's gate fulfills Jesus' words: "Lift up your eyes, and
   see that the fields are white for harvest" (John 4:35). Here,
   the redeemed are not symbols but substance—the living
   fruit of divine labor. Each soul bears witness to the patience
   of the Sower and the triumph of the Reaper who "thrust in
   His sickle, for the harvest of the earth is fully ripe"
   (Revelation 14:15). The great assembly thus becomes a
   living parable of God's victory: the Church gathered, the
   seed of faith brought to its full fruition. Charles Spurgeon
   compared the Lord's joy to that of a farmer rejoicing over
   his sheaves (*Metropolitan Tabernacle Pulpit*, 1859): "Those

who sow in tears shall reap with shouts of joy" (Psalm 126:5).

5. **The Worship of Heaven**: In depicting Heaven's worship, my purpose was to convey existence itself as adoration, not a sequence of ceremonies. "Let everything that has breath praise the Lord!" (Psalm 150:6). In Heaven, worship is not bound by moments or methods—it is continuous life in God's presence, where every thought and movement reflects His glory. Perpetua's experience reveals that praise there is not performed but *lived*; it is the soul's natural response to perfect love. Jonathan Edwards described Heaven as "a world of love," where praise is the very air the saints breathe (*Heaven Is a World of Love*, 1759): "They shall be His people, and God Himself shall be with them and be their God" (Revelation 21:3).

6. **Transitional Space and Judgment**: The radiant wall of light at Heaven's gate marks the final boundary before entering the full glory of God—a place of both completed arrival and ongoing anticipation. Scripture promises the believer's immediate presence with Christ ("Today you will be with Me in paradise," Luke 23:43) and also declares that "we must all appear before the judgment seat of Christ" (2 Corinthians 5:10). These truths point to a moment of transition: the redeemed stand within Heaven yet have not entered its deepest light. The wall represents that sacred threshold where the redeemed move from Heaven's welcome into God's full presence—where worship becomes as natural as breathing. Here, judgment comes not in fear but in joy, for "there is now no condemnation for those who are in Christ Jesus" (Romans 8:1). This is the judgment of reward, not rejection—when "each one will receive his praise from God" (1 Corinthians 4:5). Though "each one's work will become manifest... the fire will test what sort of

work each has done" (1 Corinthians 3:13), that fire reveals glory, not guilt. What endures is that which has been sanctified by grace and refined by holy love. When believers stand before the judgment seat of Christ, their sins are not charged against them but seen through mercy's light, magnifying the grace that has already removed them. As C. S. Lewis wrote, "It would be wicked to call the good that meets us then 'forgiveness' if we did not also see, with blinding clarity, all that we have been forgiven" (*Mere Christianity*, 1952). The redeemed behold that truth—their failures covered by mercy, their stories crowned with love—and "the righteous shall shine forth as the sun in the kingdom of their Father" (Matthew 13:43).

THEOLOGICAL / LOGICAL CONCLUSION

Perpetua's passage through the gate completes the redemptive arc begun at the river, uniting resurrection, revelation, and worship into a single act of grace. The believer rises in a glorified body, "sown in dishonor, raised in glory" (1 Corinthians 15:42–44), "conformed to Christ's glorious body" (Philippians 3:21). The trumpet declares transformation, announcing that the mortal has been redeemed into immortality. Before the *bēma* of Christ, grace becomes sight; faith's story is unveiled not for condemnation but for celebration, for "there is now no condemnation for those who are in Christ Jesus" (Romans 8:1). Sin is acknowledged only to magnify mercy, and every life shines with the beauty of its redemption. Perpetua's radiant seal embodies innocence restored and holiness perfected—Eden recovered and surpassed (Genesis 2:25; Revelation 19:8). The harvest of God is gathered, worship becomes existence, and eternity begins its endless song. As C. S. Lewis wrote, "Joy is the serious business of Heaven" (*Letters to Malcolm: Chiefly on Prayer*, 1964).

CHAPTER 5: THE VALLEY

OVERVIEW

The valley bursts with Edenic splendor—meadows, trees, and living creatures alive with praise—where Perpetua meets saints from across the ages and joins in joyful activity that reveals the beauty of God's creative heart.

INTERPRETIVE PROCESS

1. **Eden Restored, Personified, and Glorified**: The valley unfolds as living proof that Heaven is more than a crystal city or radiant cathedral—it is Eden restored, alive, and glorified beyond mortal conception. The garden first planted by God (Genesis 2:8–9) has not been replaced by walls of stone but transformed into the living heart of His eternal creation. In that first paradise, "every tree was pleasing to the sight and good for food," but here the trees of life bear fruit each month "for the healing of the nations" (Revelation 22:2). The shadow has given way to substance; what was temporal now shines with imperishable splendor. The river of life flows clear as crystal, "proceeding from the throne of God and of the Lamb" (Revelation 22:1), winding through landscapes radiant with His glory. Hills breathe praise, valleys shimmer with holiness, and every current of light declares, "The Lord is God; He has made His light to shine upon us" (Psalm 118:27). This is creation transfigured—the cosmos awakened to its true design. The "very good" of Genesis (1:31) has become the "all things new" of Revelation (21:5). As Isaiah foretold, "The wilderness and the dry land shall be glad; the desert shall rejoice and blossom like the rose" (Isaiah 35:1). Charles Spurgeon called Heaven "the garden of God, where His

230

presence blooms unendingly" (*The New Park Street Pulpit*, 1859). In this garden made eternal, creation itself fulfills its purpose—reflecting the unbroken fellowship between God and His redeemed, beauty serving as the language of worship.

2. **Fellowship Across Time**: Perpetua's conversations with figures from history—Joseph, Hubert, and others—embody the unity Jesus prayed for in John 17:21: "that they may all be one." These meetings echo the Mount of Transfiguration (Matthew 17:1–8), where Moses and Elijah stood beside Christ, revealing fellowship across the ages. Such encounters illustrate Wayne Grudem's summary that in Heaven, believers from every era will enjoy perfect and joyous fellowship together in God's presence (*Systematic Theology*, Zondervan, 1994). The valley thus becomes a meeting place of centuries—Eden's family restored.

3. **Purposeful Activity**: Heaven will not be a place of idle drifting but of joyful purpose. The labor of Eden—cultivating, naming, and tending—finds its eternal fulfillment in the valley. "The Lord God took the man and put him in the garden of Eden to work it and keep it" (Genesis 2:15); so too the redeemed will continue to reflect God's image through creativity, discovery, and the glad exercise of dominion now freed from curse. Every action in Heaven—crafting, exploring, building, or feasting—is worship, a way of saying with our hands what our hearts already sing. Revelation 19:6–9 celebrates fellowship; Revelation 20:4 speaks of reigning; and Matthew 5:12 affirms reward. Alistair Begg explains that heavenly service will be "the glad overflow of hearts at rest, not dull repetition" (*Made for His Pleasure*, 1996). Thus, the work once begun in Eden reaches its completion in Heaven—labor transformed into praise, purpose into unending joy.

4. **The Delight of God**: God Himself rejoices in His creation. "He will rejoice over you with singing," declares Zephaniah 3:17, and all creation joins that song: "Let the field exult, and everything in it" (Psalm 96:12). The shimmering herds, chiming streams, and star-flecked meadows of the valley echo His gladness. Timothy Keller took note that Heaven is not mere compensation for earthly loss but the fulfillment of everything God intended (*The Reason for God*, Dutton, 2008). In this joy, creation reflects its Maker perfectly—the happiness of God shining through all He has made.

5. **Animals in Heaven**: When God created living creatures, He called them "good" (Genesis 1:20–25). Formed before humanity, they filled the air, land, and sea with motion and music—an early chorus in creation's song of praise. Isaiah foresaw their harmony restored: "The wolf shall dwell with the lamb, and the leopard shall lie down with the young goat" (Isaiah 11:6). Paul echoed the same hope: "Creation itself will be set free from its bondage to decay" (Romans 8:21). The presence of animals in the valley—majestic, playful, and at peace—reveals the kindness of the Creator and the completeness of His redemption. Speaking of this very restoration, John Wesley wrote of animals that "whatever affections they had in the garden of God will be restored with vast increase; being exalted, together with their human friends, in a state of everlasting happiness" (*Sermon 60: "The General Deliverance," 1782*). Thus, even the animal world will share in the liberty of glory, for Heaven's joy is not confined to humankind alone. Heaven's living symphony proclaims the goodness of God's compassion, as all creation joins in the song of renewal: "Let everything that has breath praise the Lord!" (Psalm 150:6).

THEOLOGICAL / LOGICAL CONCLUSION

The valley reveals the completion of God's creative design—Heaven's order perfected, Eden's purpose fulfilled and glorified. What began in a garden (Genesis 2:8–9) finds its consummation beside the river of life, where "the tree yields its fruit each month for the healing of the nations" (Revelation 22:2). Here, creation's original calling—to display God's goodness through joyful stewardship—is magnified beyond imagination. The redeemed now serve, reign, and rejoice within a world that pulses with divine life. "Let the field exult, and all that is in it; then shall all the trees of the forest sing for joy before the Lord, for He comes" (Psalm 96:12–13). Every relationship bears the fragrance of perfect love, and every task becomes an act of worship, for "we are His workmanship, created in Christ Jesus for good works, which God prepared beforehand" (Ephesians 2:10). Perpetua's awe before this renewed creation is not poetic fantasy but theology made visible—the Creator's "very good" work transfigured into everlasting delight. As J. I. Packer wrote, "Heaven's glory consists in a richer revelation of God than we have ever known, and our hearts find their rest in wonder" (*Knowing God*, 1973).

CHAPTER 6: THE CITY

OVERVIEW

The New Jerusalem shines with jasper walls, pearl gates, and the vast Tree of Life, where Jesus is omnipresent and reunions abound, reflecting both divine majesty and the perfect community of Heaven.

INTERPRETIVE PROCESS

1. **City's Design**: My interpretation of the New Jerusalem
   draws directly from Revelation 21:11–21, where John
   describes a city "having the glory of God, its radiance like a
   most rare jewel, like jasper, clear as crystal." The cube-
   shaped form (21:16) reflects not mere symmetry but divine
   intentionality—a geometry that mirrors God's perfection
   and completeness. In ancient Israel, the Holy of Holies
   shared this same cubic design (1 Kings 6:20), signifying the
   fullness of God's presence within sacred space. So too, the
   New Jerusalem functions as the eternal dwelling place of
   God among His people (Revelation 21:3). The
   measurements—roughly 1,400 miles in every direction—are
   staggering, yet profoundly meaningful. If such a city were
   set upon our earth, its summit would soar more than 1,300
   miles beyond the boundary of outer space, a height that
   defies comprehension. These measurements represent both
   artistry and revelation: a design so vast it reflects the infinite
   imagination of the Creator. The city's beauty is not symbolic
   excess but ordered glory, built to display both God's
   grandeur and His intimacy. Hebrews 11:10 speaks of
   Abraham awaiting "the city that has foundations, whose
   designer and builder is God." I interpret these dimensions
   literally—not as speculation, but as testimony to Heaven's
   divine craftsmanship, where structure itself proclaims
   redemption's completeness. As Randy Alcorn notes, "The
   vastness of the city displays the vastness of God's
   redemptive plan" (*Heaven*, Tyndale, 2004).

2. **Unseen Layers**: Scripture hints at realities beyond
   perception. Paul spoke of being "caught up to the third
   heaven" (2 Corinthians 12:2–4), implying layers or realms
   unseen. Perpetua's vision of terraces, portals, and radiant

plazas reflects those ascending dimensions—a poetic portrayal of infinite discovery. Psalm 104:24 declares, "O Lord, how manifold are Your works!"—and in Heaven, each work unfolds without end. C. S. Lewis suggests we will never exhaust Heaven's joys; every door leads further into knowing God (*Letters to Malcolm*, 1964).

3. **The Omnipresence of Jesus**: In Heaven, Christ's presence permeates all existence. My interpretation emphasizes that Paradise is not merely where God dwells—it is the eternally joyous atmosphere His presence creates. "I am with you always" (Matthew 28:20) finds its everlasting fulfillment here. Every street glows with His nearness; every conversation is illuminated by His love. Colossians 1:17 declares that "in Him all things hold together," and so in that heavenly home, all joy coheres in Christ. Theologically, this harmonizes holy transcendence and intimate nearness —Jesus enthroned in glory yet personally known by every soul in every timeless moment. D. A. Carson observed that "the glory of Heaven is not simply the absence of sin but the presence of the God whose love defines every joy" (*The Difficult Doctrine of the Love of God*, 2000). I interpret His laughter among the redeemed and His majesty upon the throne as two expressions of one truth: Heaven's life is relational because its Lord is the embodiment of love (1 John 4:8)

4. **Reunions and Relationships**: My interpretation of heavenly relationships rests upon Scripture's promise that the redeemed "will always be with the Lord" (1 Thessalonians 4:17). Perpetua's reunions with Mago, Felicity, Lucius, and Sabina embody the restoration of community that sin and death once severed. Revelation 7:9 envisions a multitude "from every nation, tribe, people, and language," revealing the unity of the redeemed family across

ages. While Jesus taught that marriage, as an institution, does not continue in Heaven (Matthew 22:30), love itself is not abolished but glorified. Earthly affections are not erased but perfected. C. S. Lewis wrote, "Our natural affections will be purified and immortalized; love will possess us wholly" (*The Four Loves*, 1960). Martyn Lloyd-Jones affirmed that in glory, "self is gone, and therefore love reigns perfectly" (*The Kingdom of God*, 1992). Thus, I depict heavenly relationships as eternal communion without rivalry or loss—each love transfigured, yet every affection preserved.

5. **The Tree of Life**: At the city's center towers the Tree of Life, "bearing twelve kinds of fruit" (Revelation 22:2). If the river flowing beneath it spans 200 meters, the trunk would rise 4.35 miles high and crown a canopy covering 1,241 square miles; for a half-mile river, its breadth might reach 1.63 miles and its height 14.3 miles. These are straightforward geometric estimates assuming an ordinary tree form scaled to the text's setting—not metaphorical placeholders. Their literal magnitude is meant to awaken awe at God's creative power. Psalm 36:6 declares, "Your righteousness is like the mighty mountains," and such vastness fittingly communicates Heaven's scale of holiness. Terraces, bridges, and dwellings woven among its branches suggest not fantasy but divine architecture—a living cathedral sustaining all. Alistair Begg notes that Heaven's abundance will be the glad portion of those who now rest from labor and live forever in the fruit of God's grace (*Made for His Pleasure*, 1996).

6. **Eden's Continuity and Age in Heaven**: The presence of young people—such as the child playfully chased by Jesus—reveals God's mercy toward the innocent. Scripture suggests that those who die before an age of accountability are received into His presence, their souls covered by divine

grace (2 Samuel 12:23). In Heaven, that grace takes form in glorified bodies—transformed to express eternal joy rather than mortal age. Jesus said, "Unless you become like little children, you will never enter the kingdom of Heaven" (Matthew 18:3–4), reminding us that childlike purity reflects the very nature of the redeemed. While Scripture does not specify the age we will appear, it assures us that all decay and decline belong to the curse—and the curse is no more (Revelation 22:3). Yet the absence of decay does not mean the absence of growth. God designed humanity to mature, to learn, and to flourish as an act of divine artistry. To suggest that Heaven excludes such growth would not align with the biblical vision of life abundant (John 10:10). The redeemed will continue to deepen in wisdom and wonder, ever expanding within the perfection of glory. Thus, the vitality of youth becomes a symbol of everlasting life— innocence restored, vigor perfected, joy unending. John MacArthur writes, "God's grace ensures that the innocent find rest in His presence, and all the redeemed are perfected in beauty and strength" (*The Glory of Heaven*, Crossway, 1996,).

THEOLOGICAL / LOGICAL CONCLUSION

The City of God embodies both architecture and affection—Heaven's community built of living light. Its design reveals God's intellect; its fellowship reveals His heart. In my interpretation, the New Jerusalem is not an allegory but the fulfillment of a divine promise: redeemed humanity dwelling with the omnipresent Christ in perfect harmony. Every wall, jewel, and gate speaks theology through beauty—its vast dimensions and radiant symmetry proclaiming both the mind and imagination of God. The Tree of Life anchors this reality, its unimaginable scale and fruitfulness bearing witness to divine generosity and to the growth that continues even within perfection. Reunions echo His mercy; laughter echoes His joy; every relationship flourishes as creation itself expands in praise. Augustine described this destiny as "the most blessed society of all the saints and of the holy angels, united in one eternal city, where God shall be all in all" (*The City of God*, XXII.30). Jonathan Edwards likewise affirmed that "the saints in Heaven shall see and know more of God in one moment than they could in a thousand years on earth" (*Works*, 1754). Together, these truths reveal Heaven as the generous and creative work of God—His wisdom displayed in its design, His presence in its people, His glory in their joy. In that radiant dwelling, every gate stands open, every tear is forgotten, and every heartbeat joins the unbroken hymn of glory to the Lamb who reigns forever.

CHAPTER 7: THE THRONE

OVERVIEW

The throne radiates divine majesty—encircled by emerald light and alive with worship. God's threefold presence fills the scene: Father enthroned, Son revealed as the Lamb, and Spirit blazing like living fire. Before this glory, Perpetua joins the redeemed in ceaseless adoration and glimpses the relentless mercy still pursuing her family on Earth.

INTERPRETIVE PROCESS

1. **The Throne's Description**: My interpretation of the throne draws from Revelation 4:2–3, which portrays "a throne in heaven... its appearance like jasper and carnelian, and around the throne an emerald rainbow." I see this not as poetic flourish but as theological revelation. The rainbow—first given to Noah (Genesis 9:13–16)—anchors the scene in covenant mercy, reminding the reader that God's

sovereignty never operates apart from His compassion. Surrounding the throne are the four living creatures—the lion, the ox, the man, and the eagle—imagery drawn directly from Ezekiel's vision (Ezekiel 1:10; 10:14) and repeated in Revelation to signify the fullness of creation in perpetual worship before its Creator. Together they represent the entire created order acknowledging divine holiness, their unceasing cry of "Holy, holy, holy" (Revelation 4:8; Isaiah 6:3) echoing through eternity. A. W. Tozer called the throne "the blazing center of reality from which holiness radiates to the ends of creation" (*The Knowledge of the Holy*, 1961). My interpretation follows that logic—the throne as both the origin and orientation of all existence. To behold it is to encounter the heart of the universe: sovereignty encircled by grace.

2. **The Threefold Presence**: At the center of Heaven stands the mystery that defines all others—the throne of God, where love and majesty exist as one. Here, the Father, the Son, and the Spirit are not three powers sharing a space but one glory expressed in three persons of being. The Father reigns in sovereign splendor; the Son, revealed as the Lamb, reigns in redeeming grace; the Spirit burns before them as living flame—the light in which they are known and adored. The vision is not of separation but of shared radiance, where the power that rules the universe is the same love that binds it together. Jesus' words, "I and the Father are one" (John 10:30), find their ultimate fulfillment here, and the seven blazing lamps before the throne (Revelation 4:5) reveal the Spirit as the breath of their communion. Christ seated "at the right hand of God" (Hebrews 1:3) is not representative of spatial distance but of eternal unity—the Father glorified in the Son, the Son glorified in the Father, and the Spirit glorifying both. As R. C. Sproul observed, "To behold the throne is to perceive the Trinity in perfect communion—the

Father reigning, the Son redeeming, the Spirit illuminating" (*The Holiness of God*, 1985). The throne is thus not the seat of a monarch but the home of relationship itself—the everlasting pulse of love from which all creation lives and to which every heart will one day return.

3. **God's Pursuit of the Lost**: In this vision, Perpetua glimpses the mercy of God still reaching toward those she left behind, and I interpret that moment as Heaven's echo of divine pursuit. The throne does not merely symbolize judgment but the active compassion of a God who seeks. "Surely goodness and mercy shall follow me all the days of my life" (Psalm 23:6) reveals a love that chases rather than waits. Peter reminds us that the Lord is "not wishing that any should perish, but that all should reach repentance" (2 Peter 3:9). Even now, Christ is interceding for us (Romans 8:34). Charles Spurgeon wrote, "When the shepherd seeks his lost sheep, he does not sit upon the hill and call, but goes after it until he finds it" (*The Good Shepherd*, 1881). Likewise, John Stott declared that "the love of God is a pursuing love, following us until grace has the final word" (*The Cross of Christ*, 1986). My interpretation therefore views the throne not as distant majesty but as the seat of mercy in motion—the place from which redemption continues to reach outward even as worship rises upward.

4. **The Worshipful Crescendo**: Perpetua's awe before the throne culminates in the great chorus of Heaven—the sound of creation restored to perfect harmony. Revelation 5:11–14 records "ten thousand times ten thousand" voices crying, "Worthy is the Lamb who was slain!" I understand this moment as Heaven's natural order renewed—the cosmos itself becoming a choir. Ezekiel 28:13 hints that before rebellion, the realm of glory was musical, crafted for praise. Worship, then, is not Heaven's duty but its atmosphere.

Donald Bloesch described it as "movement, not monotony—
the rhythm of divine joy made audible" (*The Last Things*,
2004). Psalm 16:11 gives its melody: "In Your presence
there is fullness of joy." Worship in Heaven is not static
adoration but living participation in God's life—the soul
joining the music of His glory.

5. **The Crystal Sea**: Before the throne spreads "a sea of
   glass, like crystal" (Revelation 4:6)—a surface as clear as
   ice yet alive with reflection. My interpretation sees this
   not as an ornament but as symbol and structure: the
   boundary between Creator and creation now made
   transparent by perfect grace. Exodus 24:10 describes a
   similar pavement "like sapphire stone, clear as the sky
   itself," linking the two visions across covenants. The
   crystal sea represents purity undisturbed—God's holiness
   revealed as serene rather than unapproachable. Jonathan
   Edwards wrote that "Heaven is the place where the beauty
   of God shines with ineffable luster, like light reflected
   from a sea of glass" (*Works*, Vol. 2, 1758). The redeemed
   stand upon that sea not by merit but by mercy, upheld by
   the holiness they adore. It is, in essence, the reflection of
   divine calm—the stillness of infinite perfection inviting
   unending praise.

THEOLOGICAL / LOGICAL CONCLUSION

The throne of God is the center of Heaven's gravity—the axis of reality. Around it, worship and wonder orbit without fatigue. Here the
triune God is revealed in blazing unity; His pursuit of the lost proves
His heart; His holiness becomes music. The crystal sea mirrors His
purity; the creatures cry His glory; the Lamb bears His love. As
Perpetua joins the chorus, Heaven's song swells into eternity. John
MacArthur affirms that all worship in Heaven revolves around the
sovereign Lord on His throne (*The Glory of Heaven*, Crossway, 1996). In

that everlasting anthem, awe and affection meet, and the redeemed find the joy for which they were created.

CHAPTER 8: THE ETERNAL HOME

OVERVIEW

Perpetua and her friends enter homes prepared for them by Jesus Himself—each radiant with individuality, joy, and divine care. From this sanctuary, the redeemed glimpse Earth's continuing story, their hearts rising in prayer and thanksgiving as God's redemptive plan unfolds.

INTERPRETIVE PROCESS

1. **Observing Earthly Lives**: My description of Heaven's "observatories" is grounded in the scriptural tension between separation and awareness—the redeemed removed from Earth's sorrow yet still rejoicing in its redemption. Revelation 5:8 portrays the prayers of the saints ascending like incense before God, revealing communion rather than distance between Heaven and Earth. Jesus taught that "there will be more joy in Heaven over one sinner who repents" (Luke 15:7), confirming Heaven's active awareness of salvation's progress. This awareness is not mere curiosity but active participation in divine joy. The redeemed, fully aligned with the will of Christ, echo His intercession for those on The Choosing Ground (Hebrews 7:25). John Calvin affirmed that "the prayers of the saints are the breath of the Spirit through which Heaven and Earth are joined" (*Institutes of the Christian Religion*, III.20). Thus, I portray Perpetua and her companions not as spectators but as

participants in the mercy that still moves through time—worshippers whose praise harmonizes with the unfolding of God's redemptive plan. In Heaven, love does not grow passive; it becomes worshipful agreement with divine compassion.

2. **Personalized Homes**: When Jesus promised, "In My Father's house are many rooms" (John 14:2), He revealed the personal nature of Heaven. I interpret these homes not as uniform mansions but as living reflections of redeemed identity—masterpieces of divine craftsmanship shaped by grace. Each home bears the signature of its Maker, uniquely designed for the soul it shelters. The splendor of ivory arches and golden walls is not luxury but language—the visible form of divine affection. Psalm 139:14 declares, "I am fearfully and wonderfully made," and in Heaven that truth becomes architecture. Augustine observed that "the dwellings of God's city correspond to the measure of every soul's love" (*City of God*, XXII.30). My depiction follows that insight: each home is as individual as the heart it was built for, yet all share one foundation—Christ Himself. These sanctuaries display that God's understanding of His children is both infinite and intimate, transforming personal history into eternal artistry.

3. **God's Character in His Gifts**: The feasts, gardens, and treasures of Heaven represent more than abundance—they reveal the heart of the Giver. "Every good gift and perfect gift is from above" (James 1:17), and in Heaven that promise becomes perpetual. I interpret these gifts not as material reward but as the expression of divine generosity: the Father's delight in giving joy. Matthew 7:11 reminds us that if earthly fathers know how to give good things, "how much more will your Father in heaven give good things to those who ask Him." Every blossom, melody,

and meal in Heaven testifies to His nature. J. C. Ryle wrote, "Heaven is the perfection of holiness and happiness because it is the manifestation of God's infinite kindness" (*Holiness*, 1877). My depiction embraces that truth: Heaven's gifts are the overflow of divine character. They are not earned but shared, not stored but enjoyed—grace translated into beauty. In Heaven, generosity is not an event but an atmosphere; joy is not temporary but structural.

THEOLOGICAL / LOGICAL CONCLUSION

Heaven's homes are the Father's joy made tangible—each dwelling an extension of divine personality. These sanctuaries reveal God's character in form and function: personal, generous, relational, and endlessly creative. The saints' awareness of Earth magnifies His pursuing mercy; their individualized dwellings celebrate His intimacy; their feasts and songs proclaim His kindness. Jesus Himself walks among them—the Friend who prepared each room and the King whose presence sanctifies every threshold. Here, gratitude becomes instinct, fellowship becomes worship, and beauty becomes revelation. Abraham Kuyper expressed it well: "Heaven's homes are the crowns of God's grace, displaying His boundless mercy in form and fellowship" (*The Work of the Holy Spirit*, 1900). In this eternal home, every heart at last understands what it means to be perfectly known, wholly loved, and finally home.

CHAPTER 9: ABUNDANT LIFE

OVERVIEW

The company attends the great garden feast, joins historical saints, glimpses Earth through Heaven's lens, and begins planning the ongoing rhythm of eternal life—each activity saturated with joy, wonder, and worship, revealing God's inexhaustible generosity.

INTERPRETIVE PROCESS

1. **Ongoing Supper**: The garden feast reflects the "marriage supper of the Lamb" (Revelation 19:7–9) and Jesus' promise that "many will come from east and west and recline at table with Abraham, Isaac, and Jacob in the kingdom of heaven" (Matthew 8:11). Luke 14:15 rejoices, "Blessed is everyone who will eat bread in the kingdom of God." The repetition of such imagery implies not a single event but a perpetual fellowship—Heaven's feast ever renewed in divine celebration. Each loaf, fruit, and fragrance manifests the joy of Psalm 16:11: "In Your presence there is fullness of joy." Marcus' worshipful baking, his bread golden with light, becomes a fitting response to divine artistry, echoing George Whitefield's portrayal of Heaven's banquet as "radiant with God's joy" (*Select Sermons*, Sermon 14, 1740). The redeemed do not merely dine; they participate in eternal thanksgiving, feasting upon the very goodness of God.

2. **Food and Gifts**: Heaven's edible bounty—sapphire berries, radiant fruits, heavenly manna—reflects Revelation 22:2's abundant harvest, embodying God's intent to lavish good gifts upon His children (Matthew 7:11). For those wondering whether delights like a thick, juicy steak will grace Heaven's table, rest assured that, whatever tastes and textures await, they will surpass earthly satisfaction in every way. These elements proclaim a theological vision where God's generosity and artistry converge, crafting a paradise of transcendent nourishment and delight. Herman Bavinck notes that Heaven's bounty reflects "God's unending kindness" (*Reformed Dogmatics*, Vol. 4, 1901).

3. **Darkness and Night**: The holy darkness that follows the garden feast is not the loss of light but the fullness of its purpose—a sacred dimming through which the Lamb's radiance shines all the more. Revelation 4:8 speaks of creatures worshiping "day and night," revealing that even in eternity there is rhythm, not monotony. Genesis 1:4 declares that God "separated the light from the darkness," and "it was good." The first night was not curse but cadence—a divine pause in the song of creation. So too in Heaven, these serene shadows amplify glory, casting jeweled hues across crystal pathways and deepening awe in eternal worship. The darkness is not needed for rest but given for reflection. Charles Spurgeon observes in *The Treasury of David* that the light of God can be gentle as well as splendid; His glory inhabits every shade (on Psalm 139).

4. **Historical Meetings**: The company's encounters with figures like Esther and Paul echo the fellowship of Hebrews 12:1's "great cloud of witnesses." The redeemed across centuries form one living household of faith, each story woven into another. Even in Eden, where God walked with Adam in perfect nearness, He said, "It is not good that the man should be alone" (Genesis 2:18). From the beginning, God designed humanity not only for fellowship with Him but also for fellowship with one another. In Heaven, that design reaches its fullness. The relationships fractured by sin are restored, and every bond reflects the love of Christ—without jealousy, distance, or fear. Esther's courage, Paul's endurance, and Perpetua's faith converge in shared wonder as the family of God becomes whole. The laughter of saints from every nation harmonizes with Revelation 7:9's multitude. John Owen described this unity as "the perfection of love, where every soul delights in another's glory, and all in the glory of Christ" (*The Glory of Christ*, 1684). In that perfected communion, every heart is fully

known and wholly loved. The joy of fellowship is no longer tiring or partial, but peaceful, mutual, and eternal.

5. **Observing Earthly Lives**: The redeemed share in Heaven's awareness of God's continuing work on Earth. Jesus said, "There is joy before the angels of God over one sinner who repents" (Luke 15:7), revealing that Heaven celebrates every act of mercy unfolding below. Revelation 5:8 portrays the prayers of the saints rising like incense before God, forming a bridge of love between Heaven and Earth. Catherine of Siena wrote in *The Dialogue* that these prayers are woven by God into the lives of those still on their journey (Dialogue 41, 1378). This vision does not suggest anxious watching but joyful participation—the redeemed rejoicing as divine grace reaches new hearts and generations yet to come. Their gladness reflects the Son's own intercession (Hebrews 7:25), a shared harmony of gratitude and hope that never fades.

6. **Eden's Continuity**: When the company makes plans for exploration and creation, they mirror Eden's purpose restored. Humanity's first calling—stewardship and delight (Genesis 1:28; 3:8)—is now fulfilled without toil or decay. Every garden cultivated, every song composed, every craft imagined becomes worship, expressing the chief end of man: to glorify God and enjoy Him forever. Revelation 22:3–5 captures this: "His servants will worship Him… they will reign forever and ever." The Edenic commission continues, purified of corruption, bursting with boundless beauty. Richard Baxter writes that Heaven's life is not idleness but communion with the living God, where service is joy and joy is service (*The Saints' Everlasting Rest*, 1650).

247

THEOLOGICAL / LOGICAL CONCLUSION

In Heaven, the redeemed live in the fullness of God's goodness, where every moment overflows with His grace. The feast never ends; it continues to unfold in ever-deepening joy. Even mystery itself—the "darkness that is light" (Psalm 18:11)—invites the soul into greater wonder. Fellowship with the saints of every age becomes a living hymn, each shared joy proclaiming Christ's finished redemption. The redeemed rejoice with those who repent, their praise rising with the prayers of Earth, for mercy still binds Heaven and Earth together in praise. Everything in Paradise—every purpose, every work, every song —reveals the wisdom and love of the Creator in perfect harmony. As Athanasius wrote, "The life that God bestows is participation in His own immortality, and so it knows no decay" (*On the Incarnation*, 318 AD). Indeed, Heaven is life without lack, joy without fading, and worship without weariness—an eternity where every breath resounds with the gladness of God.

POST-CREDIT SCENE: UP, AROUND, AND THROUGH

This scene presents my interpretation of everyday heavenly living— existence as worship, adventure, and delight. Perpetua and Mago's exhilarating ascent up the celestite cliffs and their eager venture into radiant forests fulfill Eden's first command to "subdue" and "have dominion" (Genesis 1:28), now perfected in Heaven's sinless realm where "no longer will there be any curse" (Revelation 22:3). In a sense, Perpetua and Mago are Adam and Eve as they were intended to be—humanity's first calling restored and glorified, stewardship now expressed as joy. Their exploration is not labor but love, their dominion not rule but reverence.

Pippa, the tiny *miulume* with fur like starlight; the eagle gliding in playful majesty; and Billy, the mountain goat bounding along the ledge —all testify to the Lord's boundless imagination. Each living thing praises Him simply by existing, its joy harmonizing with the music of the redeemed.

Then comes the Voice—gentle yet thunderous, vast yet tender: "Come and see, My children." It carries the same affection that resounded over the Jordan—"This is My beloved Son, in whom I am well pleased" (Matthew 3:17)—and the everlasting delight of Zephaniah 3:17, where God rejoices over His people with singing.

Together they climb higher, laughter carried on the wind, drawn ever onward by divine love—up, around, and through—into the endless gladness of God.

But do not think of this as their story alone—it is yours, it is mine, it is how every soul, called and chosen in Him, will spend eternity: exploring, rejoicing, and forever ascending into the joy of the Lord.

EMBRACING HEAVEN'S MYSTERY WITH HUMILITY

Some may question the imaginative details woven throughout this vision—layered cities, observatories, radiant feasts—wondering if they drift beyond Scripture. Admittedly imaginative, these depictions remain anchored in four guiding principles: Scripture, God's character, Eden's continuity, and otherworldly imagery.

Scripture grounds every scene, from Revelation 21:11–21's jasper walls to Revelation 22:2's vast Tree of Life. Each vision stands on the bedrock of God's revealed truth. God's character—His generosity (Matthew 7:11), creativity (Psalm 104:24), and relational love (John 15:15)—breathes life into each portrayal, ensuring Heaven's wonder never strays from His heart. Eden's continuity flows through it all: the purposeful dominion of Genesis 1:28, the intimate walk of Genesis 3:8, now restored in perfection where humanity once again stewards creation in joy. And through it all, otherworldly imagery, drawn from Revelation's transcendent language, invites us to imagine beyond mortal scale—to perceive a glory that exceeds human vocabulary.

Across these chapters runs not a simple storyline, but a progression into ever-deepening glory. Each vision draws the reader further into the life of Heaven itself—

- From arrival in radiant light and resurrection (*The Glory*),
- To welcome and transformation (*The Gate*),
- To relationship and belonging (*The Valley* and *The City*),
- To worship and intimacy (*The Throne*),
- To home and communion (*The Eternal Home* and *Abundant Life*),
- And finally to adventure—the endless discovery of God's creative joy (*Up, Around, and Through*).

Each chapter is a deeper step into participation—arrival, welcome, relationship, belonging, and adventure—revealing Heaven not as still-ness, but as eternal movement into the heart of God. The soul's journey is an ascent through love, an ever-widening awareness of divine beauty, each revelation preparing for the next.

While I have sought to honor multiple eschatological perspectives, Heaven's timeless nature frees us from the confines of earthly sequence (Psalm 90:4; 2 Peter 3:8). The observatories, though imagi-native, arise from Revelation 5:8's prayers and Luke 15's rejoicing, suggesting heavenly awareness of God's ongoing redemptive work. The seals of light reconcile the language of heavenly garments with the shameless glory of perfected existence.

This work intentionally avoids speculative mass events—such as the Rapture or the final return of Christ—to focus instead on the immediate experience of individual believers after death. It is the story of your loved ones, your friends, and, ultimately, your own soul. These interpretations are presented not as mere imagination but as carefully investigated theology—grounded in Scripture, informed by history, and written with humility before the mysteries of eternity.

C. S. Lewis once wrote, "We are not forbidden to imagine Heaven. If we are allowed to imagine the joys of Heaven, we are also allowed to imagine their degree and kind. The only danger is of imagining them too feebly" (*Letters to Malcolm*, 1964). My prayer is that this vision helps you imagine Heaven not faintly but fully—alive with color, movement, and love—without shrinking God's promises into something tame. Heaven is not an abstraction but a home where every longing finds rest (Psalm 107:9), every tear is healed, and every purpose redeemed.

As Paul wrote, God "is able to do far more abundantly than all we ask or imagine" (Ephesians 3:20). And as Dr. Woodrow Kroll puts it, Heaven is the eternal reward for those who trust in Christ, where God's glory shines without end (*Facing Your Final Job Review*, 2008).

May Perpetua's journey rekindle your faith, her joy renew your worship, and her witness strengthen your courage to trust the Savior —for Heaven awaits: a gift beyond Earth's shadow, a promise beyond description, a reality more radiant than we dare to dream.

APPENDIX B
A THEMATIC ANALYSIS
OF HELL'S VISION

We have journeyed with Emperor Septimius Severus through the desolate wasteland of Hades and the searing torment of the Lake of Fire. This descent, rooted in the unyielding truth of Scripture, unveils a reality that demands our attention—not to terrify, but to awaken. My heart has borne the weight of crafting this vision, striving to reflect the eternal consequences of rejecting God's grace as revealed in texts like Revelation 20:14–15 and Luke 16:23–24. Unlike the chapter-by-chapter interpretive analysis of Appendix A, Appendix B offers a thematic exploration of Hell, focusing on six key elements: the atmosphere of Hades, the nature of divine judgment, the Lake of Fire's fiery desolation, human form and behavior, demonic form and behavior, and human-demon interaction. Each theme is anchored in Scripture, supported by esteemed theologians, and extended through logical conclusions drawn from God's Word. I have aimed to illuminate Hell's stark reality, urging you to choose the path of life before it's too late.

This interpretation is grounded in two principles:

1. Scripture as the infallible foundation.
2. The biblical and logical extension of human and demonic corruption when stripped of God's common grace (Matthew 5:45).

Unlike Dante's *Inferno*—a renowned allegorical work blending mythology and speculation (e.g., nine circles, pagan guides)—this vision adheres more precisely to Scripture, grounding Hell's anguish in mankind's inherent evil (Psalm 51:5) and divine warnings (Revelation 20:14–15). Texts like Isaiah 59:2, Romans 3:10–18, and Matthew 25:41 shape the narrative, while the depravity described in Jeremiah 17:9 and 1 Peter 5:8 informs the behavior of souls and demons. Though Hades and the Lake of Fire's atmospheric desolation may stem from God's design as a consequence of sin, fallen human and demonic behavior significantly amplify this anguish. Theoretically, if mankind were inherently good, unity, love, and companionship could mitigate the harsh climate. Instead, mankind's inherent evil (Psalm 51:5), without God's grace, ensures no harmony, making Hell's true torment man-made.

HISTORICAL ANALYSIS

A Song of Light & Fire: An Uncensored Journey Through Hell centers on the life—and everlasting death—of Emperor Septimius Severus, who ruled Rome from AD 193 to 211, founding the Severan dynasty. Born in AD 145 in Leptis Magna (modern-day Libya), Severus rose to power following the assassination of Emperor Commodus in AD 192, which sparked the Year of the Five Emperors. He secured the throne through military campaigns, defeating rivals such as Didius Julianus—a senator who briefly purchased the imperial title in AD 193—and Pescennius Niger by AD 194, leveraging his legions' loyalty and strategic alliances.

Severus' reign was marked by brutal purges of the Senate to consolidate power, particularly after defeating Pescennius Niger in AD 194 and Clodius Albinus in AD 197. Historical sources, such as Cassius Dio's *Roman History* (Book 76), record that Severus executed twenty-nine senators who had supported Albinus, despite promising clemency, as a means to eliminate threats and instill fear. These executions were often public—sometimes following staged trials—and demonstrated Severus' dominance over the senatorial class, which he marginalized in favor of equestrian officers. This historical backdrop explains the realism of Severus' threats in Chapter 1, where he commands the governor of Britannia to crush Pictish resistance or see his family executed. Such threats were credible; Severus had already established a precedent of ruthless violence against dissenters, including senators and their households. The Senate's fear, reflected in the cautious dialogue of attending senators in the narrative, mirrors historical accounts of this oppressive atmosphere. As historian Anthony Birley notes in *Septimius Severus: The African Emperor* (1999), Severus' authoritarian rule left the Senate "subdued and humiliated under his shadow."

The narrative includes the following historical elements, drawn from primary sources such as Cassius Dio's *Roman History*, the *Historia Augusta*, and archaeological evidence:

- **Persecution of Christians (AD 193–211):** Chapter 1 situates Severus in Carthage in AD 203, overseeing the martyrdom of Perpetua and her companions as recorded in *The Passion of Perpetua and Felicity*. Severus' edict in AD 202 banned conversions to Christianity, intensifying persecutions intended to enforce emperor worship and preserve Roman unity. The depiction of executions during a festival honoring his reign reflects this decree.
- **Success in Britannia (AD 208–211):** Chapter 1 references Severus' campaign in Britannia, where he sought to subdue Pictish tribes and reinforce Hadrian's Wall. Cassius Dio (Book 77, *Roman History*) corroborates these efforts, describing arduous military expeditions north of the wall that lasted until Severus' death in AD 211.
- **Other Military Successes:** Chapter 2 highlights Severus' triumph over Parthia (AD 197–198), when he sacked the Parthian capital Ctesiphon and expanded Roman control in Mesopotamia. Cassius Dio (Book 76) documents this victory, which bolstered Rome's eastern frontiers and secured the emperor's reputation for relentless conquest.

Julia Domna, Severus' wife, appears prominently in Chapters 1 and 2. Born in Emesa (modern-day Homs, Syria), she married Severus in AD 187 and became a politically influential empress known for her intelligence and patronage of philosophy. In Chapter 1, she is depicted at the Carthage amphitheater—her composed demeanor reflecting her historical reputation as the empire's stabilizing presence. Chapter 2 shows her at a Roman feast, her restrained tension consistent with the documented skill she exhibited in navigating imperial politics. Barbara Levick's *Julia Domna: Syrian Empress* (2007) supports this characterization, describing Julia as "the silent power behind the emperor's throne."

Cassius Dio, the senator-historian, appears in both chapters as an observer of Severus' tyranny. Born around AD 163 in Nicaea, Dio served under multiple emperors and chronicled their reigns in *Roman History*. In Chapter 1, he flatters Severus in the Carthage amphitheater to avoid his wrath—a behavior consistent with Dio's survival during the emperor's purges. In Chapter 2, he raises a toast at the imperial feast, masking dread beneath polished rhetoric. Dio's cautious diplomacy aligns with his historical reality, as he recorded the Senate's degradation under Severus in Book 76 of *Roman History*.

Didius Julianus, a senator born around AD 133, briefly ruled after purchasing the throne from the Praetorian Guard following Commodus' death. His short reign (66 days) ended when Severus seized power and executed him in the imperial palace—a scene described in the *Historia Augusta*. In Chapter 3, Didius reappears as a damned soul in Hades, his uneasy reunion with Severus reflecting the tension of their earthly rivalry.

Publius Septimius Geta, Severus' father, is referenced at the close of Chapter 6. A prosperous equestrian from Leptis Magna, Publius elevated the family's standing by holding municipal office and securing local influence, paving the way for his son's imperial ascent—a background supported by North African inscriptions and municipal records.

Caracalla and Geta, the sons of Septimius Severus, inherited the empire upon their father's death in AD 211, ruling jointly from

Rome. Their uneasy partnership soon collapsed into hostility, culminating in Caracalla's orchestration of Geta's murder within the imperial palace later that same year. Caracalla then ruled alone until his assassination in 217, remembered for granting Roman citizenship to nearly all free men and for his notorious cruelty. Both brothers appear in Chapter 3, where their rivalry and its deadly outcome cast a shadow over Severus' judgment in Hades. The film *Gladiator II* dramatizes this turbulent chapter of Roman history, portraying the bitter struggle between Severus' sons and the violent legacy of their father's empire.

Scholarly references grounding these depictions include Birley's *Septimius Severus: The African Emperor* (1999), Levick's *Julia Domna: Syrian Empress* (2007), and Michael Grant's *The Severans: The Changed Roman Empire* (1996). Grant observes that "Severus' relentless military campaigns and unyielding rule likely hastened his physical decline," making the novel's depiction of his death by heart failure plausible. In Chapter 2, Severus' sudden collapse at a Roman feast—with crushing chest pain and left-arm paralysis—reflects clinical signs of cardiac failure, aligning historical probability with narrative authenticity.

IMAGINATIVE ANALYSIS

Part Two of *A Song of Light & Fire* paints a harrowing portrait of Hell, weaving scriptural truth with imaginative elements to highlight the eternal consequences of spurning God's grace. While most scenarios—from Hades' gray desolation to the Lake of Fire's searing torment—are drawn directly from biblical texts (such as Luke 16:22–24 and Revelation 20:14–15) or their reasoned implications, carefully selected creative elements have been inserted to better communicate the raw truth of unrestrained depravity and torment. These additions, though not directly referenced in Scripture (for example, the sacred scroll, the orb, the Crown of Ash, and the character of Maximus), are rooted in biblical principles, historical contexts, and predictable human behaviors. They vividly portray Hell as an active realm of desperation, deception, and pride, with conflicting impulses to hide, escape, or dominate. This section explores these imaginative inclusions, highlighting their theological purpose and grounding in both Scripture and history.

MAXIMUS: A VOICE OF TRUTH

In Chapter 2, Maximus, a fictional Roman tribune turned preacher, stands boldly before Emperor Septimius Severus, proclaiming the Gospel of Christ in the imperial palace. Though imagined, Maximus mirrors the Apostle Paul, who testified with fearless faith before Governor Festus (Acts 25:10–12) and, according to early church tradition, later faced Nero and was beheaded for his witness (2 Timothy 4:16–17). Like Paul, Maximus calls Severus to repentance (Acts 26:20), his words burning with conviction as he confronts imperial pride. His testimony symbolizes the light of truth shining upon The Choosing Ground—where souls decide between life and death (Deuteronomy 30:19). Severus' rejection of this message marks his spiritual fall, sealing his descent into Hades (John 3:18). Rooted in the historical Severan persecutions of Christians, Maximus echoes the courage of the early martyrs. As Charles Spurgeon observed, "The martyr's voice, like Paul's, slices through stone hearts with Christ's unyielding truth" (*Sermons*, 1861). This imagined character thus amplifies the real and timeless call to repent before it is too late.

SYMBOLS OF AMPLIFIED DESPERATION

The sacred scroll (Chapter 4), orb (Chapter 5), and Crown of Ash (Chapter 7) are fictional relics pursued by souls in Hades and the Lake of Fire, symbolizing desperate hopes for escape or dominion. These elements are not arbitrary creations but represent the logical extension of fallen human behavior, magnified in a realm stripped of divine grace. Scripture warns of chasing false hopes apart from God, as in Isaiah 44:20: "He feeds on ashes; a deluded heart has led him astray." The scroll, rumored to unlock Hades' gates, reflects the deceitful promise of self-salvation, echoing the futility of idolatry condemned in Jeremiah 10:14–15. The orb, said to bring freedom, personifies shifting lies that perpetuate despair, mirroring the vanity of human pursuits described in Ecclesiastes 1:14. The Crown of Ash, promising power and rule, embodies pride's delusion, paralleling Satan's boast to "ascend above the heights of the clouds" (Isaiah 14:13–14).

In Hell, where God's common grace (Matthew 5:45) and moral law (Romans 2:14–15) are absent, human depravity (Psalm 51:5) spirals without restraint. Earthly crises—where social order collapses under fear and scarcity—offer faint glimpses of this truth: when restraint vanishes, evil multiplies. In Hell, the same principle reigns absolutely. The damned, gripped by unending thirst (Luke 16:24) and terror of demonic oppression (Revelation 9:1–11), claw for any illusion of control. Carl Jung observed this psychological impulse: "Man's unconscious is driven to create symbols of salvation, projecting desperate hopes onto illusory forms when severed from the divine source" (*The Archetypes and the Collective Unconscious*, 1959). John Calvin similarly wrote, "Man's heart, apart from God, grasps at shadows, finding only ruin" (*Institutes of the Christian Religion*, 1559). These reflections illuminate Hell's psychological chaos—a realm where every lie and lust is magnified beyond measure, where the pursuit of self-salvation becomes its own torment.

HELL'S ACTIVE DESPERATION

Hell is not a passive prison but a realm of motion and madness, where souls writhe in perpetual unrest. The rich man's plea in Hades (Luke 16:23–24) reveals conscious desperation, while Jesus' repeated phrase, "weeping and gnashing of teeth" (Matthew 13:42), depicts anguish in motion—an eternal striving that never achieves rest. In *A Song of Light & Fire*, Severus' relentless pursuit of false relics mirrors humanity's ancient rebellion in Genesis 6:5, where "every intention of the thoughts of his heart was only evil continually." Without divine order, torment becomes interactive—souls wounding, deceiving, and betraying one another in endless futility.

Philip Zimbardo, reflecting on the Stanford Prison Experiment, noted that "under conditions of extreme stress and fear, people regress to primitive, aggressive behaviors" (*The Lucifer Effect*, 2007). In Hell, such regression becomes absolute. With divine restraint removed, human cruelty flourishes unchecked. Jonathan Edwards described this state as "the soul plunged into misery of its own making, its passions ungoverned, its torment self-inflicted" (*The Justice of God in the Damnation of Sinners*, 1734). This understanding frames Hell not merely as a punishment imposed but as a moral collapse exposed—the natural end of unrepentant pride.

LOGICAL CONCLUSION

The imaginative elements of Maximus, the sacred scroll, the orb, and the Crown of Ash enhance the depiction of Hell by illustrating its inner logic: that without God, every pursuit collapses into despair. Maximus embodies the silenced truth of the Gospel rejected by pride. The relics embody the futility of self-salvation. Together, they reveal Hell as an environment of endless striving and disunity—a stark contrast to Heaven's ever-deepening harmony (Revelation 21:3–4). By blending imagination with scriptural fidelity, this vision calls every reader to recognize the eternal stakes of The Choosing Ground and to choose the light of Christ while mercy still speaks (John 8:12).

THEME 1: THE ATMOSPHERE OF HADES

Hades, as depicted in Chapters 3 and 4, is a gray, earthlike wasteland —a decayed shadow of Severus' Roman palace, stripped of light, color, and vitality. This portrayal draws directly on Scripture's evocative descriptions, particularly Job 10:21–22, which speaks of "the land of darkness and deep shadow, the land of gloom and chaos." Theologically, the restrained imagery in these passages suggests that Hades is a hauntingly familiar realm—a warped echo of creation, retaining its earthly form but emptied of divine presence. Hermeneutically, the lack of fiery imagery (which is reserved for the Lake of Fire) implies a place that is recognizably terrestrial yet lifeless, intensifying its psychological torment as an interim state before final judgment.

Wayne Grudem notes, "Scripture's reticence on Hades' form, compared to its vivid eschatological imagery elsewhere, suggests a realm familiar to human experience, yet wholly bereft of divine light" (*Systematic Theology*, 1994). I envisioned a crumbling Rome—cracked columns, dry fountains, and ashen air—to capture this desolation, reflecting the anguish of the wicked whose sin has decayed all that was once beautiful.

Near-death testimonies across centuries and cultures—ancient Near Eastern, medieval European, modern African, and Western— when carefully vetted for consistency with Luke 16 and Job 10, often describe Hades as a gray, oppressive, lifeless void, drained of hope and pulsing with despair. While such accounts must be weighed against Scripture, their recurring imagery of shadowed familiarity lends experiential reinforcement to the biblical portrayal. The atmosphere of Hades, then, reflects the absence of God's sustaining grace. While God's design establishes its desolation as a consequence of sin, human malice—suspicion, hatred, and betrayal—amplifies its suffering, ensuring that torment in Hades is both divinely just and self-inflicted.

Scripture even notes that Jesus Himself "descended into the lower regions, the earth" (Ephesians 4:9), affirming that this realm is not abstract but rooted in recognizable, created reality—a physical, conscious plane deprived of the Creator's light.

SCRIPTURAL FOUNDATION

Job 10:21–22 anchors this depiction: "Before I go—and I shall not return—to the land of darkness and deep shadow, the land of gloom like thick darkness, like deep shadow without any order, where light is as darkness." Luke 16:23–24 vividly reinforces this, portraying the rich man "in Hades, being in torment," who lifts up his eyes and begs for water—a tangible, conscious setting deprived of relief. Psalm 88:3–6 laments, "My soul is full of troubles, and my life draws near to Sheol. You have put me in the depths of the pit, in the regions dark and deep," evoking isolation and despair. Ezekiel 32:24 describes Elam "gone down to the world below... bearing their shame with those who go down to the pit," further supporting a recognizable, earthly dimension to this realm of conscious shame. Psalm 18:4–5 depicts the "cords of Sheol" entangling the psalmist, a powerful image of oppressive captivity. Psalm 143:7 pleads, "Answer me quickly, O Lord! My spirit fails! Hide not your face from me, lest I be like those who go down to the pit," highlighting the anguish of divine absence. Isaiah 57:20 declares, "The wicked are like the tossing sea; for it cannot be quiet, and its waters toss up mire and dirt," portraying ceaseless unrest. Isaiah 59:2 states, "Your iniquities have made a separation between you and your God," establishing the root cause of this isolation, while Jeremiah 17:9 explains the human role in perpetuating it: "The heart is deceitful above all things, and desperately sick; who can understand it?"

Modern corroboration can be seen in documented near-death accounts, such as those studied by Dr. Maurice Rawlings in *Beyond Death's Door* (1978), which describe "gray wastelands" and "the absence of light" consistent with the biblical view of Hades as separation from God's presence.

THEOLOGICAL SUPPORT

C. S. Lewis, in *The Great Divorce* (1945), envisions a gray, endless town where "nothing is ever finished," capturing the monotony and spiritual decay that characterize separation from God. John Calvin affirmed, "Hades is a place of separation from God, where the soul, though conscious, languishes in His absence," describing it as a realm of divine withdrawal (*Institutes of the Christian Religion*, 1559). Jonathan Edwards wrote, "Hades holds the wicked in misery, a foretaste of eternal wrath," emphasizing its function as an intermediate state of conscious suffering (*The Eternity of Hell Torments*, 1739). J. C. Ryle observed, "Hades is a realm of gloom, where God's absence torments the soul more than fire ever could" (*Expository Thoughts on the Gospels*, 1856). These voices together affirm that Hades, though not yet the Lake of Fire, is a real and dreadful domain—a bleak prelude to the final judgment.

LOGICAL CONCLUSION

Scripture's imagery of darkness, isolation, and separation portrays Hades as an earthlike realm bereft of God's presence—a place of tangible despair where light itself feels heavy and hollow. The absence of divine grace, rather than overt flames, defines its torment. The human heart, deceitful and unrestrained, intensifies the suffering, producing suspicion, betrayal, and sorrow. Thus, Hades is both punishment and revelation—God withdrawing His presence, and humanity left to the full consequence of its own corruption. This realm stands in direct contrast to Heaven, where God's nearness restores harmony and joy (Revelation 21:4). Hades reminds every soul on The Choosing Ground that existence without God, however familiar its form, is existence without life.

THEME 2: THE NATURE OF DIVINE JUDGMENT

In Chapter 5, Severus stands before the throne of God, his life exposed in unrelenting light. Every secret act, word, and motive is revealed; his name is absent from the Lamb's Book of Life (Revelation 20:15). Angels, acting as executors of divine justice, carry out the decree. This moment portrays not arbitrary vengeance but perfect righteousness— judgment that is at once revelatory and retributive. Scripture declares, "We must all appear before the judgment seat of Christ" (2 Corinthians 5:10), and that "books were opened... and the dead were judged by what was written in the books" (Revelation 20:12). The vision presented in *A Song of Light & Fire* echoes this solemn reality: the throne surrounded by blazing holiness, the celestial chant of "Holy, holy, holy" (Revelation 4:8), and the overwhelming awareness that divine justice flows from divine purity.

This judgment scene reflects a truth central to Christian theology —that judgment is not capricious wrath but moral necessity. God's holiness, by its very nature, exposes and opposes sin. As Jonathan Edwards wrote, "God's judgment is according to truth, revealing every deed in His holy light" (*Sinners in the Hands of an Angry God*, 1741). Similarly, John Calvin affirmed, "The judgment seat of Christ lays bare the secrets of men's hearts" (*Institutes of the Christian Religion*, 1559). The event is revelatory before it is punitive—an unveiling of what already is. In that light, the Lake of Fire becomes not merely the place of punishment but the visible outworking of truth itself: the soul shown for what it has chosen to be.

In this unveiling, angels play an active role. Jesus Himself taught that "The Son of Man will send His angels, and they will gather out of His kingdom all causes of sin and all law-breakers, and throw them into the fiery furnace" (Matthew 13:41–42). The participation of angels underscores the order and holiness of divine justice—God's decrees are neither chaotic nor impersonal but enacted through His appointed servants. Revelation 14:10–11 confirms that "they will be tormented... in the presence of the holy angels and in the presence of the Lamb." Thus, the angels' presence does not mitigate wrath but magnifies its righteousness.

Revelation 20:12–15 offers the foundation for this vision: "The dead were judged by what was written in the books, according to what they had done... and if anyone's name was not found written in the book of life, he was thrown into the lake of fire." This is judgment by revelation. Romans 2:5–6 explains, "Because of your hard and impenitent heart you are storing up wrath for yourself... He will render to each one according to his works." Ecclesiastes 12:14 adds, "God will bring every deed into judgment, with every secret thing, whether good or evil." Hebrews 9:27 concludes, "It is appointed for man to die once, and after that comes judgment."

In *A Song of Light & Fire*, this moment is rendered with literary fidelity to theology: Severus' arrogance collapses before divine majesty. His empire, power, and logic—all the fortresses of human pride—disintegrate in the light of omniscience. The words, "You chose self over Me" (Matthew 25:41), summarize the moral center of divine justice. Punishment, in this sense, is not imposed from without but drawn forth from within.

R. C. Sproul wrote, "God's justice is perfect, punishing those who reject His mercy" (*The Holiness of God*, 1985). John MacArthur likewise observes, "Angels, as ministers of God's wrath, execute His righteous judgment, casting the unrepentant into eternal fire, fulfilling Scripture's solemn warning" (*The Glory of Heaven*, 1996). Judgment, therefore, is not an emotional response but a moral equilibrium—the fulfillment of every divine promise, warning, and act of patience.

At the throne, Severus' defiance finds no defense. Pride, which defined his life, becomes his sentence. As the angels seize him, the full meaning of his rebellion comes into view—not as misunderstood ambition but as cosmic treason. He is cast into the Lake of Fire, where his final descent mirrors the fall of every soul that refuses grace.

LOGICAL CONCLUSION

Divine judgment is the consummation of truth: sin revealed, justice executed, holiness vindicated. It is both the unveiling of reality and the fulfillment of consequence. The throne scene in *A Song of Light & Fire* captures this duality—God's light revealing what was hidden, His justice confirming what was chosen. Angels enforce this decree, not in cruelty but in obedience to perfect holiness. Severus' condemnation is thus the echo of his own rejection of grace.

This theme establishes the hinge upon which all eternity turns. Judgment divides Heaven from Hell as moral revelation divides truth from deceit. What begins as rejection on The Choosing Ground culminates here in exposure before the throne, leading to either eternal communion or eternal exile. Divine judgment, therefore, is not only the end of rebellion but the beginning of eternal order—an order that will deepen endlessly into either glory or despair.

THEME 3: THE LAKE OF FIRE

The Lake of Fire, portrayed in Chapters 6–8, represents the culmination of divine judgment—the final realm of separation where rebellion meets its eternal consequence. Scripture names it "the second death" (Revelation 20:14), not as annihilation, but as conscious existence cut off from the source of all goodness, life, and joy. If Hades is the prelude to exile, the Lake of Fire is exile completed—the absolute void of God's presence.

In *A Song of Light & Fire*, this realm is imagined as a vast, molten abyss—rivers of lava cutting through jagged obsidian, sulfurous air thick with decay, and scab-like crusts forming over restless fire. Its atmosphere is not merely punitive but theological: the absence of divine attributes. Without the sustaining presence of God's light, all that remains is the inversion of His nature—life becomes death, beauty becomes distortion, and fellowship becomes isolation. Augustine described this reality with piercing clarity: "Hell's torment is the absence of God's love, a fitting consequence for rejecting His eternal goodness" (*City of God*, Book XXI, c. 426 AD).

This vision aligns with the biblical narrative. Revelation 20:14–15 declares, "Then Death and Hades were thrown into the lake of fire. This is the second death, the lake of fire... and if anyone's name was not found written in the book of life, he was thrown into the lake of fire." Jesus warns in Matthew 25:41, "Depart from me, you cursed, into the eternal fire prepared for the devil and his angels." This realm was never created for humanity but becomes the inheritance of all who persist in rebellion. Mark 9:48 describes it as the place "where their worm does not die and the fire is not quenched," a striking image of endless decay and restless consciousness. Paul adds in 2 Thessalonians 1:9 that the wicked "will suffer the punishment of eternal destruction, away from the presence of the Lord and from the glory of His might." These texts do not describe annihilation but separation—an unending awareness of loss.

In the narrative, Severus' descent into this realm mirrors the trajectory of pride's fall. The emperor who once commanded armies now trembles before the dominion of justice. He reaches for command —orders the flame, resists the angels, shouts defiance—but every word echoes as futility. His attempts to rule the fire are swallowed by it. This mirrors Revelation 14:10–11, which speaks of the condemned who "have no rest, day or night." Their restlessness is not imposed but intrinsic; the same rebellion that defied God now devours itself. Augustine wrote, "The soul apart from God seeks rest and finds none, for it has forsaken the fountain of life" (*Confessions*, Book IV). In Hell, this restless striving becomes eternal identity.

The Lake of Fire therefore embodies divine justice not as chaos but as moral equilibrium. It is not fire without order, but holiness without mercy. As the writer of Hebrews declares, "Our God is a consuming fire" (Hebrews 12:29). For the redeemed, that fire refines; for the unrepentant, it consumes. The same holiness that sanctifies Heaven scorches Hell. The fire reveals; it does not purify. The condemned are not annihilated because their existence serves a solemn purpose: the eternal vindication of God's righteousness (Psalm 89:14).

J. C. Ryle affirmed this when he wrote, "In the eternal fire, the loss of God's joy leaves only sorrow and evil to consume the soul" (*Expository Thoughts on the Gospels*, 1856). Randy Alcorn echoes this: "The Lake of Fire, the second death, is the eternal void of God's goodness, where the unrepentant dwell in unrelenting despair" (*Heaven*, 2004). Together, these insights frame the Lake of Fire as the anti-Heaven— the final realization of what life apart from God truly means.

In *A Song of Light & Fire*, I envisioned the geography of this realm to reflect that truth. The molten plains and burning caverns are not merely external scenery but the physical manifestation of inner corruption. The heat symbolizes unrelieved desire; the darkness, unbroken isolation. Where Heaven's landscape expands endlessly into glory, Hell's closes inward into self. This is not speculative license but logical theology: sin, left unchecked, eternally collapses upon itself.

LOGICAL CONCLUSION

The Lake of Fire is the consummation of separation—the final fulfillment of rebellion's trajectory. Scripture's portrait of this realm is consistent and deliberate: it is the domain of absence, the inversion of all that God is. Where Heaven deepens eternally in fellowship, Hell deepens eternally in estrangement. Its fire does not destroy but defines: it reveals the moral physics of existence apart from grace.

In the story of Severus, this descent marks the completion of the arc that began with defiance. His rejection of the Gospel led to Hades' shadow, to judgment's throne, and finally to the Lake of Fire's endless despair. The arc of Hell is the mirror opposite of Heaven's ascent—ever-deepening isolation instead of communion, ever-diminishing light instead of radiance, ever-narrowing self instead of expansion into glory.

Where Heaven unfolds in arrival, welcome, relationship, belonging, and adventure, Hell collapses through rejection, exile, judgment, and despair. The Lake of Fire thus stands as the final declaration of divine justice: that existence without God, however proud its beginning, ends in unending ruin.

***

THEME 4: HUMAN FORM AND BEHAVIOR IN HELL

Scripture teaches that human existence beyond death remains conscious, embodied, and moral. In Hell, that continuity persists—but without redemption or restraint. The body, once created as a vessel for divine purpose, becomes a vessel of judgment. The soul, having rejected grace, continues to live in full awareness of its ruin. In *A Song of Light & Fire*, these truths appear vividly in the tormented figures of Severus, Livia, and others who endure thirst, burns, and unrelieved agony. Their suffering is not symbolic—it is judicial. The durability of their bodies becomes the canvas upon which divine justice is revealed.

This state is shown most clearly in Jesus' account of the rich man and Lazarus (Luke 16:23-24). The man is "in Hades, being in torment," fully conscious of thirst, pain, and memory. His awareness proves that Hell's inhabitants think, feel, and recall. Daniel 12:2 declares that "many... shall awake, some to everlasting life, and some to shame and everlasting contempt." Revelation 14:11 intensifies this: "The smoke of their torment goes up forever and ever, and they have no rest, day or night." Hell does not destroy the body—it preserves it to bear the full weight of sin's consequence. Jonathan Edwards affirmed, "The bodies of the damned will be tormented with exquisite pain, their senses alive to every pang, with no end or dulling of their misery" (*The Justice of God in the Damnation of Sinners*, 1734). Likewise, R. C. Sproul observed, "Hell is an eternity of unrelieved suffering in body and soul, where the damned endure God's wrath without ever growing numb to their pain" (*Essential Truths of the Christian Faith*, 1992).

This bodily endurance reveals divine symmetry: as Heaven perfects virtue through grace, Hell perfects vice through its absence. Every soul becomes the harvest of its own sowing. Paul warns, "Do not be deceived: God is not mocked, for whatever one sows, that will he also reap" (Galatians 6:7). In Hell, this law finds its ultimate expression— every selfish act becomes bondage, every deceit becomes chain, and every proud ambition becomes torment. Romans 1:28-32 catalogs the descent of sin—envy, strife, malice, arrogance—and in Hell, these traits consume both the self and others.

In *A Song of Light & Fire*, the alliances among the damned—Severus and Didius, Publius and Livia—exist only to betray and collapse. Without the restraint of the Spirit, human community degenerates into suspicion and violence. The "weeping and gnashing of teeth" (Matthew 13:42) is not passive misery; it is the clenched jaw of hatred that cannot forgive or repent. John Owen described this condition: "The heart is a fountain of corruption, from whence issue all manner of filthy streams, if not restrained by grace" (*The Mortification of Sin*,

1656). John Flavel echoed it: "Without God's restraining grace, man's corruption breaks forth into wickedness, with no escape from the torment of an undying body" (*The Method of Grace*, 1681).

Even in judgment, conscience remains. Romans 2:15 reveals that "their conscience also bears witness, and their conflicting thoughts accuse or even excuse them." Memory becomes its own fire—each mercy refused, each truth rejected returns as a living flame. The damned remember God's goodness, yet are incapable of loving Him. Their remorse is not repentance; it is sorrow without transformation.

Psychologically, this condition fulfills C. S. Lewis's haunting line: "The doors of Hell are locked on the inside" (*The Problem of Pain*, 1940). Freedom, idolized in life, becomes captivity in death. The will that once demanded autonomy now has nothing left to rule but itself. The sinner's rebellion persists eternally, but its orbit grows smaller with every turn—self feeding endlessly on self.

Severus embodies this tragedy. His mind remains sharp, his pride intact, his ambition undiminished—but his heart cannot bow. The emperor who once commanded legions now commands nothing but ruin. His refusal to surrender becomes the very essence of his punishment. In Hell, defiance is not quenched—it is perfected.

LOGICAL CONCLUSION

Human form and behavior in Hell reveal the moral order of eternity. The body, imperishable yet dying, bears witness to divine justice. The soul, conscious and intelligent, perpetuates its own anguish through pride and hatred. Hell is therefore not a static prison but the full harvest of rebellion—a moral and spiritual ecosystem where every unrepented choice echoes forever.

In Heaven, grace transforms the body into glory and the will into love. In Hell, freedom hardens into defiance and the body becomes the instrument of its own ruin. Thus, the downward arc continues—from rejection on The Choosing Ground, to despair in Hades, to exposure in judgment, and finally to the Lake of Fire's endless isolation.

Where Heaven ascends in ever-deepening communion, Hell

descends in ever-deepening isolation. The same holiness that perfects the righteous condemns the rebellious. Every breath in Hell affirms one immutable truth: the heart apart from God becomes its own executioner.

THEME 5: DEMONIC FORM AND BEHAVIOR

The demons of *A Song of Light & Fire* are portrayed not as mythic curiosities but as theological realities—fallen intelligences whose rebellion continues beyond time. Scripture names them "angels who did not stay within their own position of authority" (Jude 6) and depicts their nature through images of serpents, locusts, and dragons (Revelation 9:3; 12:9). Each image reveals function rather than form—deceit, destruction, and domination.

Their appearance—ashen wings, distorted features, eyes like coals—conveys what theologians from Augustine to Aquinas have long affirmed: evil deforms but does not annihilate. Augustine wrote, "Evil has no positive nature; the loss of good has received the name 'evil'" (*City of God*, 426 AD). What was once created to reflect divine beauty becomes a grotesque caricature of it. Their bodies are mirrors of their morals: twisted by pride, bound by fury.

In Hell, their malice is unrestrained, for God's common grace no longer tempers their nature. During life on the Choosing Ground, divine sovereignty limits evil's reach (Matthew 5:45); but in Hell, that restraint is gone. Their hatred runs rampant, and they lash out without boundary or purpose. C. S. Lewis captured this truth succinctly: "The Devil's kingdom is held together only by mutual hatred; it cannot stand" (*The Screwtape Letters*, 1942). Their violence, envy, and rivalry are not ordered—they are chaos embodied.

The demons are not rulers of Hell but prisoners of the same rebellion that consumes them. Revelation 9:11 calls their leader *Apollyon*—"the destroyer." They destroy not to rule, but because destruction is all that remains. John Calvin observed, "Satan and his hosts labor to ruin God's creation, yet in the end they are ministers of their own torment" (*Institutes of the Christian Religion*, 1559). Their existence is a tragic inversion of divine purpose—forever active, forever collapsing.

The hierarchy within their ranks—alphas ruling briefly, slaves rebelling endlessly—illustrates this chaos of pride. Alliances dissolve because pride cannot share power. Isaiah 14:13–15 captures their delusion: "You said in your heart, 'I will ascend to heaven... I will make myself like the Most High.' But you are brought down." Pride remains the pulse of their existence. Charles Spurgeon remarked, "Hell is full of proud spirits who would rather reign in misery than serve in joy" (*Sermons*, 1861).

Their speech patterns—half-truths, riddled promises, self-exalting boasts—echo the serpent's voice from Genesis 3: "Did God actually say...?" The same whisper that deceived Eve now resounds through Hell, deceiving the damned with lies of false hope and counterfeit crowns. Revelation 16:14 warns of "spirits of demons, performing signs," even amid judgment. They remain persuasive, but their persuasion births only despair.

In literary terms, these dialogues deepen the psychological realism of Hell. The demons' words perpetuate rebellion and amplify fear, ensuring that pride and deception feed on one another. Timothy Keller captured this dynamic when he wrote, "Evil promises freedom while delivering slavery; it persuades until it possesses" (*The Reason for God*, 2008).

Ultimately, the demons of *A Song of Light & Fire* represent the dark inverse of Heaven's angels. Where Heaven's seraphim cry "Holy, holy, holy," Hell's fallen cry only "Mine." Their unity is hatred; their worship is mockery; their purpose is decay.

THEOLOGICAL AND LOGICAL CONCLUSION

The demonic form and behavior in Hell reveal the inevitable collapse of all good once severed from God. They are not restrained, not governed, and not free. They rage within their own ruin, consuming and consumed. Every torment they inflict rebounds upon them, every lie they tell deepens their despair.

Within the broader arc of *A Song of Light & Fire*, the demons mirror the descending path of the damned—beginning in pride on The Choosing Ground, facing exposure at judgment, and ending in the Lake of Fire's eternal conflict. Just as Heaven ascends in ever-deepening harmony, Hell descends in ever-deepening chaos.

Hell's demons are the embodiment of self-destruction. Their rebellion, once defiant, now sustains their torment. They exist as witnesses to a universe that cannot survive without God's presence—and as warnings to all who still live within it.

THEME 6: HUMAN & DEMON INTERACTION ON EARTH VS. HELL

On The Choosing Ground—that brief window of mortal life—humanity and demons coexist within boundaries established by God's sovereign restraint. Satan and his hosts prowl the Earth as tempters, but not as rulers; their influence remains limited by divine permission. In Job 1:7, the Lord asks Satan, "From where have you come?" and the adversary replies, "From going to and fro on the earth." Even in this exchange, the parameters of his freedom are defined. God's presence and providence act as barriers, ensuring that demonic influence operates only within the limits of His will. As Paul wrote, "No temptation has overtaken you that is not common to man. God is faithful, and He will not let you be tempted beyond your ability" (1 Corinthians 10:13).

This divine restraint, however, is entirely absent in Hell. Once the soul passes beyond death and judgment, it enters a realm no longer sustained by God's common grace (Matthew 5:45) or His moral law written on the heart (Romans 2:14–15). There, demonic malice erupts without limit. What was once temptation becomes torment. What was once whispered deceit becomes open violence. The demons of Hell are not cunning manipulators but ravenous beasts, their hatred unchecked, their rage absolute.

This contrast is vividly illustrated through Severus' encounters. On Earth, demonic influence came through pride, ambition, and deceit—an emperor convinced of his own divinity, driven by invisible persuasion. In Hell, those same forces reveal their true nature: not subtle, but savage. Slave demons tear at the damned with clawed hands and lionlike teeth (cf. Revelation 9:7–8), while alpha demons whip and devour, their grotesque laughter echoing through caverns of despair. These are not allegorical torturers—they are beings of ancient intelligence, consumed by hatred and freed from all restraint.

Scripture draws the same contrast. In Mark 5:1–20, a legion of demons inhabits a man, driving him to self-harm among tombs, yet even that legion trembles before the authority of Christ. In Acts 19:13–16, another possessed man overpowers false exorcists, revealing that apart from divine authority, humanity is powerless against demonic rage. On Earth, as these passages reveal, demonic activity is restrained by Christ's lordship. But Revelation 9:1–11 portrays a time and place where that restraint is gone—the abyss, where locust-demons "were allowed to torment," symbolizing an unbounded fury.

In Hell, the absence of God's presence removes all barriers. The same beings who once lured men into pride now turn their malice upon those they deceived. Their cruelty is indiscriminate; their torment, self-sustaining. Irenaeus observed this grim reversal: "On Earth, God's presence restrains the adversary's malice, but in Hell, His absence allows evil to torment the condemned unchecked" (*Against Heresies*, Book V). George Whitefield echoed the same: "Satan's earthly deceptions are restrained by God's grace, but in Hell, the absence of His joy unleashes relentless sorrow" (*Select Sermons*, sermon 14).

Humanity's role in this chaos is tragically consistent. Even in torment, the damned cling to pride, jealousy, and self-deception. In *A Song of Light & Fire*, Publius forms a fleeting alliance with demons, grasping at false promises of power or escape through the Crown of

Ash. This interaction, and others, illustrate the perpetual cycle of rebellion—man trusting his own strength, demon exploiting that trust, both falling deeper into despair. Isaiah 44:20 describes the futility of such pursuits: "He feeds on ashes; a deluded heart has led him astray."

John Calvin summarized the divide between Earth and Hell with characteristic precision: "God's sovereignty limits Satan on Earth, but in the place of His absence, demonic evil consumes souls with death and despair" (*Institutes*, Book II). R. C. Sproul likewise affirmed, "Hell is the void of God's goodness, where human rebellion and demonic savagery amplify sorrow unchecked" (*The Holiness of God*, 1985).

The result is a horrifying moral symmetry. On Earth, demons tempt humans to sin; in Hell, they torment those who followed them. Both are consequences of separation from God—one partial, the other complete. The same pride that resisted grace on The Choosing Ground now resists repentance in the abyss.

LOGICAL CONCLUSION

The contrast between Earth and Hell reveals the terrifying progression of unrestrained evil. On The Choosing Ground, God's restraining grace and moral law limit the adversary's reach, allowing for repentance and redemption. In Hell, that grace is gone, and with it, every vestige of order. Demons, once deceivers, become destroyers; humanity, once tempted, becomes prey. Their interactions—driven by hatred, pride, and despair—perpetuate the very torment they suffer.

Where Heaven's communion grows ever more radiant, Hell's chaos spirals endlessly inward. Both realms manifest God's justice: Heaven through union with His presence, Hell through separation from it. And as every demonic assault and human betrayal resounds through that dark eternity, it declares the same unyielding truth—life apart from God is not freedom but ruin.

COMPARISON & CONTRAST: LIFE IN HEAVEN VERSUS LIFE IN HELL

Eternal existence in Heaven and Hell, as depicted in *A Song of Light & Fire*, presents a profound dichotomy, each realm reflecting the ultimate consequence of choices made on The Choosing Ground (Deuteronomy 30:19). While both are eternal, their nature, purpose, and experience stand in stark opposition, underscoring the urgency of embracing Christ's salvation (Romans 10:9). The following contrasts, drawn from scriptural revelation and the narrative arcs of Perpetua and Severus, illuminate the divergent realities of these eternal abodes.

- **Bodily Form:** In Heaven, believers receive glorified bodies— imperishable and radiant—reflecting souls cleansed and beautified by the Savior's blood (1 Corinthians 15:42–44; 1 John 1:7). Perpetua's transformed form, vibrant and eternal, exemplifies this divine gift (*Part One*, ch. 4). In Hell, the damned bear corrupted bodies, destined for unending torment, mirroring the soul's unrepentant corruption (Luke 16:24; Revelation 20:10). Severus' tormented frame, wracked by thirst and burns, embodies this anguished state (*Part Two*, ch. 3).
- **Clothing:** Heavenly inhabitants wear seals of light, symbolic of the righteousness imputed through Christ (Revelation 7:9; Philippians 3:9). These radiant garments celebrate the redeemed's purified identity (*Part One*, ch. 4). In Hell, clothing consists of filthy rags, representing human righteousness, which Scripture deems worthless (Isaiah 64:6). The tattered, soiled attire of Severus and others reflects their futile self-reliance (*Part Two*, ch. 4).
- **Reunions:** Heaven is marked by joyful reunions, where the redeemed—like Perpetua with Mago and Felicity—embrace in eternal fellowship, united in Christ's love (1 Thessalonians 4:17; *Part One*, ch. 6). Hell, conversely, hosts awkward, estranged encounters, as seen in Severus' tense

reunion with Publius, marred by betrayal and isolation (*Part Two*, ch. 7).

- **Environment:** Heaven's environment is a radiant paradise, with crystal rivers, golden streets, and the Tree of Life exuding divine beauty (Revelation 22:1–2; *Part One*, ch. 5). Hell is a desolate wasteland, with Hades' gray ruins and the Lake of Fire's molten caverns steeped in gloom and torment (Job 10:21–22; Revelation 20:14; *Part Two*, chs. 3–6).
- **Languages:** In Heaven, languages unite in divine harmony, where the redeemed from every nation communicate seamlessly—their diverse tongues transformed into a singular expression of worship through a gift of understanding (Revelation 7:9; 1 Corinthians 12:10; *Part One*, ch. 4). In Hell, languages fragment into a cacophony of confusion, with barriers akin to Babel's curse isolating souls, as Severus struggles with foreign tongues, amplifying discord (Genesis 11:1–9; *Part Two*, ch. 5).
- **Community:** Heavenly community thrives in harmonious worship, as diverse believers from every era unite in adoration of the Lamb (Revelation 7:9; *Part One*, ch. 7). Hell's community is fractured, characterized by suspicion and violence, as souls like Severus and Livia form fleeting, treacherous alliances (Romans 1:28–32; *Part Two*, ch. 4).
- **Purpose:** In Heaven, purpose is fulfilled in eternal worship and creative stewardship, as the redeemed engage in joyful activities reflecting God's glory (Revelation 22:3–5; *Part One*, ch. 9). In Hell, purpose is absent, replaced by futile pursuits —such as the sacred scroll or Crown of Ash—deepening despair (Isaiah 44:20; *Part Two*, chs. 4–7).
- **State of Mind:** In Heaven, the redeemed experience profound peace, hope, and joy, their hearts filled with the assurance of God's love and eternal security (Philippians 4:7; Psalm 16:11; *Part One*, ch. 3). In Hell, the damned are consumed by suspicion, regret, anger, sadness, and constant fear, their minds tormented by unrelenting despair

and dread (Isaiah 57:20–21; Revelation 14:11; *Part Two*, ch. 3).

- **Physical Well-Being:** In Heaven, the redeemed experience delightful sensations of pleasure, with taste and touch heightened in glorified bodies—savoring the Tree of Life's fruit and the crystal river's purity (Revelation 22:2; Psalm 16:11; *Part One*, ch. 5). In Hell, the damned endure unrelenting thirst and agony, their corrupted bodies wracked by burning torment and unquenched suffering (Luke 16:24; Revelation 14:10–11; *Part Two*, ch. 3).
- **Angelic Beings:** In Heaven, angels are radiant, holy beings serving as ministers of God's glory and protectors of the redeemed, their presence enhancing worship and fellowship (Isaiah 6:2; Ezekiel 10:1–2; Hebrews 1:14; *Part One*, ch. 7). In Hell, fallen angels—or demons—are grotesque and malevolent, with corrupted forms, preying on the damned with unrelenting malice, amplifying torment and chaos (Revelation 9:7–8; 1 Peter 5:8; *Part Two*, chs. 6–8).
- **Divine Presence:** Heaven is saturated with God's presence, His Shekinah glory filling every breath with joy and awe (Revelation 21:3; *Part One*, ch. 3). Hell is defined by God's absence—a void of divine grace that amplifies torment, choking on sulfur and ash (2 Thessalonians 1:9; *Part Two*, ch. 3).

These contrasts, and a host of others, underscore the eternal divergence between Heaven and Hell. Heaven, as Perpetua's journey reveals, is a realm of restoration, where glorified bodies, radiant attire, and joyful fellowship reflect the soul's redemption through Christ's blood (John 3:16). Hell, as Severus' descent illustrates, is a domain of desolation, where corrupted bodies, filthy rags, and estranged encounters mirror the soul's unrepentant corruption (John 3:18). As Dr. Woodrow Kroll affirms, "Hell is as terrible as Heaven is blissful. The Bible makes it clear that the choice you make in this life determines your eternal destiny" (*Facing Your Final Job Review: The Judgment Seat of Christ, Salvation, and Eternal Rewards*, Crossway, 2008).

CONCLUSION

This thematic analysis unveils a Hell grounded in Scripture's warnings and defined by moral logic. It follows the full arc of damnation as portrayed in *A Song of Light & Fire*—a descent that mirrors, in reverse, the ascent of Heaven's glory. Each movement within that arc marks a deepening separation from God: the rejection of Christ, the imprisonment of Hades, the revelation of judgment, and the Lake of Fire, culminating in ever-deepening anguish.

It begins with rejection, where pride refuses grace and the soul exalts itself above its Maker. It descends into Hades, the gray wasteland of consciousness and regret—where light is memory but not hope, and every echo of Earth mocks the absence of God. Then comes judgment, when all deeds are unveiled and the soul faces truth without excuse (Revelation 20:12–15). Finally, the condemned are cast into the Lake of Fire, the second death, where existence continues but life does not—where awareness survives without connection, and will survives without peace. This is the end of rebellion: not annihilation, but eternal isolation.

Severus' story traces this descent step by step. From imperial pride to infernal ruin, from the throne of Rome to the caverns of the damned, his journey embodies the logical consequence of rejecting divine mercy. The same pride that ruled empires now rules only ashes. The same intellect that commanded armies now gnaws on regret. Hell's torment, though ordained as justice, is magnified by human corruption—its anguish intensified by the souls who create their own chaos. This is why Hell's torment is not only divinely decreed but man-made, the ultimate fruition of sin unchecked (Psalm 51:5).

In contrast, Perpetua's ascent reveals the counter-arc of Heaven— ever-deepening glory. Her passage through the River of Life, her welcome at the Gate, her reunion with loved ones, and her joyful commission in the luminous forests of Paradise reveal not stagnation but expansion—the infinite unfolding of divine presence. Heaven grows brighter as Hell grows darker. Heaven moves outward in love as Hell collapses inward in despair.

Jonathan Edwards summarized this divine symmetry: "The damned, stripped of restraint, plunge into misery of their own making, while the redeemed rise ever higher into joy unending" (*The Justice of God in the Damnation of Sinners*, 1734). Likewise, R. C. Sproul observed, "Hell is the absence of God's goodness, and that absence is itself the essence of judgment" (*The Holiness of God*, 1985). Their insights affirm the vision expressed throughout this appendix—that Heaven and Hell are not arbitrary opposites, but necessary reflections of divine justice and human choice.

Thus, *A Song of Light & Fire* concludes its descent as it began its ascent: with a summons. Let Severus' fall serve as warning, and Perpetua's ascent as promise. For one path leads to ever-deepening despair, and the other to ever-deepening light. Heaven and Hell are not destinations of chance but trajectories of the soul—set forever by the choices made in this life, upon The Choosing Ground, before the gates close and eternity begins.

BIBLIOGRAPHY
(SOURCES AND RESOURCES)

The following sources, including Bible translations, theological works, historical texts, psychological studies, and literary works, were cited, referenced, or paraphrased in *A Song of Light & Fire: An Uncensored Journey Through Heaven and Hell*. They are organized by category to reflect their contributions to the book's depiction of Heaven, Hell, and historical contexts.

BIBLE TRANSLATION

- *English Standard Version (ESV)* — 2001, 2007, 2011, 2016, Crossway

THEOLOGICAL WORKS

- *Against Heresies*, Book V, ch. 24. Irenaeus. c. 180 AD. In *Ante-Nicene Fathers*, Vol. 1. 1885.
- *The Archetypes and the Collective Unconscious*. Carl Gustav Jung. 1959. Princeton, NJ: Princeton University Press.
- *The Christian Life*. Sinclair Ferguson. 1981. Edinburgh: Banner of Truth.
- *Christian Theology*. Millard J. Erickson. 1998. Grand Rapids, MI: Baker Academic.
- *The City of God*. Augustine. 426 AD.
- *The City of God*, Book XXI. Augustine. 426 AD.
- *The Consolation of Philosophy*. Boethius. 6th century.
- *Confessions*. Augustine. 4th century.
- *The Cross of Christ*. John Stott. 1986. Downers Grove, IL: InterVarsity Press.
- *Desiring God*. John Piper. 1986. Sisters, OR: Multnomah.
- *The Dialogue*, Dialogue 41. Catherine of Siena. 1378.
- *The Difficult Doctrine of the Love of God*. D. A. Carson. 2000. Wheaton, IL: Crossway.
- *Essential Truths of the Christian Faith*. R. C. Sproul. 1992. Wheaton, IL: Tyndale.
- *Exegetical Fallacies*. D. A. Carson. Grand Rapids, MI: Baker Academic.
- *Facing Your Final Job Review: The Judgment Seat of Christ, Salvation, and Eternal Rewards*. Woodrow Kroll. 2008. Wheaton, IL: Crossway.

BIBLIOGRAPHY

- *The Four Loves.* C. S. Lewis. 1960. London: Geoffrey Bles.
- *Heaven.* Randy Alcorn. 2004. Wheaton, IL: Tyndale House.
- *Heaven Is a World of Love.* Jonathan Edwards. 1759.
- *The Glory of Christ.* John Owen. 1684. London: Nathaniel Ponder.
- *The Glory of Heaven.* John MacArthur. 1996. Wheaton, IL: Crossway.
- *The Great Divorce.* C. S. Lewis. 2009. New York, NY: HarperOne.
- *The Great Evangelical Disaster.* Francis Schaeffer. 1984. Wheaton, IL: Crossway.
- *The Holiness of God.* R. C. Sproul. 1985. Wheaton, IL: Tyndale.
- *Holiness.* J. C. Ryle. 1877. London: James Clarke.
- *The Holy Spirit.* Sinclair Ferguson. 1996. Downers Grove, IL: InterVarsity Press.
- *The Justice of God in the Damnation of Sinners.* Jonathan Edwards. 1734.
- *The Kingdom of God.* Martyn Lloyd-Jones. 1992. Wheaton, IL: Crossway.
- *Knowing God.* J. I. Packer. 1973. Downers Grove, IL: InterVarsity Press.
- *The Knowledge of the Holy.* A. W. Tozer. 1961. New York, NY: Harper & Row.
- *The Last Things.* Donald Bloesch. 2004. Downers Grove, IL: InterVarsity Press.
- *Letters to Malcolm: Chiefly on Prayer.* C. S. Lewis. 1964. London: Geoffrey Bles.
- *Made for His Pleasure.* Alistair Begg. 1996. Chicago, IL: Moody.
- *Mere Christianity.* C. S. Lewis. 2001 ed. New York, NY: Harper.
- *On the Incarnation.* Athanasius. 318 AD.
- *Pathway to Freedom.* Alistair Begg. 2000. Chicago, IL: Moody.
- *The Problem of Pain.* C. S. Lewis. 1940. London: Geoffrey Bles.
- *The Prodigal God.* Timothy Keller. 2008. New York, NY: Dutton.
- *The Reason for God.* Timothy Keller. 2008. New York, NY: Dutton.
- *Reformed Dogmatics*, Vol. 4. Herman Bavinck. 1901. Grand Rapids, MI: Baker Academic.
- *Romans.* John Stott. 1994. Downers Grove, IL: InterVarsity Press.
- *The Saints' Everlasting Rest.* Richard Baxter. 1650.
- *Sermon 60: "The General Deliverance."* John Wesley. 1782.
- *Sermons.* Charles Spurgeon. 1861. London: Passmore & Alabaster.
- *The New Park Street Pulpit.* Charles Spurgeon. 1859. London: Passmore & Alabaster.
- *Sinners in the Hands of an Angry God.* Jonathan Edwards. 1741.
- *The Treasury of David.* Charles Spurgeon. 1880. London: Passmore & Alabaster.
- *The Whole Christ.* Sinclair Ferguson. 2016. Wheaton, IL: Crossway.
- *The Work of the Holy Spirit.* Abraham Kuyper. 1900. Grand Rapids, MI: Eerdmans.
- *The Revelation of Jesus Christ.* John Walvoord. 1966. Chicago, IL: Moody.
- *The Justice of God in the Damnation of Sinners.* Jonathan Edwards. 1734.

BIBLIOGRAPHY

- *The Saints' Everlasting Rest.* Richard Baxter. 1650.
- *The Whole Christ.* Sinclair Ferguson. 2016. Wheaton, IL: Crossway.
- *Works,* Vol. 2. Jonathan Edwards. 1758.

HISTORICAL SOURCES

- *Annals,* Book XV, Tacitus, c. 116 AD
- *Apologeticus,* Tertullian, c. 197 AD
- *De Spectaculis,* Tertullian, c. 200 AD
- *Ecclesiastical History,* Book VIII, Eusebius, c. 324 AD
- *Historia Augusta,* unknown author, c. 4th century
- *Julia Domna: Syrian Empress,* Barbara Levick, 2007, Routledge
- *Letters,* Book X, Pliny the Younger, c. 112 AD
- *Roman History,* Cassius Dio, c. 229 AD
- *Septimius Severus: The African Emperor,* Anthony Birley, 1999, Routledge
- *The Passion of Perpetua and Felicity,* unknown author, c. 203 AD
- *The Severans: The Changed Roman Empire,* Michael Grant, 1996, Routledge

PSYCHOLOGICAL STUDIES

- *Beyond Death's Door,* Maurice Rawlings, 1978, Thomas Nelson Inc.
- *The Archetypes and the Collective Unconscious,* Carl Gustav Jung, 1959, Princeton University Press
- *The Lucifer Effect,* Philip Zimbardo, 2007, Random House

LITERARY WORKS

- *Letters to Malcolm: Chiefly on Prayer,* C. S. Lewis, 1964

GLOSSARY OF TERMS

This glossary explains key words and ideas in the book to help you understand its message, whether you're new to Christianity or growing in faith. Some terms, like *Eden* and *salvation*, come directly from the Bible, while others, like "lumora fruit" and "rakers," are imaginative elements I've created to bring biblical truths to life in the story. Each definition includes a Bible verse where relevant, pointing you to God's Word as the foundation for everything in this book.

- **Alpha Demons**: In the book, these are powerful fallen angels in Hell, depicted as towering, fiery beings with charred skin and blazing wings (chapters 6–8, Part Two). They represent the strongest demons, ruling over lesser ones and tormenting souls, as part of the eternal punishment described in Revelation 20:10, where the devil and his angels face unending torment in the Lake of Fire.
- **Angel**: A spiritual being created by God to serve Him and help people, often described as a messenger of God in the Bible (Hebrews 1:14). In Heaven, angels like Neriah guide and worship alongside God's people (Part One), appearing as radiant beings with wings and countless eyes, reflecting God's holiness (Isaiah 6:2–3). Some angels rebelled against God and became demons.
- **Bēma**: A Greek word meaning "judgment seat" or "raised platform." In the New Testament, it refers to the place where Christ will evaluate believers' lives—not to condemn, but to reward faithfulness (2 Corinthians 5:10). In the book, the bēma is portrayed as a radiant threshold where grace is revealed and believers receive confirmation of redemption rather than fear of punishment (Part One, chapter 5).

- **Book of Life**: A heavenly record mentioned in the Bible, listing the names of those who have accepted God's gift of salvation through Jesus Christ (Revelation 20:12–15). If your name is in this book, it means you're welcomed into Heaven; if not, Scripture warns of eternal separation from God in Hell.
- **Christ/Christ Jesus**: Another name for Jesus, meaning "the anointed one" or "Messiah" in the Bible (John 1:41). He is the second member of the Trinity—God the Son—who became human, died on the cross, and rose again to save people from their sins, welcoming believers into Heaven as their Savior and King.
- **Common Grace**: The kindness God shows to everyone, whether they believe in Him or not—like the beauty of a sunrise, the love between friends, or the sense of right and wrong we all feel (Matthew 5:45). In Hell, this kindness is completely absent, leaving only despair and torment.
- **Cross**: The wooden structure on which Jesus was crucified, as described in the Bible (John 19:17–18). His death on the cross paid the price for humanity's sins, offering forgiveness and salvation to all who trust in Him, making it a symbol of God's love and sacrifice.
- **Crown of Ash**: An imaginative element in the book, representing a false hope in Hell (chapter 7, Part Two). It's a rumored crown that promises power over demons but leads to betrayal and torment, reflecting the Bible's warning about chasing empty promises instead of God's truth (Isaiah 44:20).
- **Demon**: A fallen angel who rebelled against God and now works against Him, often seeking to harm people and lead them away from God (1 Peter 5:8). In the book, demons in Hell, like slave demons and alpha demons, torment souls with claws, fangs, and fiery whips, reflecting their evil nature (Revelation 9:1–11).

- **Death**: The cessation of earthly existence and opportunity, marking the end of the biological body we currently inhabit, as described in the Bible (Hebrews 9:27). However, it is not the end of spiritual life, which endures eternally. For those who reject God's mercy, death in the eternal sense continues in an unending cycle of demise in Hell, a perpetual state of spiritual separation and torment (Revelation 20:14).
- **Eden**: The garden described in the Bible's first book, Genesis, where God placed the first humans, Adam and Eve, in a perfect, joyful relationship with Him and nature (Genesis 2:8–9). It was a place of beauty and peace before sin entered the world. Heaven is described as a restored and even better version of Eden, fulfilling God's original plan for humanity.
- **Eternal Life**: The unending life promised to those who trust in Jesus (John 3:16). It is an ever-present, joyous "now," where time converges in God's timeless presence, filled with perfect connection, worship, and happiness in heaven, free from pain, sorrow, and fear.
- **Faith**: Trusting in God and believing in Jesus as your Savior, even when you can't see Him (Hebrews 11:1). It's the choice to rely on God's promises, like the promise of eternal life, and to follow Him with your heart and actions, which leads to salvation.
- **Fallen Angels**: Angels who rebelled against God, led by Lucifer, and were cast out of Heaven (Jude 1:6). They became demons, including alpha demons and slave demons in the book, and now oppose God, facing eternal punishment in the Lake of Fire alongside unrepentant humans (Matthew 25:41).
- **Forgiveness**: God's act of erasing your sins when you repent and trust in Jesus (1 John 1:9). It means He no longer holds your wrongs against you, restoring your relationship with Him and freeing you from the punishment of sin, leading to eternal life in Heaven.

- **Glory**: The radiant beauty and greatness of God, often described as a bright light in the Bible (Exodus 24:16–17). In Heaven, God's glory fills everything, bringing awe and joy to His people, as seen in the Shekinah glory and the shining New Jerusalem.
- **God the Father**: The first member of the Trinity, who is the Creator of all things and the loving Father of those who trust in Jesus (John 1:12). In the book, He is the source of all goodness, welcoming believers to Heaven (Part One) and pursuing the lost on Earth (Part Two, chapter 7), showing His desire for all to be saved (2 Peter 3:9).
- **Gospel**: The Good News of Jesus Christ, which means that God loves you, sent His Son to die for your sins, and rose again so you can be forgiven and have eternal life with Him (John 3:16). It's the message that by trusting in Jesus, you can be saved from Hell and welcomed into Heaven.
- **Grace**: God's undeserved kindness and love toward people, shown in two main ways in the Bible. First, "common grace" is the goodness He gives everyone, like rain and sunshine (Matthew 5:45). Second, saving grace is the gift of salvation through Jesus, offered to all who believe in Him (Ephesians 2:8–9), which rescues us from sin and Hell.
- **Hades**: A temporary place of torment after death for those who reject God, based on descriptions in the Bible (Luke 16:23–24). It's a gray, hopeless realm where souls wait before the final judgment, experiencing the consequences of living apart from God's kindness.
- **Heaven**: The eternal home where God lives with those who trust in Jesus, described in the Bible as a place of perfect joy, beauty, and peace (Revelation 21:1–4). It's where believers go after death to be with God forever, free from pain and sorrow, as seen in Part One with Perpetua's journey.
- **Hell**: The place of eternal torment for those who reject God's mercy, as described in the Bible (Revelation 20:14–

15). It's a fiery realm of suffering, including Hades and the Lake of Fire in the book (Part Two), where people and demons are separated from God's goodness forever.

- **Holy Spirit**: The third member of the Trinity, who is God living with and in people (John 14:16–17). The Holy Spirit guides believers on Earth, helping them understand God's truth, and in Heaven, is worshipped as God, filling His people with joy and love.

- **Judgment**: After death, every person stands before God to account for their life's choices, as described in the Bible (Revelation 20:12–15). For those who trust in Jesus, it's a celebration of God's grace; for those who reject Him, it leads to eternal separation in Hell.

- **Lake of Fire**: The final place of eternal torment for those who reject God's mercy, as described in the Bible (Revelation 20:14–15). It's a fiery, cavernous realm where both humans and demons face unending separation from God's goodness, often called the "second death" because it's the permanent end of hope.

- **Lucifer**: Another name for Satan, the leader of the fallen angels who rebelled against God (Isaiah 14:12–15). In the book, Lucifer appears in Hell as a deceptive, beautiful figure who turns malevolent, tormenting Severus (chapter 8, Part Two), reflecting his role as the enemy of God and humanity (1 Peter 5:8).

- **Lumora Fruit**: An imaginative element created to communicate the vibrant taste and texture of Heaven, evoking the sensory delight of God's eternal paradise (chapter 5, Part One). Lumora fruit tastes like light, inviting readers to savor the richness of Heaven's delights, reflecting the Bible's promise of a paradise beyond imagination, filled with delights God has crafted for His people (1 Corinthians 2:9).

- **Moral Law**: The sense of right and wrong that God places in every person's heart, as described in the Bible (Romans

2:14–15). It's part of God's common grace, acting like an inner compass that guides even those who don't know Him to feel guilt for wrongdoing or joy in doing good, pointing them toward His truth. In Hell, this moral law is no longer felt, leaving only chaos and selfishness (Part Two, introduction).

- **Miulumes**: An imaginative element crafted to convey God's gentle spirit and the small, heartwarming surprises that reflect His tender care (chapter 5, Part One). Miulumes are tiny, purring creatures in celestial groves, embodying the Bible's promise of a paradise beyond imagination, filled with God's happy delights (1 Corinthians 2:9).
- **New Jerusalem**: The heavenly city described in the Bible, where God lives with His people forever (Revelation 21:1–22:5). It's a place of incredible beauty—with walls of jasper, gates of pearl, and streets of gold—symbolizing the ultimate fulfillment of God's promise to make everything new and perfect.
- **Rakers**: An imaginative term in the book for humans in Hell who betray others to serve demons (chapter 7, Part Two). They spy for powerful demons, hoping to escape torment, but their actions only deepen their suffering. This reflects the Bible's warning about the selfish, deceitful behavior that grows without God's kindness (Romans 1:28–32).
- **Redeemer**: A title for Jesus, meaning the one who rescues humanity from sin by paying the price for their salvation (Galatians 3:13). In the book, Jesus as the Redeemer offers freedom from Hell through His death on the cross, restoring believers to a relationship with God and welcoming them into Heaven (Part One, chapter 6).
- **Redemption**: God's act of saving people from sin and Hell through Jesus' death on the cross and resurrection (Ephesians 1:7). It means being bought back by God,

forgiven, and restored to a relationship with Him, leading to eternal life in Heaven.

- **Repentance:** Turning away from living for yourself and choosing to trust and follow Jesus as your Savior and Lord (Acts 3:19). It's more than feeling sorry—it means agreeing with God about what needs to change in your life, surrendering to His righteous judgment, and yielding your heart to be transformed by His grace, resulting in a life that seeks to honor Him (2 Corinthians 7:10).

- **Reprobate:** A term describing those who, hardened by persistent rejection of God's truth, are given over to a depraved mind, choosing sin over righteousness (Romans 1:28). In the book, reprobates are depicted as souls unyielding in their defiance, consumed by self-destruction and eternally separated from God's grace, their hearts sealed against redemption (Part Two, chapter 5).

- **Resurrection:** The act of rising from the dead, as Jesus did on the third day after His crucifixion (Luke 24:6–7). The Bible promises that those who trust in Jesus will also be resurrected to eternal life in Heaven, receiving new, glorified bodies free from pain and death (1 Corinthians 15:42–44).

- **Sacred Scroll/Orb:** Imaginative elements in Hell, representing false hopes that souls chase to escape torment (chapters 4–6, Part Two). Severus searches for a scroll and later an orb, believing they'll free him, but they lead to more betrayal and pain. This mirrors the Bible's warning about chasing empty promises instead of God's truth (Isaiah 44:20).

- **Salvation:** God's gift of being saved from Hell and welcomed into Heaven, offered through Jesus' death on the cross and resurrection (John 3:16). It means being forgiven for your wrongs by trusting in Jesus, choosing to follow Him, and receiving the promise of eternal life with God.

- **Satan:** The leader of the fallen angels, also called Lucifer or the devil, who rebelled against God and now opposes Him

(1 Peter 5:8). In the book, Satan appears in Hell as a deceptive figure who torments Severus (chapter 8, Part Two), reflecting his role as the enemy who seeks to destroy humanity by leading them away from God.

- **Savior**: A title for Jesus, meaning the one who saves people from their sins and Hell (Luke 2:11). In the book, Jesus is the Savior who welcomes believers like Perpetua into Heaven (Part One) and offers salvation to all, including Severus, who rejects it (Part Two).
- **Seals of Light**: An imaginative depiction of the "clothing" worn by people in Heaven, inspired by the Bible's description of white robes (Revelation 7:9). Unlike earthly clothes that cover shame, these seals glow with God's glory, celebrating each person's unique story and faith in a paradise where there's no shame (Genesis 2:25).
- **Shekinah Glory**: A term describing the visible presence of God, like a radiant light or fire seen in the Bible (Exodus 24:16–17). In Heaven, it's the awe-inspiring glow of God's love and holiness that surrounds His people, filling them with wonder.
- **Sin**: Any thought, action, or choice that goes against God's perfect way, separating us from Him (Isaiah 59:2). It's not just "bad things" like lying or stealing—it's also living for yourself instead of God, which the Bible says leads to spiritual death (Romans 6:23). Jesus offers forgiveness for sin through His sacrifice on the cross.
- **Slave Demons**: In the book, these are lesser fallen angels in Hell, depicted as gangly, clawed creatures with glowing eyes (chapters 6–8, Part Two). They serve more powerful demons and torment human souls, reflecting the Bible's description of demons as evil beings who oppose God and harm those separated from Him (Revelation 9:1–11).
- **The Blood**: A term referring to Jesus' blood shed on the cross, which the Bible describes as the means of forgiveness and salvation for humanity (Ephesians 1:7). In the book, the

blood of Jesus is the payment for sin that allows believers to be saved, as seen when Perpetua enters Heaven (Part One, chapter 6), while its absence in Severus' life leads to his judgment (Part Two, chapter 5).

- **The Choosing Ground**: A name for Earth in this book, showing its purpose as a temporary stage where every person decides their eternal future (Deuteronomy 30:19). It's the time you have in this life to choose whether to follow Jesus into Heaven's joy or reject Him and face Hell's despair.

- **The Lamb**: A title for Jesus, symbolizing His role as the perfect sacrifice for humanity's sins, as described in the Bible (John 1:29). In the book, Jesus as the Lamb welcomes believers like Perpetua into Heaven (Part One, chapter 6) and judges the unrepentant like Severus at the throne (Part Two, chapter 5), fulfilling His role as both Savior and Judge (Revelation 5:12).

- **Throne of God**: The majestic seat of God in Heaven, described in the Bible as surrounded by radiant light and worshiping creatures (Revelation 4:2–8). In the book, it's where God's glory shines in Heaven (Part One, chapter 7) and where judgment happens (Part Two, chapter 5), showing His power and holiness.

- **Tree of Life**: A symbol in the Bible of eternal life and abundance, first seen in the Garden of Eden (Genesis 2:9) and restored in Heaven (Revelation 22:2). It grows on both sides of the River of Life in the New Jerusalem, bearing fruit that reflects God's unending provision and healing for His people.

- **Trinity**: The Christian belief that God exists as three persons in one—God the Father, God the Son (Jesus), and God the Holy Spirit (Matthew 28:19). In Heaven, this unity is fully revealed, showing God's love and power in a way that fills His people with awe and joy.

- **Worship**: The act of praising and honoring God with your heart, words, and actions (John 4:23–24). In Heaven, worship is a joyful, eternal response to God's glory, seen in singing, feasting, and every moment of life with Him (Part One, chapters 7–9), reflecting the love and awe His people have for Him.

ABOUT THE AUTHOR

Cory Rosenke is a theologian, counselor, and storyteller whose inspiration springs from his passion for God's Word, a fascination with history and philosophy, and a perspective molded by the pressure and grace of human experience. An adventurer at heart, he carries the warmth of a pastor and the rigor of a scholar into every page, weaving narrative and biblical insight into journeys that stir both mind and soul.

An alumnus of Western Seminary, Cory's path has been anything but ordinary—shaped by the rhythm of ranch life, the grit of the carpenter's bench, and the reverent halls of study. Each pursuit has left its mark, forging a distinctive voice that confronts empty philosophy and lifeless dogma with vibrant faith and authentic humanity.

His 2024 release, *The Magnetic Heart of God*, revolutionized readers' understanding of what it means to be human by unveiling "the five cravings of the soul"—security, identity, independence, significance, and innocence—as keys to our deepest motivations and longings. Similarly, *A Song of Light & Fire* breaks new ground by uniting rigorous theology with imaginative storytelling, leading readers on a life-changing odyssey through Heaven and Hell.

Cory's calm yet authoritative voice brings clarity to complexity and grace to brokenness. With a style that bridges ancient yearning and modern soul-searching, he invites readers into discoveries both timeless and transformative. And this is only the beginning. With more works already underway, Cory continues to rekindle forgotten flames of truth—while unveiling fresh insight for a world in desperate need of faith, hope, and wonder.

www.ingramcontent.com/pod-product-compliance
Lightning Source LLC
Chambersburg PA
CBHW051820040426
42447CB00006B/291